WHAT
BLACK EDUCATORS
ARE SAYING

WHAT

BLACK EDUCATORS

ARE SAYING

Edited by

NATHAN WRIGHT, JR.

HAWTHORN BOOKS, INC.   PUBLISHERS   NEW YORK

To those who die daily almost forgotten, with the
hope that they and others somehow may live.

WHAT BLACK EDUCATORS ARE SAYING

FOREWORD

IN THESE ESSAYS, some of the nation's leading black educators speak of the urgent need for humanizing the nation's schools.

Those who represent power have a vested interest in keeping society as it is, with the minimum necessary adjustments. It is thus that parents, who represent disproportionate power in relation to their children, work to "hold the line." Only as our young people break the bonds of a built-in "parental oppression" are they liberated. As so many of us may testify who as parents have watched adolescents grow, in this way also our homes experience rare moments of rehumanization and fulfillment. So it is as well in the institutional life of larger communities.

Power positions yield only to the clearly expressed and determined voice of those whom power would unconsciously abuse. Thus, the victims of a culture of oppression must always speak out—clearly, creatively, and with unmistakable candor—if human possibilities are to be extended, if the lives of all are to find their due fulfillment.

The men and women whose essays follow are all humanly inspired voices to which we must listen for our own growth and for the enhancement of the nation's peaceable and orderly progress. Some voices may jar us, others may comfort, but all should teach us. As we listen carefully to their intent, we will perhaps be impelled to share more fully in their earnest striving not for the lesser good of human betterment but for nothing short of the greatest good of complete human liberation and fulfillment.

The alternative at the very least is wantonly wasted human potential.

In a way that is not typical of America as a whole, the black communities throughout the nation have traditionally sent their ablest men and women into the field of education. Hence any educational enterprise which does not employ disproportionately large numbers of black people in its work of definition, management, teaching, research, and leadership may have greatly impoverished itself.

The especially sensitive and accomplished men and women whose essays are included here represent the nation's best resource for guidance and direction in the most critical urban concerns that face us today. Listen well to these beautiful brothers and sisters. Then call upon them and others like them for the ready and substantial insight with which they may inform your work.

NATHAN WRIGHT, JR.

CONTENTS

Part III: The University Scene

Part IV: Educational Redefinition

Part V: Community Involvement and Action

PART I

THE BLACK EDUCATOR

EDUCATION FOR BLACK HUMANISM: A WAY OF APPROACHING IT*

by Preston Wilcox

"If we react to white racism with a violent reaction, to me that is not black racism. If you come to put a rope around my neck and I hang you for it, to me that's not racism. My reaction is the reaction of a *human being,* reacting to defend himself and protect himself. This is what our people haven't done, and some of them, at least at the high academic level, don't want to. But most of us aren't at that level."—*Malcolm X at a Harvard Law School Forum, December 16, 1964*

THE ROLE OF THE BLACK REVOLUTIONARY INTELLECTUAL

IT IS WORTHY of observation that the intellectual power behind the educational revolution which is slowly penetrating the black community emanates from outside the traditional ivory-tower setting. Malcolm X's oratorical indictment of white America brought to public visibility the degree to which black Americans had been conditioned to oppress themselves of the mythical superiority of whites.[1] His public indictment of whites refurbished what Garvey had begun some years earlier. Frantz Fanon linked psychiatry with sociology as a means to reveal the oppressive nature of the relationship between the colonized native and the colonial settler.[2] Harold Cruse demonstrated with scholarly precision that the black-white conflict was cultural in form and not merely political in the fragmented and narrow sense. White hyphenated groups had substituted their values for those of the WASPs and had become antiblack oppressors also.[3] Eldridge Cleaver pulled back the covers of the integrated bedroom and revealed human interaction on one level, and mutual

*Dedicated to the Malcolm El Shabazz Community College, Chicago, Illinois.

self-destruction on the other.[4] Martin Luther King, Jr., climbed to the mountaintop—only to be assassinated. He was too human to survive without the collective support of his black brothers.

Malcolm X's "moment of truth" occurred in a jail cell.[5] Frantz Fanon's writings surfaced after his death; he wrote about a revolution through which he lived. Harold Cruse's book turned a literal unknown into a nationally known writer. Martin Luther King's now-famous *Letter from a Birmingham Jail* moved his potential to contribute to the liberation of blacks to a higher plane.[6] Eldridge Cleaver, too, wrote from inside a jailhouse. These men held in common a desire to liberate the masses, not only themselves. What Malcolm X had to say about white racism and tricknology was matched by Martin Luther King's essays on white America's violence. Harold Cruse's excoriating attack on WASPisms was equaled by Eldridge Cleaver's analysis that America was organized to protect the white vagina. Frantz Fanon put it all together from afar.[7]

Of interest and perhaps not ironic is that white America viewed Malcolm X as being antiwhite; Martin Luther King as being violent; Harold Cruse as being envious; Eldridge Cleaver as an irreversible rapist; and Franz Fanon as a revolutionary. The peculiar ability of this nation to assign to black men equal status as it relates to antisocial behavior and to deny them the accreditation of humanness has compelled an increasing number of black men to begin to define themselves on their own terms—*to rid themselves of the need to be defined in a positive sense by white America.*

Malcolm X's real message was that *one's right to be human is nonnegotiable.* Martin Luther King was engaged in a struggle to protect his *right to be nonviolent.* Harold Cruse's message was that if he was required to reject himself and to substitute the values of the oppressor for his own, he would choose to be *who he was himself.* Cleaver—a convicted rapist—knew too well that *the system produced rapists;* and, as Dick Gregory has commented, the goal of a humane society is to deal with those factors which create *the need for people to rape each other.* Fanon's "plunge-the-knife concept" required that the native commit a double murder in order to liberate himself, by killing the settler and his old self at the same time. He believed that one had to be reborn in order to liberate himself anew.

On one level, the above-mentioned brothers might be called black *revolutionary* intellectuals since they taught as they acted, as they organized, and as they developed others—and seldom within the traditional classroom. The black community was *their* black university. Street corners, stadiums, churches, dance halls, storefronts, picket lines, the stage, bars, courtyards of jails—and even bedrooms—were their classrooms. The content of the curriculum was real life: the Birmingham bus strike, the Memphis strike, the March on Washington, the New York school integration struggle, Selma, Alabama, the Freedom Rides, the Huey Newton case, the Harlem Renaissance, and the Algerian revolution made learning and doing inseparable; apprehension and comprehension indivisible; intellect and emotion one; and thought and action a single effort. For all of them the authentic role of the black teacher was that of *convincing black people of their essential educability, potential, and humanity.* Malcolm X and Martin Luther King had a peculiar love for their brothers: it was undying. Malcolm died when he did because he refused to have the audience searched as they entered the hall which was to become his tomb. Martin Luther King died while surrounded by his brothers, but a part of his mystique was that no black man could really be free on earth—unless he was willing to die for that in which he believed.[8]

Booker T. Washington, the first black man anointed into national prominence by white America, chose a system of enslavement over extinction. He failed to realize, as Malcolm X did, that one's philosophy of survival affected his attitude and his behavior—toward the world and himself.[9] Booker T. Washington must have felt that black people would be given freedom by appealing to the white conscience and by the subordination of their own black consciousness. Despite his contributions, his model of education was an exaggerated imitation of that of his oppressors. His students learned to line up when whites spoke—without being "too uppity."[10]

W. E. B. DuBois, an acknowledged black intellectual, never fully understood the impact of white institutional racism. Had he been able to do so, he would not have urged the full integration of black students into white racist institutions. My point is that he lacked the current level of comprehension: that authentic blackness is not the replica of whiteness.[11] Neither is it solely a reaction to white rejection. Rather it is a soul-searching, excruciatingly difficult attempt to undo four hundred years of de-Africanization, dehumanization, and colonization—to reach deeply into the instinct and belief systems of black people in order to restore them to a self-defined level of *experienced* humanity, *figurative* Africanization, and *literal* collective liberation. Sister Edwina Chavers Johnson makes the same point in this fashion:

> The African descendants in America, having passed through three phases of education in America, i.e., de-Africanization, dehumani-

zation, and (finally) an inferior-caste status, through application of self-determination and the establishment of a voluntary self-separated school system, can educate themselves.[12]

THE DESIGN FOR MISEDUCATION—VEILED

Sister Johnson's optimism as an African American, when placed beside the wish-fulfillment of the white oppressor, helps to push the issue of education for black humanism into perspective. When Miss Ophelia asked St. Clare in *Uncle Tom's Cabin* why he didn't free his enslaved persons, one of his responses was as follows:

> The capitalist and aristocrat of England cannot feel that as we do, because they do not mingle with the class they degrade as we do. They are in our houses, they are the associates of our children, and they form their minds faster than we can, for they are a race that children will always cling to and assimilate with. If Eva, now, was not more angel than ordinary, she would be ruined. We might as well allow the smallpox to run among them, and think our children would not take it, as to let them be uninstructed and vicious, and think our children will not be affected by that. Yet our laws positively and utterly forbid any efficient general educational system, and they do it wisely, too; for just begin and thoroughly educate one generation, and the whole thing would be blown sky high. *If we did not give them liberty, they would take it.*[13]

A careful reading of St. Clare's response, Sister Johnson's analysis, and Jerry Farber's *Student As Nigger* suggests an essential agreement about:

1. The oppressive nature of WASP-oriented educational processes. The white radical student rebellions are a case in point.

2. The latent belief by blacks and even racist whites of the essential educability of blacks.

3. The white control of integrated education as merely a tool to avoid integration of the curriculum content and to redistribute control over curricular matters. A multicultural control over the discrete cultural aspects of the program itself. As resolved at the Third International Black Power Conference:

> Black persons working within white institutions, if [authentically] black, should be working for the best interests of the black community, to whom they are ultimately responsible. The point here is that the physical locale of the black man should have no relationship to his role or perception of himself as a black man.[14]

What black men fully understand, and what white men cannot allow themselves to believe, is that the myth of white supremacy remains a *myth* perpetrated to foster the privileges of white skin. Indeed, if white men were in fact "superior" to black men, and black men believed it, there would be no need for white institutional racism, white backlash, White Citizens' Councils, Minutemen, or a white-controlled police system, protecting the white people from black people even within the ghettos.

Had an authentic black man written William Whyte's *Organization Man*, he would have probably named it *The White Uncle Toms*. Daniel P. Moynihan's *The Negro Family* would have addressed itself to how white families maintain themselves economically within white enclaves surrounding the inner city by the exploitation of black men, their families, and their communities. He would have named his statement *The Victimization of Black Families*. A rational policeman would question the gambling on Wall Street in the way that he "questions" in order to bribe the local numbers runner. A nonracist health service would render abortion readily accessible within less-chance communities as it is within lily-white America. The sociologists who identify such role models as pimps, prostitutes, hustlers, and racketeers within less-chance communities would look for the same behavioral characteristics on Wall Street, in the state capitals, and in the nation's capital. The use of God to raise money regardless of the salvation of the donors has turned the nation's religious institutions into corporate structures devoid of legitimate relationships to their original purposes.[15]

Motherhood has become a symbol for the propagation of wars, not peace. The vagina has become the world's most vaunted war machine. It is no accident that the sons of black mothers were the first to decide not to fight in Vietnam. It is no irony that authentic blacks are attempting to articulate and codify a nondestructive relationship between males and females—a relationship that assigns roles not on bedroom or athletic criteria but on the basis of the collective survival needs of black people. (Collective survival within the black world can never be achieved as long as institutionalized conflict and colonialism exist within male-female relationships.)

Recall the recent report by the National Advisory Commission on Civil Disorders, which dealt with the issue of racism while remaining silent on the issue of sex.[16] This occurred despite Gunnar Myrdal and Emory S. Bogardus' listing of sex as the number one discrimination in "rank order of discriminations" among a list of six items (sex, social equality, use of public facilities, political disfranchisement, discrimination by public servants, and economic exploitation).[17] The black man's rank order is just about parallel but inverse to that of the white man.[18]

Is it any wonder that the public schools are just getting around to sex education courses? The fact that such courses are directed more toward birth control than they are toward sexual liberation compounds the issue. A white-middle-class black differential as it relates to children born out of marriage is the tendency of whites to reject the causal act and the resultant child; lower class blacks tend to accept the child and they reject *only* the causal act.[19] But the deeper question relates to why children born out of wedlock are labeled "illegitimate" and treated as though they were less human, through no fault of their own. They have a God-given right to be born—it seems—and after that God is usually dead as far as they are concerned.

There are many other issues which, when submitted to serious intellectual scrutiny by liberated minds, reveal the application of *scientific colonialism* by white America.[20] Arthur R. Jensen's recent report, which suggested that blacks, on the average, are genetically inferior to whites in I.Q., is an example of the above. Jensen blithely dismissed the consequences of *white institutional racism, WASP-oriented I.Q. tests, environmental deprivation, and the absence of the requisites for serious scientific study of the subject.* That he had a need in 1969 to produce such evidence was much more consonant with white America's need to continue to justify its inhumane actions against black people.[21]

Finally, much of the testimony dealing with racism suggests that whites are versatile. They have the ability to benefit in economic terms from the reality of racism and at the same time, they are able to participate meaningfully in the salvation of black people! The same people who had "trained" black people into a system of enslavement (since the white man knew that black people were not natural-born enslaved persons) now want to *plan* their emancipation![22] It was SNCC which first challenged this assumption:

> It must be offered that white people who desire change in this country should go where that problem [racism] is most manifest; the problem is not in the black community. The whites should go into white communities where whites have created power for the express [purpose] of denying blacks human dignity and self-determination.[23]

SNCC was offering whites an alternative: to become either a part of the problem *or* a part of the solution, but not both. One sees in this white do-gooder behavior a linking of capitalism and racism. Far too many whites—and black-skinned people—are "doing well by doing good"—exploiting by getting paid to keep blacks in their places. Those with black skins who start a "movement" or a militant action in order to get a job are in the same bag. The resultant underdevelopment of black people has been characterized by James Boggs as follows:

(1) They [blacks] have been systematically excluded from supervisory, planning, and decision-making roles which could have given them practical experience and skills in organizing and planning and administration.

(2) They have been systematically excluded from the higher education which would have given them the abstract and conceptual tools necessary for research and technological innovation at *this* stage of economic development, when productivity is more dependent on imagination, knowledge, and the concepts of systems, i.e., on mental processes, than it is on manual labor.[24]

The inseparability of capitalism and racism has had educational consequences for black people, but as James Forman put it:

Where do we begin? We have already started. We started the moment we were brought to this country. In fact, we started on the shores of Africa, for we have always resisted attempts to make us slaves and now we must resist attempts to make us capitalists.[25]

THE RESPONSE FOR THE BLACK COMMUNITY

What does all this mean in educational terms? What are the implications for the education of black people? How is the redefining taking place?

One example is seen in the work of the National Association for African American Education. At its first meeting in June 1968 it engaged the following issues: higher education, blackening the curriculum, black educator, black student, school and black community, materials of instruction. When it met in August 1968 in St. Louis, it followed through on the above themes but in the context of nation building: internal relationships, external relationships, and the role of the NAAAE.[26] Unlike most organizations, the NAAAE does not exclude on the basis of ideology, social class, age, occupational status, and/or organizational affiliation. It defines the black educator as follows:

Students, parents, community leaders, clergymen, businessmen, activists, moderates, college professors, teachers, educational ad-

ministrators, and all those who are actively involved in the educational liberation and survival of black people.[27]

During the period of August 20 to August 24, 1969, the NAAAE
conducted its first anniversary meeting in the form of a five-day Black
University. The theme was "The Fire This Time: New Black Perspectives, Creative Black Solutions." Stated in functional terms, an effort was
undertaken to codify on a collective basis the intellectual and technical
requisites to promote the physical and mental health of black people.
Brother M. Lee Montgomery, Academic Dean Brother, for the August
encounter, sketched out a paradigm containing the following four
threads:[28]

Childhood	replaces	preschool education
Youth	replaces	elementary education
Young adult	replaces	secondary education
Adult	replaces	higher education

Education was discussed then, not only as it occurs traditionally within
the classroom, but in terms of its uses as a liberating force for black
people. The four age levels above were discussed as they relate to families, neighborhoods, and cities. In other words, black educators are required to define new models for black manhood, womanhood, families,
communities, etc.

The aim of the meeting was to engage the enrollees in a reasoned,
planful, well thought out approach that:

1. Builds black competence as it develops self-concept.
2. Develops operational unity internally even as it constructs models
for meaningful collective action.
3. Employs education as a liberating force.
4. Produces a winning attitude as overwhelming odds are confronted.
5. Views struggle as being educational.
6. Engages the black community in living for that for which it is
willing to die.
7. Constructs models for meaningful collective action.
8. Builds an authentic sense of nationhood.[29]

The key is a recognition that the education of black people must go
on inside and outside of the classroom; that "credentials" are not a
prerequisite to learn from and/or teach each other; and that the experience must encourage all black people to acquire the skills to humanize
their own existence and to protect their rights to be who they *need* to
be. Values, too, become important concerns—as my readers shall see.

The revolutionary aspects of a search for black humanism are clear. Brother Paul Henry has put it this way:

> The moral imperative involved is apparent. When a society is organized to destroy other cultures and it is also willing to destroy its own culture to save the system, this madness must be stopped. Therefore, it is the Afro-American who must oppose this dehumanizing policy simply because it is black people who are first to be annihilated.[30]

To fail to educate for black humanism is merely to gradualize the destruction of black people and to turn black people against each other. To fail to respond to this imperative is to educate blacks to participate in the destruction of their own identities and cultures—and to substitute the oppressors' values for their own.

Education for black humanism asserts that:

1. All black children are human and educable.
2. Blacks hold in common African descendancy and victimization by white institutional racism.
3. To subscribe to racism and capitalism is to participate in one's own destruction and that of his own people, the largest oppressed class in America.
4. Education which effectively overlooks the aspirations and technical survival requirements of the black masses is irrelevant.
5. Education for blacks is essentially a retooling process: rehumanization, re-Africanization and decolonialization; i.e., authentic black men enjoy only one kind of freedom as a conceptual whole: a respect for native cultural differences, a resistance to all kinds of oppression, and recognition of one's right to defend his right to become who he wants to become as long as the expression of that right does not demand the oppression of others.
6. Black men have a right and an obligation to define themselves and the terms by which they will relate to others.
7. Education must become a process that educates for liberation and survival—nothing less.

SOME SPECIFICS

Cooperative Economic Relationships

A cardinal principle in the humanizing process is the humanization of the *socioeconomic relationship* among black people. As Fanon writes:

If there is an inferiority complex, it is an outcome of a double
process:
  —primarily economic;
  —subsequently, the internalization, or, better, the epidermaliza-
tion—of this inferiority.[31]

Early in their lives black people must be *conditioned,* yes, conditioned,
to relate to each other on a *cooperative economic shared-decision-making
basis.* Instead of savings bank clubs wherein students save individually
—and become embryonic capitalists who learn how to postpone their
gratifications—they must be helped to save jointly in credit unions as a
means to begin to deal with their day-to-day problems collectively.

Reparations—Economic Contact with White America

The reality of white institutionalized racism strongly suggests that
white philanthropy—the control of recipients via gift giving—should be
politicalized into a form of black restitution: the total control of such
funds when obtained by black people. James Forman's thesis is based on
this premise: white philanthropy developed on the backs of black men
must be replaced by a *new* socioeconomic contrast between blacks and
whites.[32] Booker T. Washington established the first one. He agreed to
train black people into menial roles as the price of benefitting from white
philanthropy. The black bourgeoisie chose social integration and entre-
preneurism, with a small *e,* as a price for social integration. Authentic
black people are choosing to control, define, and manage their own
socioeconomic development through the use of reparations—not white
philanthropy. They are asking for justice in payment for their slave
labors, not noblesse oblige. They are choosing to compete with white
America in building a humane system rather than to compete for white
patronage.

Black students should learn early that the public welfare system was
established to contain the have-nots who subscribe to and are the victims
of capitalism. Black students are entitled to the accrued benefits in terms
of interest from the original pledge of forty acres and a mule. It is their
earned and documented right; it is not charity.

Self-Concept

The fact of life for black students is that they receive a thousand daily
encounters which suggest to them that they are, in fact, inferior to whites.
Education of black students must convince them as they are being edu-

cated of their essential worth despite their residence within a white racist society. Authentic black students should be evaluated on the basis by which they *accept themselves;* view their skin color as being a *permanent* condition linked to a rich cultural heritage, and perceive white defined integration as Brother Joseph Pentecoste notes:

> Integration as a theory is basically a willingness to give up one's own attributes and lose racial self-identity by merging with the dominant group.[33]

Importantly, the economic aspects of integration should also be understood. The tendency to establish lily-white suburbs and golden ghettos at the expense of the black poor is the point being made.

A black person with a healthy self-concept values integration with other black people socially and economically, establishes a reparations contract with the white system, and functions black whether within the white or the black world. A black man within a white capitalistic institution is engaged in efforts to redistribute the flow of wealth into *black-controlled cooperative enterprises.*

Pluralistic Decision Making

Black students who are helped to understand the reality of racism will also come to understand the requirement to identify those decisions which cannot be made about their lives by anyone—parents, teachers, employers, police, etc.—outside of themselves. This is particularly the case in the instance of white racists or the institutions that they operate. Black people must acquire the internal insights and ability to accredit their own actions; to ordain themselves, to certify their own humanity; to liberate themselves from a need to blindly comply with rules set outside of themselves.

Persons who respect black people will not want to make decisions about their lives. Rather they will want to transmit the skills and knowledge to them, to enable them to make decisions about their own lives. One's humanity, similarly, cannot be determined by someone else; its existence can only be confirmed outside of oneself.

Self-Liberation

Ultimately the education of black people must free them from psychological dependence on others: it must teach them to think and act on their own. This ability does not rest solely on intellectual talents but on one's ability to rid himself of a need to be controlled by those who have power over him. One's ability, then, to think for oneself derives from several aspects:

1. Resolution of his parental relationships, i.e., getting his mother off his mind.
2. Resolution of his relationships with the opposite sex, i.e., male strength and feminine assets should become liberating instruments rather than weapons.
3. Resolution of his attitude toward whites, i.e., ridding himself of a need to be equal to whites but developing a desire to be "equal to the occasion."
4. Resolution of his materialistic needs, i.e., liberating himself from an ability to be controlled by someone else's purse.
5. Resolution of his religious hangups, i.e., freeing himself from the need to be saved by first finding his own salvation within himself.

A Reordering of Values

Education should provide students with an opportunity to select, design, and articulate their own values and to discern their impact on their behavior and attitudes—and relationships with others. In an earlier paper, I identified the following values which require re-examination and ordering:[34]

1. Black people must forget their *isolation* from white people and deal with their *alienation* from black people.
2. Black people must replace their *need to belong* with a sense of *functional marginality* as it relates to their membership in this society.
3. An effort must be made to distinguish *needs* from *wants;* the economic consequences are crucial.
4. Peer and mutual relationships across age, class, and sex lines should come to be valued more than superordinate and/or subordinate relationships.

Brother Bob Rhodes has posed this question with great clarity. He stated:

We must create a new value system and determine:

1. How to create value;
2. How to allocate value; and
3. Upon what criterion do you create values and allocate values?

When one combines all of these specifics—cooperative economic relationships, reparations, self-concept, pluralistic decision making, self-liberation and a reordering of values—into a conceptual whole, one finds that as the student learns he alters his relationship to the teacher, his family, his community, and to the society in which he lives. Importantly, he solves problems as he learns problem solving. He no longer separates thought from action. He no longer submits himself to be "fitted in." He learns to acquire the skills to force society to include him *on his own terms!*

NOTES

1. Alex Haley (editor), *The Autobiography of Malcolm X* (New York: Grove Press, 1964).
2. Frantz Fanon, *The Wretched of the Earth: A Negro Psychoanalyst's Study of the Problems of Racism and Colonialism* (New York: Grove Press, 1963).
3. Harold Cruse, *The Crisis of the Negro Intellectual* (New York: William Morrow, 1967).
4. Eldridge Cleaver, *Soul on Ice* (New York: McGraw-Hill Book Company, 1968).
5. Alex Haley, *op. cit.*, Chapter 10, pp. 153–69.
6. Martin Luther King, Jr., *Letter from a Birmingham Jail* (April 16, 1963).
7. Frantz Fanon, *ibid.*
8. Louis E. Lomax, *To Kill a Black Man* (Los Angeles: Holloway Publishing Co., 1968).
9. Booker T. Washington, *Up from Slavery* (New York: Dell Publishing Co., 1965), p. 180.
10. Christopher Jencks and David Reisman, "The American Negro College," in *Harvard Educational Review* (37:1, 1967), p. 21.
11. Preston Wilcox, "It's Not a Replica of the White Agenda," in *College Board Review* (No. 71, Spring 1969), pp. 6–10.
12. Edwina C. Johnson, "An Alternative to Miseducation for the Afro-American People," see pp. 200–207.
13. Harriet Beecher Stowe, *Uncle Tom's Cabin* (New York: Washington Square Press, Inc., 1963), pp. 237–38. Italics mine. See also Jerry Farber, "Student as Nigger," in *Renewal* (9:5, May 1969).
14. Preston Wilcox (editor), *Report of Education Workshop #1: Control of Schools Within the Black Community,* Third International Black Power Conference, Philadelphia, September 1968.
15. See James Forman, "Total Control As the Only Solution to the Economic Problems of Black People: The Black Manifesto," in *Renewal* (9:6, June 1969), pp. 9–13.

16. *Report of the National Advisory Commission on Civil Disorders* (New York: E. P. Dutton & Co., 1968). The omission of sex as an important variable may have occurred because very few black people who were involved directly in the black restoration and liberation movement were heard.

17. Gunnar Myrdal, *An American Dilemma: The Negro in a White Nation* (New York: McGraw-Hill Book Company, 1964), pp. 60–61. See also Emory S. Bogardus, "Race, Friendliness and Social Distance," in *Journal of Applied Psychology* (1927), pp. 272–87.

18. Myrdal, *ibid.*, p. 61.

19. Kenneth B. Clark, *Dark Ghetto* (New York: Harper & Row, 1965), pp. 72–73.

20. Johann Galtung, "The Lessons of Project Camelot: Scientific Colonialism," in *Transition 30* (1967), pp. 11–15.

21. Arthur R. Jensen, "How Can We Boost I.Q. and Scholastic Achievement?" in *Harvard Educational Review* (39:1, Winter 1969), pp. 1–117. See also Victor Cohn, "Report to Dispute Negroes Are Genetically Inferior in I.Q.," in the *Washington Post* (May 15, 1969), p. A5.

22. For a statement on the training of enslaved persons, see Kenneth M. Stampp, *The Peculiar Institution: Slavery in the Ante-Bellum South* (New York: Vintage Books, 1956), Chapter IV.

23. "Excerpts from Paper on Which the 'Black Power' Philosophy Is Based," in *The New York Times* (August 5, 1966).

24. James Boggs, "The Myth and Irrationality of Black Capitalism" (New York: Interreligious Foundation for Community Organization, April 28, 1969), p. 3. Mimeographed.

25. Forman, *op. cit.*, p. 10.

26. *Report to the NAAAE (St. Louis)* (New York: NAAAE, September 23, 1968), p. 31.

27. Preston Wilcox, *Progress Report* (New York: NAAAE, May 12, 1969), p. 3.

28. M. Lee Montgomery, *Draft: Black University* (New York: NAAAE, June 1969), p. 2.

29. Preston Wilcox, "The Rationale, The Setting, The Theme" (New York: NAAAE, June 15, 1969), p. 2. Mimeographed.

30. Paul Henry, *Memo to Walter Palmer: The Massive Decline Curve* (May 13, 1969), p. 2.

31. Frantz Fanon, *Black Skins, White Masks* (New York: Grove Press, 1967), p. 13.

32. Forman, *op. cit.*

33. Joseph Pentecoste, "Black Psychology," in *The Black Liberator* (vol. 5, June 1969), pp. 6, 4.
34. Preston Wilcox, *The School and Community with Special Concern for Higher Education: The Black and Human Position* (New York: Conference on Science, Philosophy and Religion, 1968), pp. 14–15.

SOURCE MATERIALS

Catherine Havrilesky, *Bibliography; White Institutional Racism* (New York: Afram Associates, Inc., 1969).
Toye Brown Lewis, *Black Agency Control: An Action Manual* (New York: Afram Associates, Inc., 1969).
Charles Tilly, Wagner D. Jackson, and Barry Kay, *Race and Residence in Wilmington, Delaware* (New York: Columbia University Teachers College, 1965).

THE NEW BLACK DIMENSION
IN OUR SOCIETY

by Olivia Pearl Stokes

THE MAY 1969 issue of *The Negro Digest* focused on the place and the ideological position of the black people in America today. On the front page of the *Digest* is a bronze picture of an American Negro woman dressed in the style of her African ancestors from Nigeria, with the cloth of her hat matching that of her dress. She has a smiling face, implying and signifying the hope that the black world feels in the struggle of today.

On the back page there is a picture of a little boy sitting down, looking into the future, and the heading is "Don't Despair, Little Man, Tomorrow Belongs to You," and these words follow:

> The journey has been long, and rough, but the dangers have been faced and fought, and now you can stand on the threshold of a new and brighter day. You cannot be discouraged now. Those who struggled to bring you to this moment deserve the homage of your faith and determination. Look back to them—look back in pride and love—and fine inspiration in their quiet strength and simple nobility. Your blood and muscle and genius shaped and enriched this land, and this land is yours. You were here long before Columbus, long before the Pilgrims, and—while you have no cause for shame because you were enslaved—not all your ancestors came in chains. Look back to Estevanico, who arrived in 1527 with Panfilo de Narvaez and Cabeza de Vaca; to William Tucker, firstborn Negro child (1624) in Jamestown; to Crispus Attucks, who showed other Americans that freedom was worth dying for; to Phyllis Wheatley, who, though a slave, used the brilliance of her mind and spirit to overcome it; to Nat Turner, who, though a slave, dared engineer a bloody revolt in an effort to destroy it. Look back, little man, for yours is a proud history. But, more important, look forward. Look ahead. It is a new world, and you can make your own place in it if you keep the vision and the faith of your fathers.

These two photographs and the words that are there beside them as symbols—"black world" and "don't despair, little man, tomorrow belongs to you"—express the awareness, the excitement, the exhilaration, of the black American at this moment in history.

The young and the black in our country are free now to express the moral idealism that each youth generation reaches for, but not their adults, who they feel compromise ideals for success and material well-being and vested interest.

All of us are finding the change process a very great trial if we are liberal, democratic, peace-loving, noncontroversial, middle-class Americans, according to a policy statement of the National Urban League. But even the blindest among us now know that the danger signals are flashing. Our country and our race are in trouble, not for bread but for love, acceptance, belonging. The black American is seeking the "in-position" on the economic, political, educational, and social ladders and at all levels of the American society.

The tactics of the black extremists and the black nationalists and the advocates of black power are causing the white American to increase his fear and to run for repressive measures to whip the black person into conformity of the Establishment's law-and-order processes. Within the black community, one discovers that the methodologies of black-power proponents vary from one extreme to another. There are persons who, while giving feeling assent to the description of the problem as stated by the militants, would not find the structures themselves, to bring about planned change, nor would they support the methods of the extremists. At the other extreme is the revolutionary methodology of the extremists.

The black community is probably closer together in its agreement on the need for change in the American social structure than it has ever been. No matter where a diagnostic statement is made among the middle-class Negroes, or among the extremists, there can usually be assent, and hardy support for a commonality of understanding of the dimension of the agony of blacks and poor in America.

And while the crisis has drawn blacks together, the gap between political philosophy and social-change methodology is becoming alarmingly apparent.

Many questions are being asked, and much thought is being given to such questions as, Is blackness a divine gift? (This would seem to be the thinking of sociologist Vincent Harding of Spellman College in Atlanta, Georgia.) Another burning question is, Is "separatism" a temporary step for the purpose of coalescing blacks into a unified community of people for common goals, or is it a permanent stance meaning the separation of the blacks for an independent nation? In what ways does black separation, as a permanent stance, differ from the goals of the Ku Klux Klan, or white racists, or the White Citizens' Councils? Is separation a temporary disengagement for the purpose of developing the kinds of understanding of heritage and the kinds of group goals that have been a part of the life of other nationality groups and racial peoples? If it is a temporary disengagement for the purpose of answering the questions, Who are we as blacks? What is our African heritage? What is our present situation in the American culture? Where are we going and with whom are we going?—is separation a necessary developmental period in which black persons discover their roots and build new structures, which will provide them with the kind of dignity and economic freedom that is the source of democratic strength in America?

A fundamental question is, What is the role of the black and the white in helping to further the humane quality in this racially pluralistic society? What is the black role? What is the function of volunteer organizations among black men and women, if separation is only a temporary disengagement for the period of developing group strength?

Whitney Young, Jr., says, "In our pluralistic society, basic changes must spring from a variety of sources. Programs must be shaped by the needs and the desires of the individuals they serve and be free of ideological dictates."

A statement like this leads us to raise the question of our common mission as blacks and whites in America. Could it be stated as our common aim to close the racial gap in the areas of economics, politics, education, and housing? Does closing the racial gap mean that there cannot be, or should not be, racial communities of blacks, as there are racial communities of whites? Is such an arrangement healthy in America? It has been for the whites; why can't it be for the blacks, if it is voluntary rather than imposed, either by patterns of practice or by gentlemen's agreements among the dominant group against the minority, or by law?

What actions can black Americans take, who are educated, well employed, and comfortable and who form a viable leadership group in America? Crisis demands decisive action, and middle-class Americans joining hands with their brothers and sisters at the lower economic level could prevent a paralysis of action and arrive at some positive program projections. Middle-class Americans need not be paralyzed by analysis, criticism, negation, and doubts.

1. The middle class can inject a sane voice into the mainstream and

challenge and warn whites who hold power and who embody racist attitudes and methods. It can become a parallel voice and a democratic process as a counterbalance to methods of the black revolutionaries and nationalists. Black middle America can inject a sane voice in these troubled times.

2. Black middle American volunteers and groups can formulate basic philosophy, under the democratic process, and recognize the omissions in education at this point of history and advocate teaching Americans Afro-American history and the inclusion of the problems, the issues, the contributions, and the heritage of the black American—not as history for only the blacks but as history for Americans, because the black history should be in the mainstream of the thought of white Americans. This might help to relieve some of the racist attitudes existing so widely in our culture. The formulation of a basic philosophy also would help persons understand that blacks are God's gifts, as are whites and Indians and Africans in the total world mix, and that it is His intent that man should learn to respect, understand, and appreciate the variety of human differences and contributions that are divinely created.

3. The black middle American can serve as a go-between and weld together the streams and creative forces for black advancement. It can develop support for such legal instruments as the National Association for the Advancement of Colored People's legal defense and educational fund, for projects which provide for self-determination of blacks in local areas, whether these projects be economic, political, or educational.

4. Black middle America can provide innovative strategies to bring together white Americans who are eager to join forces with blacks in the achievement of equality and dignity for blacks as well as for whites on the same parallel line when their goals and objectives are the same. One of those innovative strategies will help at the point of doing away with forced segregation. Here we have to look to black middle America to challenge white liberal America and the church to help in the process of the implementation of the civil-rights statutes on the books of this nation.

5. System analysis versus treatment: Black middle America needs to help point out that the OEO projects and many of the efforts being made on the part of whites in the black community, although they are often creative, can only treat the existing ills, and fail miserably at getting at the cause of the need for treatment. Many of the programs tend to alleviate personal agonies and pains without destroying the economic, political, and social system that makes the personal problem exist. There is great opportunity for us to understand the structures of American society and the racist nature in order to bring about change and eliminate

the kind of treatment projects which have been so popular in the war on poverty.

6. Black middle America needs to start taking its own opinion polls among black people, for only the revolutionary activities, as valuable as these may be in the social change process, are those that are picked up by mass media.

These suggestions by no means represent the total thinking and feeling of black middle America. It is true that today there are more Negroes integrated economically in top-level jobs than ever before in history. But it is also true that with the population expansion there are more Negroes at the low economic levels, because of automation and technology, than ever before. Somehow these two facts must be made known to industry and to America in general, in order that this gap can be erased and people can look to economic structures in American society that provide personal dignity and quality education for their children; homes for their families and jobs for their sustenance for their development.

The new black dimension in the American society is a fascinating, dynamic, creative, hopeful development in democracy. It is a people throwing off the imposed and designed oppression of hundreds of years and the rediscovery of their worth as persons, their coalition as a community of common interests and concerns—and their design for the future. The new blackness is an instrument of value in the American stream of democratic development.

THE BLACK TEACHER AND BLACK POWER*

by Leslie Campbell

ON A HOT, humid weekend in July we attended a gathering of over one thousand African-Americans from all over the continent of North America and beyond, and representing a multitude of organizations and points of view. The National Conference on Black Power was a momentous and historic event for all black Americans regardless of economic level, geographic location, social status, educational background, or hue of skin. This event marked the end of a nightmare and the beginning of a dream. With the convening of the conference, the nightmare of integration ended for most black Americans. The thought that black Americans could successfully intermingle and intersperse themselves into white American society, sometime in the near future, has officially died and was buried at this conference.

The dream that was born of this convention was the idea of black nationhood (here in North America) and self-determination for black people. The ideas and resolutions adopted by the conference all project toward that day when the black population of North America can say proudly, "I don't want to be part of yours, I have my own." If black power has one common meaning it most certainly means that black people have a right to and must rule and control their destinies here in America.

THE TRANSITION FOR THE BLACK TEACHER

If we as black teachers are going to further the goals of black power and prepare our youth for their role in moving toward black nationhood, we must undergo a complete change in thinking pertaining to our positions in the society. As educators we should begin to examine the existing educational structure and start revising it to meet the need of our youth

*From Afro-American Teachers *Forum*, 4th quarter, 1967.

and our communities. We must change our educational system from a traditional one to a functional one. Our schools must become tools to shape and mold our communities and our students must fully understand what and why they are being taught, and for what roles they are preparing themselves.

To institute the type of educational system that will benefit the black community and spur us toward our goal, we must institute the following changes within the present structure.

1. All African-American teachers must seek teaching positions in the black community. The black community needs competent black personnel and cannot afford to lose a single black teacher to the outside community. The old story about showing the outside community that we have competent teachers and administrators who can educate anyone regardless of racial background does not seem applicable any more. The schools in our community are in trouble, and if you are so competent, then use your talents to build your community.

2. Black teachers must protect black children against educational injustices and systematic genocide. We must begin to speak out and weed out the incompetents who are using our children to pay their rent. Any black teacher who sits back and allows miseducation to continue without speaking out is as guilty as those who are actually conducting the programs of miseducation.

3. Black teachers must begin to identify with and speak the language of the black community. Too long have black teachers aspired to reach goals that this society has denied them. They must now begin to realize that their people are most in need of their leadership and skills. However they cannot bring these to the community like a "stranger bearing gifts," but must instead join in and work with the community in such a manner as to create a unified movement in which those that have leadership ability will be selected by the many rather than the few.

THE DIFFERENCE*

by Leslie Campbell

DURING THE PAST decade the very foundation of our cherished society has been shaken to the roots by the activities of its black citizens. Throughout our land black citizens in alliance with sympathetic and guilt-ridden whites have embarked upon a course of demonstrational and organizational protest in order to revise the economic, social, and political structure of twentieth-century America. During these years we have witnessed an astounding revolution in the attitude of the masses of black people. They can no longer accept with warm smiles, the indignities, arrogance, and hypocrisy of the establishment. In simple language, black folks have gotten "mad" and "tired" of the old order and have diverted their energies toward its destruction.

The white population during this period has experienced an awakening of the mind. It has been confronted with the fact that the black man will no longer remain "invisible" and content. Under these pressures white America has squirmed in a mire of either extreme white liberalism (nigger-lover) or extreme white conservatism (legalized segregation). Token changes have been offered and accepted during the interplay between the two opposing forces. However, the goal of total reorganization and equalization in American society is, even in the eyes of most confident blacks, a long way off.

But in the light of all these changes we want to evaluate and comment upon the activities of a small, but increasing, segment of the black population, the Negro professional. Before the "black revolution of the mid-fifties" the term "Negro professional" was nothing more than a cliché used to denote those black folks that had accomplished the feat of obtaining a scholarly degree from one of America's institutions of higher learning. For all of his scholarly efforts this man received a position of importance in his inferior community and usually an income slightly higher than his downtrodden brothers. He had little or no influence in the affairs of the Establishment.

*From Afro-American Teachers *Forum*, 2nd quarter, 1968.

Suddenly along comes the "revolution" and the establishment is forced to "integrate" to try to appease the rebellious black masses. The Negro professional is catapulted into positions of relative importance and wealth. Logically he will use his position and wealth to foster the cause of his black brothers who are responsible for his advancement. Folly! The Negro professional is too secure and comfortable to realize his logical responsibility. He becomes obsessed with the amassing of material wealth and aesthetic comfort. He is too blinded to realize that his importance and stability is directly coupled to the struggle of the black masses. The creation of a schism between the Negro professional and the black masses is the last remaining weapon of the Establishment in its effort to maintain white supremacy. The creation of a Negro professional class as opposed to a Negro proletariat will allow the Establishment to play one class against the other in an effortless game in which neither will benefit.

This theory can be witnessed in practice in the recent crisis at I.S. 201. The black masses, parents and community leaders, had confronted the Establishment with a legitimate demand: Negro Supervisors for Black Schools. Seemingly, they had won a victory for improved education in the black ghetto. Then the Establishment turned to its secret weapon, the Negro professional. The Negro teachers at I.S. 201 helped transfer the victory into defeat.

How can we dismiss the white principal when the Negro teachers refuse to allow his dismissal? How can we replace the white supervisor when Negro candidates readily admit they are not qualified for positions of such responsibility? These are the echoed words of the white press and the Board of Education as they escaped with another victory for the established order.

What the black masses demand cannot be granted because the Negro professional refuses to associate himself and his success with the man on the street. Instead of leadership and direction from the Negro professional, the black masses receive deceit and betrayal. Instead of confrontation and conference, there is distrust and treason.

The I.S. 201 incident is only one where the Establishment used the schism between the black masses and the Negro professional to wipe out any significant gains. Seeing how successful the new weapon has been, we can rest assured that it will be pressed into service rather frequently.

How can we breach this gap? How can the wound be healed? How is it possible to wed black masses and black professionals into a oneness that will bring about the type of weapon profitable only to black advancement?

THE DEVIL CAN NEVER EDUCATE US*

by Leslie Campbell

FROM OUR FOREFATHERS all real knowledge and wisdom flowed; therefore the devil can never educate us.

People are constantly asking me to give my opinion on the current crisis in education and what is going to happen next. During this period of "Great Awakening," black people are learning that the devil cannot educate their children and that he never meant for their children to be educated in the first place. Let us examine the facts and background behind the miserable failure of the public schools to educate black children.

The record of the devil's administration of public schools in our community is atrocious.

THE RECORD

Our children have lower national scores in reading and math than any other racial or ethnic group. This fact has been verified by every local and national survey. We also have the highest dropout rate. Our youths become easily discouraged by the oppressive educational system and decide very early in life that they have had enough miseducation.

If you check the low percentage of quality diplomas (academic) given to black students at the conclusion of their high-school careers, you will notice additional evidence in the case against the devil. Boys High School in Brooklyn (99 percent black) reported that only 9 percent of its graduates last June were eligible for academic diplomas. With this amazingly low rate of success in educating our children it is no surprise that only 5 percent of the high school graduates of Bedford-Stuyvesant (an all black community) are prepared to enter college after graduation. It is no

*From the Afro-American Teachers Association *Forum*, November, 1960.

wonder, then, with this pattern of miseducation of our children, that our community remains totally dependent upon the devil for all vital needs and services.

FOR EXPERIMENTAL PURPOSES ONLY

For the most part, the devil has only used our children for experimental purposes. Each time black parents have questioned the devil's ability to educate, he has come up with a different experimental plan designed to help us. Consequently, he has been experimenting with our children for years under the pretense of trying to help us. Higher Horizons, Reading Readiness, Second Chance, Intensive Reading Program, More Effective Schools—these are just a sampling of the experimental programs designed by the devil to educate black children. None of these programs has proven successful educationally, but they have been successful in fooling our people into believing that he (the devil) really cares about our children's education. New York University, Yeshiva University, and other institutions of higher education have been given licenses to miseducate our children as part of the experimentation plans of the devil. When the devil's plan has failed he often phases out the program, and then it's on to another experimental project.

WHY DOESN'T HE GIVE UP?

Why does the devil persist in operating a school system in our community that is a total failure? Why doesn't he give up and admit his obvious ignorance at the task? The answer to this question lies in one word: *money.*

In the black communities of New York City over $500 million is spent yearly by the system of miseducation. School buildings in our community represent valuable real-estate holdings. If the schools in the black communities of New York were to close permanently, about thirty thousand devils would be minus their fat paychecks. $37 million are spent annually on bus services to transport our children all around the city in search of education. Devil-dominated unions enjoy an unchallenged monopoly of the multimillion-dollar contracts available from the Board of Miseducation. If you were to tabulate money spent for books and school supplies, school lunches, recreation, and after-school services, remedial and extracurricular programs, you would begin to see just how much the devil has invested in his system of miseducation.

Now that we have calculated the take, let us examine where it goes.

• Less than 2 percent of the administrators of New York City schools are black.

• Only 8 percent of the teachers employed by the devil's board are black.

• Only ten schools out of 950 have black custodians.

• The unions and companies holding fat contracts for goods and services in the schools are all owned and operated by devils.

• Conclusion: only a minute percentage (1 percent) of all monies spent for education ever finds its way into the black community. What we have operating here is a colonial educational system where the goods and services are being supplied to the colony by outsiders (devils). Outsiders reap the benefits ($) and privileges (pensions and other goodies) of this system and all the colony receives is a yearly flow of functionally illiterate youths who fulfill the need for a cheap labor force and for Vietnam War cannon fodder. The primary motive of the devil's miseducaton system is *economic,* and let us never forget this fact.

WHAT WE MUST HAVE

We are always asking what we can do about the system and the situation in which we have awakened and found ourselves.

Here are some answers I present for your enlightenment and consumption if you wish to take the first steps toward *Education* in the future:

1. All devils must go!

The colony must begin to build a school system free of any influence or contact with the devil's system. I hear some of you crying now, "But he is qualified, he has the qualification needed to educate our children." But I bitterly question the ability of the "qualified" devil who despises our children, our community, our culture, and, most of all, the goals and aspirations of our people.

If the devil is so well qualified, why hasn't he been using these qualifications positively heretofore? The truth is that the only qualifications he does possess lie in his ability to keep the system of miseducation alive and kicking.

Some of you often cry about "good, well-meaning" devils. Well, I have been in the system for eight years and for each "good" devil that I have encountered I have seen a hundred murderers of our children's minds. I am not willing to gamble with that kind of odds against me.

2. Financial independence must be achieved.

Many of us point to the school system of Washington, D.C., to illustrate that a black school system cannot succeed where the devil's system has failed. It is interesting that we never point to the Nation of Islam's schools (University of Islam) as examples of black schools that educate rather than miseducate. The key to the underlying difference between these two systems is the question of where the money comes from, and who controls the purse strings.

In Washington, D.C., blacks have been placed in the commanding positions, but these blacks are easily manipulated because their salaries are controlled by the devil's board.

The Nation of Islam operates its own schools independently and can make the decisions and changes necessary to operate its schools successfully without having to seek out the devil for financial assistance.

The Ocean Hill–Brownsville experimental project and the experimental project at I.S. 201 are doomed to failure unless they can obtain financial independence from the devils at 110 Livingston Street and elsewhere. The devil's board has already punished these black districts for their part in the present school crisis by withholding teacher paychecks and by suspension of all black educators who do not concur with their long-standing policy of miseducation.

3. We must begin to structure a system to meet our needs and discontinue imitation of the devil's system.

The present black leadership of the experimental districts now operating are always quick to point out to the news media and visiting devils that they are operating their schools by sound educational principles. "Sound educational principles" means that they are operating in the same manner as their former masters. If we really want education for our children, we must discontinue imitation of the devil's systems and begin to build anew. Discard all the old books and materials, the old traditions, old subjects, and old methods of instruction. We have many competent black people who have unique and concrete ideas on effective educational procedures for our youth. These ideas can come into fruition only when we discard the oppressive educational mechanism now stifling us and begin to go for self.

At the time of this writing, the author of this article and three colleagues are under investigation by the devil's board for alleged harassment and intimidation. It is most probable that the devil and his lackey Uncle Tom Negroes will join hands to suspend the licenses of the four black educators involved. These firings, like the firing of other black educators such as Herman Ferguson, John Hatchett, Ursala West, Ralph Poynter, and Vivian Anderson, will not deter the awakening black masses from the main task at hand: putting the devils out of our schools.

THE BLACK PSYCHOLOGIST:

PAWN OR PROFESSIONAL?*

by Jesse J. Johnson

WHEN THE ASSOCIATION of Black Psychologists first issued a call for participants on this panel, I was involved in the following situation in a northern Westchester community. The situation was as follows: A racially tense atmosphere existed in a rather large high school where blacks constituted about 13 percent of the population. There had been several recent incidents, and there were many who were apprehensive that a major explosion was imminent. There were a number of blacks who were regarded as "not deriving maximum benefit from the school opportunity" and it was felt that if a black person were brought in to counsel them, the situation might be improved. It soon became apparent that what was really wanted was someone to "quiet the natives," and there was much more importance attached to considerations of "law and order" than to the needs of the students. In this situation I clearly felt I was a pawn. There was a long list of blacks who had either been on the verge of expulsion or had actually been recommended for removal. I soon began receiving communications of the following variety: "Dr. XYZ, the school psychiatrist, was wondering if perhaps you might not think that Mamie Jones is too disturbed to function in the environment of this school and whether in fact you thought she might be better situated in a setting for the emotionally disturbed." On the other hand, I felt something of a pawn of the students. They were quick to perceive that attendance at weekly sessions with me afforded them some degree of immunity from immediate explusion from school. Any additional motivation for coming was not apparent to me. When I insisted to the administration that the students not experience a sense of coercion and advised the students that the sessions were entirely voluntary, attendance dropped sharply and the project was eventually terminated.

*Paper presented to the Eastern Psychological Association, Philadelphia, Pennsylvania, April 11, 1969.

I suppose that there may be some value in devoting the time allotted me to an analysis of the factors that contributed to the failure of this project. It is my conviction that a much better purpose would be served by sharing with you my subsequent reflections on the necessity for an organization such as the Association of Black Psychologists and establishing some broad outline as to how I feel its members can make maximum contribution to the black's struggle for human dignity. For me, two things are abundantly clear. There is an inverse ratio between the degree of involvement of the black psychologist in the struggle and the extent to which he is a pawn of the Establishment. Here I simply mean those who have power over the lives of others. There is no historical precedent for any group ever voluntarily surrendering its position of advantage to the less advantaged. Any deviation from the status quo has to be on the terms of the power group. Hence the black psychologist who has a contribution to make to the struggle on his own terms, but who has been maneuvered into a position of minimal involvement by either blacks or whites, is clearly, in effect, a pawn of the Establishment. The second conviction seems to me implicit in the first, i.e., it is extremely doubtful that any significant contribution can be expected from anyone acting as an agent of the established order. This order I feel is all too comfortable in the present hierarchical arrangement and has no real motivation for any other. Many in the vein of Martin Luther King have attempted to engender some discomfort via "pricking the conscience of America" or stirring guilt feelings in the manner of Grier and Cobb. However, as Ken Clark points out in his review of *Black Rage,* this type of activity has been in abundance since the thirties, but the evidence for any resulting fundamental structural change is hardly overwhelming. As psychologists we know that probably the last recommended way of motivating anybody to anything is by creation of feelings of guilt.

Let us recall that I alluded to the black psychologist's being rendered a pawn by the black community. I am in complete agreement with the observation that there is a substantial component of self-hate in all blacks. This has been discussed extensively by such writers as Malcolm X. It is my contention that the present estrangement of the so-called black bourgeois from the black community is clearly a form of self-hate on the part of both principals. It seems to me that E. Franklin Frazier was clearly playing into the hands of the establishment with his classic attack, and the cleavage is being perpetuated by his present-day disciples in the likes of Nathan Hare, a black. Hare's account of his personal experience with black intellectuals is must reading for all would-be racists. I submit that we can hardly afford to respond in kind to the venom of the militant who accuses us of having sold out. Some may have sold, but none are out. Those who think they are deceive themselves. All must come to recognize that self-hate may have had some survival value for us at an earlier period, as it did for those in concentration camps. However, it has no place in the present struggle. Our first order of business is to understand the dynamics of the rejection that we will probably encounter as we attempt to close the ranks. It is imperative that we work this through as we, like it or not, are all in this thing together and can ill afford to withdraw or become indifferent.

The question of how to close the ranks calls to mind one of the criticisms that Nathan Hare makes that I consider valid and that could be leveled at many black psychologists whom I know personally. The criticism is of our seeming reluctance to take to the printed page. I, a single offender, exhort my black colleagues to join me in my resolve to publish as extensively as I possibly can, immediately. I do not intend the type of publication that enhances one's professional career, as for an example articles in the American Psychological Association journals. The messages that I have in mind are intended primarily for black consumption and hence should appear in places that provide maximum exposure to blacks—*Journal of the National Medical Association, Ebony, Liberator, Freedomways, Amsterdam News,* etc. I feel that there are three broad areas where we as profesionals can provide some scientific substance to the black struggle. I feel that these efforts will contribute significantly to the repair of the schism that exists between the black professional and the black community.

The first broad area pertains to the self-concept. It seems to me that the militants appear to be the principal blacks who have a real grasp of the existential dictum that existence precedes essence, and as human beings blacks have subject qualities. Sartre distinguishes between a subject and an object in the example of a table. A table, he argues, has an "essence" which precedes its existence in that it is man-made. The concept existed previously in the mind of man and can be evaluated in terms of the fulfillment of the essence of "tableness," which one may define in advance. Sartre continues that man exists before he has an essence and it is man himself who eventually defines himself. Thus man is a subject in that he defines himself through his own activities, while objects are defined by the activities of subjects. The behavior of the black man in America has been more that of an object as he appears to have accepted a definition of himself that was provided him by those who would exploit him. The militants seem to be saying, "White America, I no longer accept your definition of me. I reject it categorically. I am free to define myself and I have the capacity, which I will exercise forthwith." The militants need to be reassured in their self-definitional pursuits, as there are many forces operative which are calculated to interfere with these efforts. Of equal importance is the necessity to get this message to the segment of the black community which seems to resist this freedom. The reasons are quite complex but it is mandatory that they exercise this freedom lest someone, not of good will, exercise it for them.

The second broad area might be labeled "psychological testing revisited." I submit that psychological tests have been in fact a most effective weapon of the powerful and the privileged, to preserve the existing hierarchical arrangement. Blacks have been led to believe that when they perform differently on these tests an inferior performance reflects an inequality created primarily by nature. The story goes, "Heredity sets the limits beyond which the environment cannot go." This arrangement was consoling to the favored, who felt that nature intended them to be entitled, and the less fortunate were expected to resign themselves to a position of disadvantage. Intellectual inequality is a fundamental assumption of the American way of life. The fundamental requirements of democracy are assumed to have been met if equal opportunity for competition exists among people who are genetically unequal. The American educational system assumes unequal capacity to learn and has developed an extensive armamentarium of psychometric techniques for identifying those thought to be more highly endowed. It is obvious that if in fact people have inherently equal capacities, our system is grounded in quicksand and reinforces arbitrary privilege. Boyer and Walsh recently reviewed the four types of evidence that are typically offered to prove that people are innately different in their capacity to learn. The following were their conclusions:

> Studies of innate intelligence, then, have not produced conclusive evidence to justify the claim for an innate difference in individual intellectual capacity. Equally there has not been conclusive evidence that the innate potential between people is equal. The research is heavily marked by the self-serving beliefs of the researchers. Psychologists have usually created "intelligence" tests which reflect their own values, predetermining that their own scores will be high. When they have discovered they are high they have often proclaimed such tests to be indicators of innate superiority.

Assumptions made about blacks on the basis of their performance on these tests have created their own self-fulfilling prophecies. We know as professionals that we aspire to *creating ability, increasing intelligence,* and *developing interests.* We know that we can help an individual to learn by changing his self-concept, his expectations of his own behavior, and his motivations, as well as his cognitive style and skills. It is imperative that we as black psychologists get this message to the millions of blacks who are fraught with frustration and despair and who have a deeply ingrained sense of incompetence. With their new-found awareness of their actual potential, they will be a much more potent source of pressure for a change in the social system. The elite will no longer be able to console themselves with the validity of their processes of exclusion.

The third broad area might be labeled "psychological invalidism." If the black community were to take seriously the preachments of the writers of the Abram Kardiner and Lionel Ovesey ilk, with their concept of the mark of oppression, or their present-day counterparts, such as Kenneth Clark (*Dark Ghetto*) and Grier and Cobb (*Black Rage*), it could only conclude that the black community abounds with psychological cripples. I doubt seriously if many blacks would recognize themselves in the portraits that have been presented of them by these writers. I feel that I can compare ghetto experiences on the West and South Sides of Chicago and Jefferson Avenue, in St. Louis, Missouri, with any of the people that these writers describe, but I do not feel that my self-concept could have been derived from their conclusions. I insist that we, as black psychologists, must get the message to the black masses that they have a choice as to whether they view themselves as having been scarred for all eternity. I have seen reviews of Claude Brown's *Manchild in the Promised Land* which dismissed the work as the type of a hustler. I am not convinced. This is exactly the type of option that I am talking about.

From the above remarks, it is obvious that I reject the conclusions of Grier and Cobb, who state, "The black intellectual must accept his exclusion from this battle." I have conviction that with continuing messages of the three types I have mentioned, the black community will cease to view us as "outsider" and eventually we will be able to meet the Man together—singing, if you like—not "We shall overcome" but "I ain't gonna be your low-down dog no more!"

HUMANIZING OUR SCHOOLS*

by Nathan Wright, Jr.

THE LATE PROFESSOR John Dewey of Columbia University, spent several generations encouraging—and warning—Americans to make our nation's educational enterprise far more humane than it was even in his day.

It has remained principally for a growing number of black educators and black student protesters—all working for the betterment of the nation's life—to give John Dewey's work some ready promise of substantial fulfillment.

Black students and educators are now commanding the attention of the nation. They are saying essentially that in America's scandalous failure to meet the basic needs of black boys and girls, we have also created unwittingly a demon which incidentally demeans and destroys in some measure the lives of us all.

If we are self-interested enough to simply listen, we may learn from our increasingly self-aware and thoughtful black educators and black student dissenters much which we need to hear for the good of all of our nation's youth. Indeed, we may even learn some invaluable lessons for the immediate benefit of those young people who are closest to us, those who live in our own households.

In no aspect of the American educational process is a doubtless unconscious but deeply structured inhumanity more evident than in our longstanding approaches to pupil progress.

The basic purpose of education is to help pupils to learn. Yet the overwhelming and growing evidence over the years points to the fact that we place a disproportionate emphasis upon testing in relation to teaching. What testing actually measures, in the most devastatingly revealing way,

*From Newark *Star-Ledger*, May 4, 1969.

is the capacity or incapacity of our teachers to help pupils to learn.

In all of our schools, our teachers should be taking a developmental or tutorial approach to the needs of all of our pupils, the so called "bright" and "disadvantaged" alike.

Bright pupils especially should be aided in extending the horizons of their interest. Teacher failure to inspire bright students—both in our inner city and suburban schools—is one of the major causes of disruptive behavior by students with "above average" capacity.

A surprisingly large number of black and white "drop-outs" are those highly imaginative and exceedingly bright students whom our schools "turn off" and then soon thereafter find cause to "thrust out."

So much of the "off beat" and anti-social behavior in youth from middle-class homes comes from the fact that our youth see their teachers —with whom they spend most of each day—as prime representatives of our society. A teacher who fails to see a pupil as one to be inspired in a thoughtful and creative way fosters directly an atmosphere in which the pupil comes to hate or reject the society which the teacher is seen to represent.

In our colleges also, we need to take a tutorial approach to the needs of all of our students. It is good to set up special tutorial programs for "disadvantaged" black youth. It would be far wiser—and helpfully decent—to take the same facilitating or tutorial approach to the needs of all students, whether above or below average and whether black or white.

No student who is willing to learn should ever be failed in a course, except for the gravest cause. The purpose of human life is to be encouraged toward the fulfillment of what it is designed to be.

Teachers who place obstacles and stumbling blocks in the paths of their students are essentially revealing a far too prevalent and institutionalized contempt for human life.

Further, because of racial attitudes which are deeply embedded in our behavior in every aspect of American life, black students have been knocked out of the learning enterprise far more extensively than have white students. Nonetheless, all students are hurt in some degree in an inherently but unintentionally evil process which fails to see its task as that of assuring every life the greatest hope of reaching its optimum potential.

Any teacher, for example, who gives a test with mystery in it reflects a latent irreverence for human life. A growing number of black teachers report that—in order to strengthen the capacity of students to learn on their own—they have their pupils prepare what they consider ideal examination questions.

A pupil who can write a good set of examination questions is one with a growing capacity to organize his own materials for study. All students might be helped TO LEARN HOW TO LEARN, if they were required to prepare for each examination ideal test questions and then these questions were discussed or critiqued in class.

Is not our humane purpose, after all—as John Dewey and so many others have sought to remind us—to encourage in all of our students the capacity for self-directed growth?

What about the test questions that are actually given? Might not the class decide on the best questions and then proceed, with the help of the teacher, to outline the answers for the benefit of all?

There could scarcely be a more efficient way to assure that all the students understand, prior to the time of testing, the basic materials at hand.

So far as the test marks are concerned, most teachers grade on a "curve," at any rate. Those pupils who handle the materials with the greatest insight or imagination would then receive the highest marks.

What if, in spite of the help already given, a pupil fails to come up to the level that either the teacher or the pupil would desire? There is no law which prevents the teacher from immediately giving the pupil further simple work to do which would assure a better mastery of the materials. Then right away the mark could be upgraded to some extent.

We need to take another very serious look at the business of "averaging" marks, as this too speaks rather clearly about the degree of humaneness in our schools.

At the beginning of a semester—in trying hard to "get the hang" of a course—students may make marks which are not up to par. Should these poor marks made early in a course be averaged with superior marks at the end of a course?

Not so, if the teacher believes that life is designed for growth.

Our teachers and administrators—and all in our society—must come to see that it is not where life comes FROM but where we may help to take it "TO" that counts. "Averaging" poor marks with good ones may often reflect our unthinking disregard of life as involving the continuous unfolding of human possibilities.

In the old days—actually within my own memory—many of our small

American church-oriented colleges assumed that any pupil who had gumption enough to come to college should graduate.

The teachers in these schools saw their task as that of helping their students to become able servants of their fellow-men. Of our black colleges, until not long ago, was this particularly true. There were not the failure rates—in regard to the development of the nation's priceless human potential, with which we are all too sadly familiar today.

In all of our schools—from kindergarten through graduate school—this thoroughly humane and deeply thoughtful spirit needs to be revived.

This—in essence—is what John Dewey meant when he sought to train educators who would give shape to a civilized and civilizing nation.

This also is no less than what our black students and educators are asking for. Suburbanites and urbanites, both black and white, would benefit from it. In so doing, the nation as a whole would prosper.

Further, what better way to honor—even at this late and urgent hour—a mighty prophet among us who saw education in the noble way that we should see it?

We are thus challenged to see education FOR ALL IN OUR SOCIETY TODAY as the great humanizing and fulfilling force in a national community of men and women whose destiny for its every part it is to be both great and free.

PART II

THE WHITE ESTABLISHMENT

URBAN SCHOOLTEACHING:

THE PERSONAL TOUCH*

by Lawrence Hawkins

IT SEEMS APPARENT at this time that schools in the inner city must play a role that is different from the role played in the suburbs. For years we labored under the impression that equal educational opportunity could be provided by merely increasing funds to provide additional people and materials for inner-city schools. At this time I am almost completely convinced that additional funds alone will not guarantee improved educational achievement. This to me is one of the most significant lessons that we have learned from Elementary and Secondary Education Act Title I projects. The provision of quantitative experiences for boys and girls without providing at the same time quality in the experiences will not improve academic achievement. Quality comes with good teacher-pupil relationships.

In the January 1968 issue of the *Phi Delta Kappan*, James Kent, in reviewing the Coleman Report, makes the following statement:

> Whatever divergent views men like Coleman, Moynihan, and Bowles may have relative to the means by which equality of education is to be achieved, they would all stress the unique importance of people—students, teachers, parents, community.
> Educators who continue to think of equality in terms of "things" such as buildings, books, and curriculum do so at their peril.

In all that is done in the name of equalization of opportunities or compensatory education, it is necessary that educators keep in mind that *what* is done is important, but *how* it is done is more important. The *quality* of relationship between the teacher and the deprived child must be one of depth. The teacher must communicate concern *for* and belief *in* the inner-city school child in such a way that the child sees himself as being able to face and solve his problems, whether they be in the

*A position paper for Urban Teachers, Cincinnati Public Schools, March, 1969.

school, in the home, or in the general community. The child must be able to see the possibility of becoming a more effective person than most of the people with whom he has contact daily.

Teachers, counselors, parents, and other pupil personnel workers are mirrors into which boys and girls look to see themselves, to see what they are. If adults reflect negative images to children, they will tend to develop negative images of themselves. If adults reflect positive images to pupils, they will tend to develop positive images of themselves and behave in positive ways. Therefore, it is very important that educators be concerned about the images that they reflect to children with whom they work daily.

Marion D. Fantini and Gerald Weinstein, in *Toward a Contact Curriculum*, emphasize major considerations for curriculum development and classroom activities. Four determinants of relevant curricular content suggested are: (1) what is taught, (2) how it is taught, (3) the learners' feelings, and (4) the learners' concerns. A lack of relevance in any of the four areas or on any of what might be called four levels may cause the curriculum to lack meaning to the disadvantaged pupil and thereby limit his quality and quantity of learning. It is pointed out that the third and fourth levels or areas are more often ignored than the first two. Another quote from Fantini and Weinstein summarizes the importance of "affective" relevance indicated in areas three and four:

> Educators are not answering the spoken and more often unspoken questions children ask themselves: "Why do I feel the way I do? What makes me do that? Do they think I'm any good?" Rather than try to supply insights to these questions, the school, instead, asks children, "What do we mean by the Common Market?" "How are animals and people different?" Ignored in the process is one of the child's most persistent questions: "What does it have to do with me?" Unless there is this connection with the child's experiential and emotional framework, the knowledge that he gains will be of little significance and may not be manifested in the types of behavior spelled out by the aims of education.

The May–June 1968 issue of the National Association of Secondary School Principals bulletin, *Spotlight*, describes a good school program as one where pupils are helped to see the "big" world, feel worthy of claiming a part of it as a goal, develop values, attitudes, and habits consistent with the goal, and see classroom work as relevant to goals set for themselves. This is another way of approaching the problem of relevance in the curriculum.

Individualized instruction is a much-worked term in discussions of teaching techniques used by successful teachers of the disadvantaged. Programmed instruction, teaching machines, auto-instruction, computer-based instruction, and individual schedules of reinforcement are related. All aspects of individualized instruction require a highly competent teacher. Miriam Goldberg in the Association of Supervision and Curriculum Development publication *Educating the Children of the Poor* emphasizes the following propositions regarding teaching practices and materials:

1. Each pupil's status in each learning area has to be ascertained. Teaching must begin where the pupil is, regardless of grade level–age differential, and materials must be appropriate to his present level. No assumptions can be made about the child's prior knowledge derived from home or neighborhood experiences.

2. Each pupil merits respect as a person, appreciation of his efforts, and understanding of his problems. The teacher must not show by word, look, or gesture that the child's inability to perform adequately or his lack of comprehension of even the most rudimentary concepts is shocking or disturbing.

3. All procedures need to be paced in accordance with the pupil's speed of learning. No assumptions should be made that the child has grasped what has been taught until he is able to demonstrate his grasp over and over again in a variety of contexts.

4. The learning situation needs to have a high degree of structure and consistency so that the child knows what is expected of him at all times and is neither confused nor tempted to test the limits through inappropriate behavior.

5. The learning situation should provide a maximum of positive reinforcement and a minimum of negative reinforcement. Self-teaching materials as well as the teacher should confront the learner with as few tests as possible in which there is a high probability of error.

6. The classroom as well as the after-school learning activities should provide as much one-to-one teacher-pupil learning contact as possible.

7. Materials should be related to the world of the learner but not limited to his immediate environment. Stories about cowboys and rockets may prove more exciting and thus a better learning medium than those about the local firehouse and the sanitation truck.

8. One additional proposition needs to be stated, derived not from evidence but from the basic values underlying education in a democracy: Although the school should start where the learner is, its responsibility is to enable him to move as far as he can go, which is often much further than he himself regards as his limit.

ESEA Title I has taught us that indigenous workers can be hired to carry out successfully many aspects of Title I projects. In some cases, teacher aides, home–school liaison personnel, social-work aides, counselor aides, health aides, and others show ability to communicate with boys and girls and parents that is superior to many of us that are certified as teachers.

An excellent example is a teacher aide in a Cincinnati project who is about fifty-five years old, only a high-school graduate, but highly interested in athletics and in children in general. He has worked in projects from the preschool level through the junior-high-school level in a highly commendable way. He has shown a unique ability to work with emotionally disturbed children of all ages and now serves in a diagnostic unit that is designed to study and make special plans for boys and girls who cannot adjust to the regular school program. At times school principals have been more reluctant to give up the help of this teacher aide than they were the help of certified persons. Many other paraprofessionals have demonstrated that there is a place for the indigenous worker in the schools of the inner city.

Teacher behavior is worked in all of the approaches to educational improvement indicated above. Interaction between teachers and pupils, curriculum improvement, individualized instruction, and the use of new human resources are all parts of comprehensive efforts to improve the educational experience of disadvantaged learners. As individual teachers see more clearly their roles and improve their teaching strategies, so does education of disadvantaged children improve.

A good teacher of educationally deprived children is one who can see value in spending his professional life working with children who will not become, except in rare cases, scientists or highly professional persons. Successful teachers in city schools must be able to perceive themselves to be worthwhile whenever they have helped any child become a more effective person than he was. Yet the sky must be seen as the limit to the best potential in every person.

We recognize that the teacher cannot be all things to all people. We know that parents and general home conditions will have a great influence upon what a child will become. However, we also believe that one person, the teacher, in spite of negative home and family influence, can make the difference in the way that a given child sees himself and correspondingly in the way that he behaves and in his capacity to become what he is designed ideally to be. There have been examples of lives that were changed completely because of the influence of *one* person, a teacher who cared.

In George Bernard Shaw's *Pygmalion,* Eliza Doolittle, when discussing with Colonel Pickering her attempt to become a lady rather than a flower girl, is quoted as follows:

You see, really and truly, apart from the things anyone can pick up (the dressing and the proper way of speaking, and so on), the difference between a lady and a flower girl is not how she behaves, but how she's treated. I shall always be a flower girl to Professor Higgins, because he always treats me as a flower girl, and always will; but I know I can be a lady to you, because you always treat me as a lady, and always will.

In a similar way, boys and girls become largely what our professional conduct toward them causes them to become. Teacher behavior and expectations are thus the most significant ingredients in urban teaching. They have been, doubtless unconsciously, the cause of much of our present condition in urban education. With a deeper self-awareness and an awareness of their crucial roles in relation to pupil learning, we may look to humanely inspired teaching as the key to educational excellence for those who attend our urban schools.

BIBLIOGRAPHY

Marion D. Fantini and Gerald Weinstein, *Toward a Contact Curriculum.* Anti-Defamation League of B'nai B'rith, New York, N.Y.

Alexander Frazier, *Educating the Children of the Poor.* Association for Supervision and Curriculum Development, NEA, 1968.

Robert Rosenthal and Lenore Jacobson, *Pygmalion in the Classroom.* Holt, Rinehart and Winston, Inc., 1968.

THE EDUCATION OF BLACK CHILDREN*

by M. Lee Montgomery

A FEW MONTHS ago Dr. Ruth Hayre, superintendent of District 4, issued a call to teachers, principals, parents, students, and community residents of the North Philadelphia area for an "Educational Goals Conference." Discussion would center on the question, "What should schools and the community be doing to better meet the needs of boys and girls in these areas?"[1] With the question so ably stated, Dr. Hayre had laid before all of us the gigantic task of making education relevant to black children, and of probing the depths of our thinking to create, develop, and deliver new substance, methods, and techniques in curriculum.

Such questions are of importance because of what is happening to black children in inner-city schools. Of all of the young men and women who do graduate, 60 percent are functionally illiterate. They are unable to read at a sixth-grade level. All this means is that they have difficulty reading and understanding the daily newspaper. And as the twenty-first century rushes upon us, we must ask ourselves, What kind of world will it be when these children grow up? Technology will surely continue to advance. Then what skills must men and women have? How will they relate to each other? What will happen to those who have not been taught how to live and mastered a skill by the twenty-first century? Will they be able to survive in a highly mechanized and depersonalized society? What will the great cities of this nation be like? Will they still be growing in inner-city density with black people? What will education be in the twenty-first century? Let us not dwell upon this, because our reason for being here is a recognition that there are some things which all of us must begin to do *now!*

We have as community and school made some steps toward opening

*Delivered at Staff Development Institute, Fitz Simons Junior High School, Philadelphia, Pennsylvania, August 20, 1968.

the lines of discovery of new methods of communication with one another. The pressures for change in curriculum, career development, and community involvement, as well as in staffing and personnel development, reflect the growing concern of parents about the education of our children. The question raised at the goals conference can be more simply stated: "What does education mean for black boys and girls?" What is education's purpose? Shall we begin with the examination of a very basic measurement instrument of the educational system—tests? We need not, at this time, enter into the discussion of the relevancy of such instruments to the life style of the black child. An aerospace engineer, Clarence Harris, states in a monograph that "both cultural bias and bias based on color can and does effect the validity of tests and, therefore, the results of administered tests."[2] That is to say, these instruments have built-in biases and the results have to be biased. We have talked briefly about tests because we use them to provide the information in order to determine the development of the child, and very rarely do we question the validity of the measurement. But we are not here to speak about the many inadequacies of current tests; we are just as concerned with what we, as community, and you, as teachers, can and must do to make education an in-depth and meaningful learning experience for each child.

CULTURAL AND ETHNIC SENSITIVITY

In order to achieve the cohesiveness that we wish, we must first do some very basic things, such as getting to know each other. We should feel very comfortable in talking with one another. This has something to do with "attitudes." This raises a concern of our attitude toward each other; toward each child. Let's be honest and recognize that there are variations in our attitudes toward each other. A gap does exist between black and white, particularly in issues of race and values. Values may relate to spiritual or materialistic goals. The frank acknowledgment of the gap is a must if we are to begin to mend the break. How do we begin? Well, again, let me repeat a recognition on the part of each of us that we must attempt to overcome our shortcomings and in the process begin to discover the new *me*.

Parents want to be partners with teachers in the education of their children. There are three major facets to this desire. The first is the desire to have their cultural differences recognized and appreciated. Thus, as teachers you must appreciate the styles of speech, the mode of dress, the natural hair, the dashiki, the beads or the medallions which are popular in or indigenous to the black culture. Rules which are superfluous and offensive to black parents and students should be modified or discarded. Second, integration into this school community involves the development of a genuine sense of community among teachers, students, and parents. A lack of this sense of community has been revealed in the past by the behavior and attitudes of teachers, students, and parents. Finally, black children desire and need to be loved for themselves and be a vital part of all activity. Every child would, if the climate of opportunity is provided, be a participant. This is not a call to limit the inputs in the educational process, but rather an effort to point out where the desire of parents and children is focused.

Alvin Poussaint has written: "For all that may be said about student, parental, and teacher desire in order to understand the black man's self-image, self-concept, and Who am I? we must go back to the time of birth and creation of the 'American Negro.' "[3]

This, of course, brings us to the matter of the black man's heritage. Everyone is getting into the act of teaching Afro-American history. And the cry is loud that anyone can teach Afro-American history. And this is probably true, but for some of us black history or Afro-American history must be taught with perspective. Ron Karenga said, "Black history demands definition, interpretation, in terms of the movements of this nation and the world. Our heroes stand as symbols of the onward movement of man."[4] Thus black people must be able to relate today's events to yesteryear's facts in a way that helps us indicate tomorrow's meanings. I've mentioned history because of the great wave of concern which flows through this land. The value of history as well as the value of the total black experience—myths, soul, etc.—in the context of our gathering here is to provide an opportunity for all of us to understand what the struggle is all about today. We cannot define for any child or adult the purpose and the meaning of his life. What we can do is create conditions in which he can find his own purpose and meaning in life.

COMMUNITY AND SCHOOL

It has long been whispered that you, teachers and administrators, should beware of community people. They are without information, ignorant, stupid, harassing, ill-tempered, and don't understand a thing about educating children. So often we—that is, those of us who have been able to acquire skills—place a limit on human resourcefulness. What parents are really concerned about is the development of human potential and the liberation of the human spirit. Now I know this covers an awful lot of ground, but let's meditate for a moment.

As parents, let us look at how our children are perceived. First, they are conceived of as slow learners and really unable to master this middle-class school system. They are told you're out of it by the attitude and behavior of the teachers. The process of alienation begins from the first encounter and tends to continue with peer groups in and out of school. Hence, these same black youth are comfortable with their friends and many times they are able to organize very sophisticated social groups (gangs) which we could view as an extension of the family. We can say this because the desire of belonging and identifying is very strong, and out of it grows group cohesiveness and loyalty. Second, we, as parents, are told that our children are beset with all of the woes of life, lack of self-esteem, and serious behavior problems. And more than that, parents are responsible for these bad kids. This is true; the point I am trying to make here is that it is most important that each of you try to understand some of the frustrations which a black parent is compelled to go through each day—the constant decimation of character, the mental as well as spiritual suffering—all of this in an effort to survive. This limits the amount of time parents can spend with children. A more important question is, What are parents really saying when they talk about "community control of schools"? They mean not only physical control, but more importantly the control of information and learning for the liberation of the human spirit. In brief, the battle is for the minds of our children. We express our concern for our survival as an ethnic people in a battle of *who controls the minds of our children*. Thus, it becomes very very clear that no parent wants to see his child develop into an inhuman being.

So the purpose of our being here today is to develop the kind of relationship which will provide an opportunity to understand why it is important for black parents to say how their children are to be educated. At best, every black child has a constant battle to keep from being shunted aside as incapable of learning. There is no question in my mind that black children are destroyed daily by innuendo, by verbal and non-verbal communications. That the child is compelled to learn only those things which relate to the dominant culture in this nation. What we are really talking about in relevancy of curriculum is that which puts life itself in the context of the learning process as the most precious input into the black child's experience.

Therefore, what we do today, tomorrow, next week and in the months to come will have an impact upon every child. Our main concern is that that impact have positive effects on the child. Black consciousness leads to black awareness leads to black power leads to self-reliance. Not everyone will understand the importance of these phrases, but somehow all should attempt to empathize with black parents and students. Of course, we will make mistakes, but I feel that the task is too great to confront it with little energy and little commitment. Today this activity demands your personal commitment to a *task.*

NOTES

1. Conference Report—a priority of the conference was to initiate a five-year plan of action.
2. "The Aerospace Scientist as a Local, National, and Worldwide Community Planner," Clarence J. Harris, General Electric, Valley Forge, Pennsylvania, page 6, Conflicts.
3. Alvin F. Poussaint, M.D., *The Negro American, His Self-Image and Integration.*
4. Ron Karenga, speech in Detroit, March 31, 1968.

THE NEW LITERATURE ON EDUCATION

OF THE BLACK CHILD*

by Edward K. Weaver

DURING THE 1960's a "new" literature emerged based in a concern for the education of the disadvantaged and especially compensatory education for black ghetto children. This literature has been written mostly by whites and, to some extent, is directed toward white audiences. Funding for the programs and projects has come from both the private and the public sectors, and the programs are usually directed by white professionals. The purpose of this article is to try to answer the following questions:

1. Are the books about the education of the black ghetto child too hurriedly written? Do they have over-all value?

2. Why is the problem of educating black ghetto children being brought to the public at this time if, as the "new" literature implies, the condition has existed for thirty or more years?

3. Does what is presented in these books reflect a form of planned retardation for black ghetto children on the part of boards of education?

4. Inasmuch as these books were written about the education of the black ghetto child in the Northern urban ghetto, should comparative studies be made of the black child in the North as against the South?

Attempts to answer these questions will be in a holistic frame—that is, all four questions will be dealt with at once. At the end of the analysis, specific answers will be given for each question. The following assumptions operate as hypotheses or biases in the remainder of this article:

1. Compensatory education (education of the disadvantaged, for the culturally deprived) is a "copout" of educators to cover up the poor quality of education and the inadequately staffed and housed schools which have been afforded the low-income and minority-group children.

2. The deprivation theory, proposed in the "new" literature, and the

*From *Freedomways*, 4th quarter, 1968.

programs for black ghetto children place the blame on the black children and their parents and thereby free the school systems, the communities, and the society from sharing the responsibility.

3. The history of neglect of the education of low-income pupils and of superior provisions for the advantaged has frozen low-income pupils into social classes, and handicapped them for life.

4. Cultural deprivation has been a conscious policy and is still a major factor excluding black children and youth from appreciating, gaining, or becoming able to utilize the full potentials of public education—the major factor perpetuating this situation is white racism as applied to the black poor.

5. The compensatory-education programs for the black ghetto child are too little, too late, and are based in theories of colonialism, dependency, power, and have been inordinately influenced by the conditions which private and public funding agencies stipulate as bases for obtaining grants. Very little funding comes directly from the public school systems themselves.

6. Many of the programs are segregated (Educational Improvement Programs, Headstart, Follow-Up, and the like) and are designed as a sop to black people. They are artificially induced and die when funds cease.

7. Compensatory-education programs for black ghetto children help to salve and ease the conscience of white citizens by making them believe that something significant is being done for the black people.

In 1492 Columbus sailed the ocean blue and "discovered" America—that is, white Europeans first learned that an America existed. In less than four centuries these white Catholics and WASP's (White Anglo-Saxon Protestants) had stolen the land from the red "savages," driven them onto reservations, brought millions of black enslaved persons from Africa, and turned the South into the biggest brothel in the history of mankind. In the 1960's the black ghetto child was "discovered" and a "new" rapidly advancing specialized field of education was invented—compensatory education for the disadvantaged. A rash of books and articles, mostly written by whites, emerged. The wretched, the black poor, the black alienated, the black misfits, had been "discovered."

For purposes of this article some seventy-five books and more than 250 articles were reviewed. Only a few, prototypes, will be specified. The over-all reaction to the "new" literature is that it is full of debate about unclarified issues. Much of the debate is about the proper designation of the area (the deprived, the disadvantaged, the alienated, the wretched, the poor, or, as one individual puts it, the depraved). Another persistent issue is whether the education of black ghetto types should be considered as a separate area of specialization within the broad spectrum of education or whether it should be considered as a problem which resides within each of the already well established areas or fields of concern and interest in education.

This article will not deal with the universe of controversial problems that educators now begin to call problems of the education of disadvantaged children and youth. Special problems of disadvantage which groups such as Mexicans, Indians, poor whites, and others encounter in the American democratic society will not be dealt with. For a central thesis of this paper is that solution of the problems of the black people in the United States and elsewhere will, at the same time, solve the problems of all the oppressed and exploited peoples in the United States. When black Americans are free and equal and have been liberated, all Americans will have freedom, equality, and liberty. For the United States has become a racist and separatist society—separate for black and separate for white.

The black people in the United States have been studied and manipulated more than any other group of Americans. Most master's and doctoral studies conducted by black scholars have dealt with aspects of the "Negro problem." Thousands of books and articles have been written about the black people in the United States. Much of this literature was produced by black sociologists, anthropologists, economists, social workers, historians, psychologists, and educators, such as W. E. B. DuBois, Horace Mann Bond, Charles S. Johnson and his colleagues, Carter G. Woodson and his colleagues, Ira De A. Reid, E. Franklin Frazier, Hylan Lewis, Lawrence D. Reddick, Ralph Bunche, Rayford Logan, Doxey A. Wilkerson, St. Clair Drake, Herman Long, Preston and Bonita Valien, Allison Davis, Mozell Hill, Kenneth B. Clark. The essential point here is that the "new" literature on the education of the black ghetto child ignores this literature. It also ignores literature and research such as the Carnegie Corporation-sponsored comprehensive study of the Negro in the United States which Gunnar Myrdal, a Swedish social economist, summarized in *An American Dilemma.* The "new" literature, in ignoring this vast scientific literature about the black people, has no roots, and indeed, sets out to be "new" by deliberately operating as if it were a new field.

When the "new" literature is read, then one who is already sophisticated in the problems and proposed solutions for the black people concludes that the "new" literature is for uninitiated whites who must be convinced that it is now necessary to do something about the poor quality of education for black children. One feels somewhat like Kenneth B.

Clark, whose perceptive comment before the National Advisory Commission on Civil Disorders (the Kerner report), stated:

> . . . in candor, . . . a kind of Alice in Wonderland—with the same moving picture reshown over and over again, the same analysis, the same recommendations, and the same inaction.

On the other hand there are some serious studies and reports which seek to deal directly with the past literature and the present situation. The work of Kvaraceus, *Dynamics of Delinquency;* of Frost and Hawkes, *The Disadvantaged Child;* of Bereiter and Englemann, *Teaching Disadvantaged Children in the Preschool;* of Riessman, *The Culturally Deprived Child;* and even the Kozol documentary, *Death at an Early Age,* on "the destruction of the hearts and minds of Negro children in the Boston Public Schools" are clearly and forcefully written and one reads these with a sense of ease and familiarity, and of identification with the material. It is almost as if one already knows or has experienced this and the book merely synthesizes, or sharply specifies—as if one has read this somewhere sometime before. Only a very, very few of the white writers of the "new" literature have the insight, capacity, or creativity to write in this way. To repeat, the "new" literature is new only for the uninitiated, the newcomer, the still uncertain white.

More basic and more useful are the works of Arthur Pearl and Frank Riessman, *New Careers for the Poor,* based primarily on the study and research at the Howard University Institute for Youth Studies; of Edmund W. Gordon and Doxey A. Wilkerson at Yeshiva University, *Compensatory Education for the Disadvantaged;* and of Harry L. Miller, *Education for the Disadvantaged. New Careers* is potentially one of the most provocative, sophisticated, and significant books to emerge from the plethora of the "new" literature in its specification and demonstration of what can be done, efficiently and quickly. The Gordon-Wilkerson book is the most comprehensive analysis and evaluation of programs and practices in compensatory education from preschool through college which is available at this time. Yeshiva also publishes the IRCD Bulletin (Information Retrieval Center on the Disadvantaged), which with ERIC (Education Retrieval and Information Center) and some other potential sources make possible consideration of cognitive and affective dimensions of behavior as a single process. The Miller book, *Education for the Disadvantaged,* is one of a series intended to cope with the information explosion affecting all of the arts and sciences and is a substitute for a bibliographical guide to the current literature—it is one of the more comprehensive analyses of current issues and research on education for the disadvantaged.

One of the factors involved in the rash of "new" literature on the education of the black ghetto child is the dilemma of the white missionary type. Peace Corps, VISTA, and Teacher Corps now attract the middle-class white youth who are dedicated and consecrated, and they have increasingly supplanted the WASP missionary types who are not quite as welcome in the Near and Far East, in Latin America, in Africa, or in the slums. What is left for white professionals? The education of the black Americans. "Discovery" of the black ghetto child and proliferation of a special educational enterprise for the disadvantaged is a financially attractive endeavor, for very large sums of money are now available from both the public and private sector for the compensatory education of the black ghetto children and youth. Moreover, the Education Professions Development Act (EPDA) will make even larger sums available for educating the disadvantaged at all levels.

The following is indicative of this kind of concern. *The Atlanta Constitution* (Vol. 101, Nos. 48 and 49) under the general headline for a series "Educating the Disadvantaged" stated under the headline (August 12, 1968) "Project Headstart Lifts Slum Children":

> Modern educators have decided the best way to attack the problems of educating the disadvantaged child is *with preschool programs designed to eliminate the causes of his deprivation. Leading the field in the race to educate children before the ravages of poverty become irreversible is the federal government's massive Project Headstart.* [Italics mine.]

On August 13, 1968, under the head "City to Test Learning in Pre-School Years," the following appeared:

> Atlanta school officials have decided the time has come to institute programs designed to measure the effects of preschool education on disadvantaged youth. *As a result the city school system this year will participate in the federally sponsored Project Follow-Through,* an attempt to give deprived children in the primary grades the same specialized care provided by the summer Headstart Program. [Italics mine.]

In passing, it should be indicated that only 225 of the thousands of children who will attend the Atlanta public schools (preschool, early childhood, kindergarten, and first grades) will be given this follow-through treatment. It was stated that school officials indicated that the school system will not have the funds itself to accommodate all of the city's disadvantaged children and the project will be regarded as in the "pilot stage" and take place in two "Negro" elementary schools. The objectives of this program, typical of hundreds all over the United States, are:

1. To help each child develop intellectually by providing programs designed to compensate for his deprivation.

2. To help each child develop socially by relating the contents of subject matter to personal attitudes and behavior.

3. To help each child avoid losing the benefits of his education by including parents as active members of the educational program.

4. The main purpose is to help each child (to teach each child) to be an independent learner. The model for the sequential program of instruction is that developed by Dr. Lassar G. Gotkin of New York University.

Miller, in *Education for the Disadvantaged*, indicates that programs for the disadvantaged may be criticized on the grounds that they do not emphasize what should be emphasized and that they are uncreative. However, the reviewers go further and state that this does not constitute the most serious charge which may be leveled against them. Educators tend to become concerned with outcomes (changes in behavior?) which are long delayed or even unmeasurable. The "new" literature and the programs they describe, such as the Educational Improvement Projects funded by Ford, are so anxious to see success for their expensive efforts and to justify the millions of dollars which are involved that the directors and advisory committees become strongly committed to whatever the project or program is alleged to be about. Moreover, the agency personnel responsible for the large grants are also strongly desirous of success for efforts and for results which may be interpreted as successful. Consequently glowing reports are written about the effectiveness of the programs for the disadvantaged but very little data are collected or published which specify how changes in behavior are induced or even the actual changes which accrue to the children as they participate in the program. Changes are reported in general mass data based on tests which may or may not be germane to the children, or their ghetto experience.

Moreover, very few teachers and even fewer administrators are prepared to believe that the one-group procedure, which is so consistently used, should be abandoned. This procedure gives such very poor evidence of program effectiveness. The result is that the "new" literature presents, as yet, very, very few reasonable grounds for the many claims and allegations of causal connections between improvement and procedure. There is an alarming lack of the classical required and necessary effort for control and comparison in the "new" literature and in the programs for the disadvantaged. Dr. Doxey A. Wilkerson, in *Education for the Disadvantaged,* identifies this deficit this way:

> The research evaluation of any program of compensatory education would seem to require (a) precise description of the educational experiences involved, (b) clear formulation of hypotheses concerning the effects of specified and controlled pragmatic activities, (c) definition of appropriate tests of such hypotheses, and (d) collection and interpretation of relevant data through technically adequate procedures. Most of the studies here reviewed do not satisfy any of these requirements, and their infirmities are less pronounced than those of many other investigations not selected for review. As a consequence currently available research in this field typically reports ambiguous outcomes of unknown or amorphous educational variables.

The result is that much of the "new" literature and, perhaps, many of the programs for the disadvantaged, are based on naïve, perhaps even intuitive, decisions and programming. This possibly accounts for many of the contradictory and premature conceptual bases and trends which the "new" literature reflects. It is also quite likely that, since a very, very few of the programs and/or projects are directed at the decision and policy-making level by black professionals, some of the contradictory and premature aspects of education for the deprived are due to inadequate experience with, identification with, or insightful understanding of the victims of compensatory education.

The most pervasive and significant of the influences on education for the black ghetto child now appears to be due to the changes which black people are making in themselves, and which they are introducing into the society. The white racists have believed that white is right and that whites can do anything they choose. The white racists still believe that they have the right to spoil things or make things right. It is this arrogance which black people now challenge, and more and more it is stated that this arrogance is what had led us into Vietnam, and is responsible for what has been done to the liberation movements all over the world, and to the liberation movement of black people here at home. Today more and more black people believe that there is no real desire or sincere program for basic social change.

Most black people cannot understand why so many white people do not accept the Kerner report, which said that the United States is a racist society. More and more black people dislike the fact that black people are still being asked to side with white people who think that if the blacks went a little slower or if they didn't express their anger, more would be accomplished. And all those clichés bug black people, like "We did it, why can't you?" or "What do you people *really* want?" When white people say, "Hasn't there been a great deal of progress in the past few years?" the black man says, "Yes, there has been a little. But I don't have to settle for a little."

So perhaps the most significant factor influencing present concern over the education of the black ghetto children and youth is now coming out into the open. For some, the summer programs and swimming pools and other activities are seen as not only a "cooling down" operation, but also as a blind alley, a kind of miasma or form of planned retardation, and as a sop to the conscience of whites. Martin Luther King, Jr., and now Ralph Abernathy, Stokely Carmichael, H. Rap Brown, LeRoi Jones, Malcolm X, the hippie movement growing out of white youth participation in SCLC in Mississippi, Resurrection City, and the black nationalist movement have all made the white man aware. A large part of this awareness is the explosion of the four-hundred-year-old myth of the "good nigger." It also is due to discovery that many black people don't even have pity for the white racists.

There is, then, very little question but that the "discovery" of the need to compensate for the disadvantage of the black ghetto child is largely response to the black nationalism sweeping the nation. While some white racists continue to say that all black people know is to burn, loot, snipe, kill and be a "tool of the Communists," some other whites are turning to compensatory educational programs "designed to eliminate the causes of deprivation" before "the ravages of poverty become irreversible."

Hence, the "new" literature postpones to another generation any real solution of ghetto problems. It also places the burden for change upon the shoulders of the black child. For it is the black ghetto child who must be changed, not the centuries-old conditions which have perpetuated disadvantage. Many black people find these programs much less than thrilling, as having not too much potential, and as a delaying tactic.

The "new" literature has been written too hastily. The problem of educating black ghetto children is being brought to the attention of our people at this time partially as a cover for the poor quality of education which has long been the fate of low-income and minority-group children. The deprivation theory places the burden on the black children and the effort to denigrate the black family, and especially the black mother, is a systematic effort to free the school systems from accepting responsibility for the miseducation of black children. The neglect of the children of the poor still continues, while superior education, facilities, and opportunities are provided for white middle- and upper-class children and youth. This means a widening gap between the black ghetto child and middle- and upper-class white children, and results in a life-long handicap to the black child by freezing him into low-class status. Cultural deprivation of the black people has been a conscious policy of the white racists and their dupes and stooges on the boards of education for more than a century. Cultural deprivation is still the major factor in the education of the black child.

Compensatory-education programs are too little and too late. Many of these programs are based in (1) a power field which does not yet involve parity for black people; (2) a content field which does not identify the kinds of changes in behavior to be induced in blacks other than as a condescending approach to the culture of the black people with no effort to structure dignity for the life-style, linguistic habits, and behaviors of black people, but rather designed to produce white middle-class conventional behavior; (3) a reward system oriented toward a racist society, rather than integration of black and white people, providing for development of individual self-respect and self-control and identity with the society and culture—a reward system which develops in each individual respect for the heterogeneity of culture and cultures, a sense of responsibility for other people, and development of the capacity to make things happen; and (4) rejection of the field of colonialism and dependency for a field of relevancy. That is, insofar as the education of the black ghetto child, or indeed for that matter the education of any child, must be in a field wherein the cognitive, affective, and psychomotor domains are relevant to the lives of the children, youth, and educational personnel. Do the program philosophy and content and the methodologies go beyond the current myths of the social and behavioral sciences, and does the educational program face the present national crisis, and does education see itself as a major force for social change for humanism and what is, in fact, education for survival? It is also true that this education must reflect serious and basic concern for the poor and wretched, for lawlessness in our society, for the degradation and attempt to destroy the cultures of people, and for increasing use of aggression, money, and war to solve conflict.

The "new" literature not only sets out to bring the ghetto school up to a par with the middle-class school; it fails to take its content from the ghetto itself. It closes its eyes to that passionate cliché of American educators, "the study of the life situation," and, while it "steals" much of the format and arrangements from the progressive-education movement and its successors, it does not yet have a rationale, philosophy, or conceptualization. It does not have research or other data to account for change which the reading and writing and speaking and listening and problem solving will induce.

One concludes, then, that the goal of the "new" literature and the programs which derive from it is to educate the black ghetto child so that he will become a black "Anglo-Saxon." It postulates that a black "Anglo-Saxon" can or should escape from the ghetto. It ignores the real estate, industry, and financial controls which conspire to block any significant outward movement from the ghetto. Its obsession that black ghetto children and their teachers must be held to the same standards as white middle-class children and teachers is based in the dogma that the black ghetto child must look forward to that tenuous future when, as a black "Anglo-Saxon," he will leave the dependent environment for the white world. Verily, the "new" literature proposes that the black ghetto child become a superchild, lifting himself through reading and language skills to a nobler and greater world of the future.

A MESSAGE TO THE ESTABLISHMENT

Interview by Frank Kent with Norma Jean Anderson*

Commissioner Kent: As you have heard black educators this past year, what do you think has been their main message?

Dr. Anderson: I feel that in various workshops that I have attended, in various conferences that I have attended across the country, the main message was that we are going to have to put ourselves together as a black group and redefine the problems that our children are having in the schools and see what we can do to remove the problems by helping the institution, because we are part of the institution.

Commissioner Kent: Helping the institution. Are we speaking of the institution of education?

Dr. Anderson: Yes. Because you are an educator and part of it, whether you want to say you are or not, you are. And at that point you have to find out what your role is within the institution in alleviating or correcting the problems that are related to the minority.

Commissioner Kent: When people talk in terms of black educators getting together, are they saying separatism, that is, that black educators must be a separate unit?

*September, 1969.

Dr. Anderson:

At the conferences that I attended (and I have attended various ones, made up of all black educators), in some of the discussion groups there were some groups who would say that we have to have our own schools. The theory here is that if you have your own school, you could have community control, and control not only of what you teach within the classroom structure, but also the policy that is set for the education of your children. At this point I think these individuals were saying that we as a group know what is best for our children; we know where the failure lies.

Commissioner Kent:

Well, does this mean that the black educators have accepted the "black community" concept? When I say that, I am talking about a physical black community as a reality of life in America and for the foreseeable future.

Dr. Anderson:

I think it is as aforesaid—that a substantial group of teachers are saying this. At the founding meeting of the Association of African American Educators in Chicago last August this feeling was voiced strongly. It wasn't necessarily the strong feeling of the whole group, because we had people from all across the United States there, bringing their own experiences and backgrounds into the picture. The feeling of many of the teachers in Chicago was that we need our own schools, because in the majority of cases we have our own schools anyway—all they lack is control, because so many of them were totally black.

Commissioner Kent:

Does this mean black educators have accepted the basic concept of the neighborhood school?

Dr. Anderson:

I think the black educators in the

Chicago school system, for example, have been realistic to the extent that there is such a large problem in that big city that hardly any of the devised methods that we have thought up so far, such as matching schools, bussing, education, parks, etc., hardly any of them can work in a city so large. They know and resolve within themselves that this is going to be. Therefore, they are concerned with what they can do best now and ask for control of policy making, control of curriculum, and control of hiring teachers.

Now in some other cities where there seems to be more hope, I think some black educators feel that they can work in a variety of ways. These are the communities where many black teachers still feel that integration may be an ultimate goal. There are teachers on our staff here in St. Paul who feel that we as a black group have to get together for staffing sessions, where you can talk about our problems, but still go through their institution's system. I think that the majority in St. Paul feel this same way.

Commissioner Kent:

What has been your experience in terms of talking with black educators about the black disruptive student?

Dr. Anderson:

They know this is a real problem; that there are disruptive students. They would be the first to say during the last few years, black students have been among the leaders in disruption, mainly because they feel that they have a cause to do this. I think, also, black students are seen first because of the signs of the times and they are beginning to be more verbal and to ask for what they think is theirs. When a group of students becomes disruptive, the black students stand out prominently because everyone is aware that there is a problem regarding the black community, which is asking for its rights. Educators feel that you can't operate a school with children being disruptive, be they black or white; there has to be some kind of control. Commissioner, what do you see as your role in helping solve the education problems in a particular school district?

Commissioner Kent: It seems to me that a department or agency such as mine has a responsibility to see that quality education is received by all. Perhaps the best way to do this is through strict enforcement of the law; and the law says desegregate. Our problem comes then at the moment, because I sense that some of the more vocal members of the black community don't necessarily want desegregation. But I don't really know that that is true— maybe privately they do want desegregation. So, the question comes to mind whether or not the argument for "community control" of our schools is real or symptomatic of something deeper.

Dr. Anderson: I agree with you on this point of not being sure whether they want desegregation or not. Some of the people that I have heard say that we should bring all the children back to the home schools, have really said this with a feeling that possibly something may be wrong with the total plan of integration within the city; that for too long have the black students and black parents too borne the brunt of all kinds of "solutions," and too long have they felt the burden of getting up early and getting home later; too long have they been separated from their friends in the community by going to different schools and having to come home and not share a common experience at school. They feel that it is about time we thought of other ways of solving the problems, such as reverse bussing back to the ghetto schools. This comes out through statements made at various times by people who have said we as black people want our own schools. They might really buy integration if it was done differently. We also have to realize that you can't integrate learning tools, and this I think is part of the theory of getting yourselves together, getting yourself experience of having quality education so that I can do arithmetic as well as the person I am going to school with, so that when I get to another school or another child comes into our area, we meet as peers and become better related to each other.

Commissioner Kent: Are black educators saying that there is something basically wrong with the present method of educating?

Dr. Anderson: Yes. Our black educators are saying, and many white educators are also saying, that some of the techniques that we have tried for inner-city children, mostly black children, because they are inner city, have been proven to be good for all children. Individualization of instruction is the key principle involved in many new approaches. This must be coupled with a worthy estimate of and regard for each and every child. Educators are finding out that children of suburbia need this kind of innovative approach too, and that only when they get this kind of an education do they prosper to the extent that they should.

Commissioner Kent: How do you as a black educator feel

	about the neighborhood concept in schools?
Dr. Anderson:	I feel that the neighborhood concept in some respects has outlived its day. I think we tend to want to keep the neighborhood concept as sacred as a sacred cow, forgetting that we do not share this concept with any other institution. For instance, we leave the neighborhood to go to church, we leave the neighborhood to buy our groceries, we leave the neighborhood to socialize, for recreation, for almost any other thing we don't stay in the neighborhood. Our best friends often live across town.
Commissioner Kent:	Let's carry this a little further. What, then, do you feel about the system of correcting racial imbalance—the present methods of correcting racial imbalance?
Dr. Anderson:	My personal conviction is that we are going to have to develop the concept of the educational park whereby the physical structure of schools is larger. We are going to have to draw from a more diverse population, and have a more diverse curriculum and interracial staffing. We are going to have to change some of the goals of education, and not feel that every child must be bound for a conventional four-year college or be a dropout. A lot of times we have dropouts that aren't out of school but are still sitting in the chairs. We need to have continuing education for all, which will prepare older youths and adults for actual livelihood skills.
Commissioner Kent:	What are black teachers saying should be done with teachers who appear to be no longer effective? Do you follow what I am saying?
Dr. Anderson:	Yes. I think they first say—using the old

cliché of sensitivity training—the first goal should be that of seeing what you can do with a teacher to get him to change his attitude; and I think we can talk about being effective. Very few have talked about their being effective in presenting the content of the course. *If a teacher is effective, the students will learn.* Where the students have not been learning—as in most of our ghetto schools—it must be admitted that, for whatever the reason, the teaching has not been effective. Essentially the problem has been an attitudinal one, that sometimes teachers do not have the right attitude about culturally different children or children who are bussed to school. If teachers don't have positive feelings toward all of their students, they can't do an effective job of teaching them.

Commissioner Kent:

In the sensitivity training sessions that you have held or conducted, have not most of your teachers resisted in becoming "sensitized" as to their own unconscious feelings?

Dr. Anderson:

No. The sensitivity programs that I have held in St. Paul have been voluntary, and this skews the results, because you tend to get the teachers who are either doing positive work anyway or those who have no particular defense mechanism set up for doing it. Therefore, we have gotten teachers who, from all results and comments we get back from them, felt that the institutes were great and made great commitments in regard to what they were going to do. I think one of the fallacies of such a voluntary institute is that we don't get teachers who need it. If they were mandatory, I might have to answer

that question "yes." I know of some instances where they have been mandatory
and they have had the result of setting up
staffs in two different camps. I don't
think they actually made teachers anti-
black or antiwhite, but I think what they
did was just expose the problem that was
already there.

Commissioner Kent: Do the teachers in the so-called ghetto
schools tend to be older than the teach-
ers in schools that surround the city?

Dr. Anderson: Not necessarily. In the system, as I have
experienced it, you have the *moderate
few* who ask for transfers. If you teach
three or four years in these schools, you
can automatically, every year, apply for
teaching in other schools, and at some
point or other, there is usually an opening in another school. So teachers can
transfer out.

Commissioner Kent: What is the quality of teaching in the
inner-city school presently? What are
black educators saying about this?

Dr. Anderson: Black teachers have said much about it.
I think black parents who are also educators have been most outspoken on the
point. In St. Paul, black teachers haven't
said too much because in our particular
system black teachers aren't put in the
inner city when they come here. They
are spread throughout the city. Since
they are spread out, perhaps for good
and for ill, there is less thinking in terms
of what is education in black ghettos. At
least this is our local situation in St. Paul.

Commissioner Kent: Would their services be better utilized by
placing them in schools where the black
students could relate to them?

Dr. Anderson: I have mixed feelings. We need to have
our black teachers and administrators as
models not only for black children but

also for white children (and for white educators too!). I think many "culturally deprived" white youths and adults should know that there is a person of stature and authority, of education and experience, to whom they can relate. I feel that in times like these we have to make a special effort to recruit black teachers for the inner city schools. These teachers should all be self-aware and self-accepting in order to build up and capitalize on the self-confidence of our black inner-city youth.

Commissioner Kent: Some time ago you were involved in a problem which existed in one of the schools in St. Paul which has a large number of black young people. As you look back on that particular problem, what would you say was the main issue? How should the school face up to its responsibilities, and what might the school have done?

Dr. Anderson: I think the main issue was and is a nationwide issue. Young people across the country were going to actively participate in solving the problem of black people today. They see this as simply having what is ours. The black children decided that they could best do this by confronting the administration with some of the negatives that have existed in the schools for some time. These weren't problems that just developed overnight; they were long-term problems that simply hadn't been solved. With help from the community, I might say these young people "did their thing." I think the administration did not really want to be aware. They were aware that nationally young people were demonstrating and walking out. I think that the administration in our particular city feels that all they had to have was an open ear; that they had only to listen to the complaints. This is why the superintendent himself was *training the staff* of the school in which the outbreak occurred. I felt, also, that the black young people who knew that they were being short-changed needed real answers to their questions and not fake answers.

Commissioner Kent: Was there a polarization of students, blacks versus whites?

Dr. Anderson: I would say there is more polarization of parents than of students. After black students presented their demands, the next day a group of black and white students presented demands. There were two groups of students working; it wasn't just one set of demands. The situation became competitive as to whose demands were going to be solved first and to what extent they were going to be solved. Because of the two sets you had two groups of people in the community working and wondering, "Is the superintendent, is the administration, going to listen to their demands and not ours?" I think the adults became more involved emotionally than did the students. If there is any polarization, it is mostly with the adults.

Commissioner Kent: Where do the black educators think the colleges presently are failing? Where are they succeeding?

Dr. Anderson: I think they feel that the teacher-preparation colleges, in addition to not preparing (or themselves employing) sufficient numbers of black teachers, are failing to provide teachers with a real concept of what inner-city schoolteaching is all about; but I think that black educators are noting that some of the colleges are changing. We had in this regard a meeting a year ago with the former chairman of the State Advisory Committee on Racial Imbalance and Discrimination. There was a committee on teacher training, and this committee recommended that we have a three-day conference with college personnel, and college policy makers. We were to invite the presidents, the teacher trainers, and the deans of the colleges of education so that we could tell it to them like it is in regard to what we thought the needs were for college training. The conference was held at the Leamington Hotel, and Dr. Nathan Wright was the main speaker. Since that particular conference we have felt that the colleges have done work for a change in inner-city schoolteachers. A major problem with all of our colleges is that they are white-oriented and white-staffed. They must change their own character first, if they are to change the character of others.

Commissioner Kent: Speaking of black studies, is there a trend toward this in the local secondary schools at present?

Dr. Anderson: No. We have black history courses being taught as electives at two schools. This is for all students, black and white, and it is on a first-come, first-served basis, trying to get seniors enrolled first. Because we had an overflow of applications for the course last semester, we took the seniors, then the juniors, feeling that if a few sophomores couldn't get into the course, they could always get it the next year. The seniors, once they have graduated, wouldn't have such a chance. All students, both black and white, need a corrective to our current limited versions of what our nation is.

Commissioner Kent:	Do you perceive a resistance on the part of the school system to make this kind of thing a mandatory course?
Dr. Anderson:	The answer in our local system has always been that if it is accepted by the State Department of Education, it is all right with us.
Commissioner Kent:	This seems to be rather a way to evade the issue than face it.
Dr. Anderson:	If someone would push it, I think there might be an evasion. Yet no one, to my knowledge, has asked for it to be mandatory.
Commissioner Kent:	When you say no one has asked for it, does this mean that probably black parents in St. Paul are not very much concerned about it?
Dr. Anderson:	Far too many educators are saying that this is not a course as important as ancient history, as the history of Europe or of the Roman Empire. Until the educators think this is important themselves, only then will they be part of the curricula that are accepted for state certification in teachers and also for accreditation for high school subjects. Added to this immediate issue is another concern related to black identity needs. In many parts of the country both students and parents are calling for the renaming of many of our schools. The names given to schools represent an important part of the educational process. They are designed to be an inspiration. Hence names should change as times and circumstances change. Even such traditional American heroes as Abraham Lincoln are being brought into question by our black youth in some cities. They are more aware than I was at their age of what they see as the biased racial or cul-

tural outlook of such men as George Washington, Thomas Jefferson, and Lincoln. To them Lincoln's emancipatory work was an expedient. Many of our young people, for example, can quote verbatim Lincoln's sentiments expressed in Springfield, Illinois, on July 17, 1858: "What I would most desire would be the separation of the white and black races."

This means that teachers of black youth and school officials must be far more sensitive to and appreciative of the feelings of black youth than in the past, if the optimum encouragement for learning is to be achieved.

Commissioner Kent: What do you see as the self-image of a typical black educator today?

Dr. Anderson: I think the black educator today has an image of being called upon to be many things to many people. By that I mean that, if any kind of question arises, he is supposed to be an "expert." If it arises concerning black problems—on poverty, social issues concerning black people, economic change, what black people are supposed to think about politics—or any question that has to do with blackness—the black teachers are to approach as if they were experts. This is the kind of weight they carry, as you know, right now. Yet official "experts" paid by most school systems are usually white, even in essentially black-related concerns. Every system in the country needs more black administrators and continuing consultants who are black.

Commissioner Kent: What are black educators saying about I.Q. tests?

Dr. Anderson: Black educators are saying that all I.Q. tests heretofore used in the schools have been culturally and so educationally unsound, and do not give a true picture of disadvantaged children, black or white. The tests are based on their past experiences and if you haven't been "fortunate" to have these experiences, you can't answer the questions correctly. Therefore they really don't give you any picture of a child's potential, which the intelligence quotient is supposed to represent.

Commissioner Kent: Maybe it is a test of achievement?

Dr. Anderson: From experience.

Commissioner Kent: Experience, right. Is there a correlation between blackness, poverty, and slow learning rates in the schools? For example, is there a notable difference between those blacks who are in poverty conditions and those blacks who have had less poverty?

Dr. Anderson: There are many individual differences. So you can't make a blanket statement that there is a tendency to be a high correlation between poverty, education, and achievement. I think a lot of it has to do with experiences. A child coming from a more affluent family can have the advantage of travel, of meeting people, and performing many different roles in life. He can talk with politicians, with the dentists, with the lawyers, and many others. In such conversation he can pick up a lot of concepts; and a whole learning experience is built on a conceptual framework. If a child doesn't have these experiences, he may have no concept of what, for example, a cemetery is. So if he reads something about a cemetery in a book, this means little to him.

A child from an affluent family is able to relate better to the written word in the textbooks. He can build his own conceptual framework and come out with kinds of solutions that you have to do with thinking. This makes a big difference in what you are able to do in school.

Some educators think that the problems of integration in schools won't be solved until they solve the housing problem. Commissioner, what kinds of concerns do you have in this area?

Commissioner Kent: Well, I think this is true in one sense, but we won't solve the housing problem until people know that they can move to any community and feel reasonably secure. Not all who live in a "black community" live there because they don't have any other choice. Some of them live there because they want to live there and would prefer to live around people with whom they can identify, and they don't feel that they can identify with white people. Consequently, I go back to thinking that perhaps the real solution to the problem is in desegregation of schools. If a child can grow up in a desegregated school atmosphere, when he becomes an adult and has to make the decision about where to live, he will feel a lot less sensitive about living in a community that may be 90 percent white or 99 percent white. So, I guess I really think that desegregated education may well be a major key to desegregating our society. Yet this seems to suggest a long-term postponement of our coming to grips with desegregation. This must be seen as only one of many simultaneous approaches.

Dr. Anderson: What all people want is respect, acceptance, and meaningful involvement (or self-determination). Our black educators, as you so well express, are address-

ing themselves in many varying ways to
these identical concerns. The new spirit
which is alive among black educators
should be seen as invaluable and listened
to by all.

SHANKERISM*

by Nathan Wright, Jr.

A NEW AND unfortunate phenomenon which will affect us all has reared its head in the New York City public-school crisis. At a quick glance it appears to have two sides, one reflecting teacher self-interest, the other reflecting racism. The picture that is thus drawn is too easy.

Albert Shanker is both a representative union leader and a man who mirrors his times. He has upheld the job-security interests of the teachers whose union he heads.

In the protection of what are seen to be his teachers' rights he is said to have raised the banner of racism. For his alleged injection of racism into the Ocean Hill–Brownsville school confrontation, Mr. Shanker is receiving criticism from all sides.

The issue raised by Mr. Shanker's behavior—that of the protection of hard-won rights by all means possible—will become an increasingly important one. This is so because social and economic change will accelerate; and battles won in the past will often impede the path of progress under the new conditions which lie ahead.

Since men are to be known by their fruits, we might label "Shankerism" the blind and stubborn holding on to the victories of the past, regardless of the consequences for the present or the future.

It is an all-too-sad fact of union life that unless a leader can press the self-interest of his followers harder than can his competitors he may not remain their leader for very long. The use of reason or temperance by union leaders is thus not always the way to the same job security for themselves which they seek for those who are their followers.

Mr. Shanker and other union leaders like him in many of our cities and towns thus may be expected to continue to thwart the educational process for young people whose well-being will require many new experi-

*From Newark *Star-Ledger*, December 8, 1968.

mental approaches. His behavior implicitly will negate the aspirations of those whom our schools are designed to serve.

Yet such effectively inhumane behavior is an unintentional but inevitable part of the present process of protecting hard-won teacher employment gains.

In practically every major town and city of the nation we are faced with the possibility of growing tension between teacher rights and pupil progress. Where the pupils are largely black and the teachers are largely white, race inevitably enters the picture.

Hence, in places like Newark and Chicago, as well as Ocean Hill–Brownsville, the pupil progress–teachers' rights tension takes on racial overtones.

This is no less true in tense school confrontations which have developed in Minneapolis and Montclair, in Boston and East Orange. You name the major town or city, and you will find that most often tensions of change are increasing the black-white ferment in the schools.

Our teachers understandably want job protection. Our parents and pupils want far more significant learning to be accomplished.

As a matter of simple justice, we cannot blame one party or the other. Something must be done to satisfy the legitimate demands of both.

Shankerism is clearly the result of the regrettable failure on the part of many institutions in our society, including the unions, to face the need for and fact of tremendous social change. For black students to learn, they must have teachers who both are sympathetic with them as persons and hold an investment in the accomplishment of the pupils' aspirations. This calls for increased flexibility in the assignments which can be given to teachers. Our unions must be open to far greater flexibility in their contractual arrangements. This may mean that we shall also need to have greater transfer ease of employees, with their tenure and pension rights intact, between one agency and another, among city, state, and federal agencies. All of us, and not simply the unions and school officials, are therefore involved. Our veteran workers in every field must not be faced with undue job insecurity.

Thoughtful men, women, and young people in our society must address themselves to hitherto untried possibilities for accomplishing job security. Otherwise we will find tasks undone on every side by virtue of entrenched skills, talents, or personnel that are no longer useful or appropriate in situations where they once were needed. This may be in large part true with many of our urban teachers.

Those who are thoughtful and responsible will also recognize that by no means can we afford to continue our present massive waste of the human potential of our youth. Yet our urban schools particularly, as the public has allowed them to be structured, are promoting unconscionable human waste. The unions should, among other things, help all of us understand that specialized teaching calls for specialized pay. Uniformity of pay in any occupation breeds mediocrity; and job security for the use of obsolete skills—whether in our schools, our railroads, our hospitals, or our mines—is public folly.

Nearly a million young people in Chicago and Greater New York—including northern New Jersey—this year bear the stamp of human waste.

The failure rate in the reasonable development of the potential of our youth in northern New Jersey and everywhere is a cause for serious concern. The lives involved must be reclaimed entirely by every possible means; and the waste itself must be stopped. The public must call for a thoughtful re-examination of our schools in the light of anticipated social and political as well as economic and technological change. Nowhere has this urgent task been done to the extent that our times demand.

Shankerism is designed to protect, and at times too crudely, the supposed self-interest of our teachers. It will assuredly continue to grow in its own understandable yet often ugly way, unless a wider public accepts the challenge to assure at once in new and creative ways both the basic rights of teachers and the claim by pupils and their parents that pupil progress is, after all, the basic purpose of our schools.

PART III

THE UNIVERSITY SCENE

FINANCING THE BLACK UNIVERSITY*

by Robert S. Browne

ALTHOUGH IT IS a less glamorous subject, perhaps, than the arts, or ideology, or the black university, financing is probably the greatest obstacle to the actual realization of the black university. This is not to minimize in any way the numerous and intransigent conflicts which a black university is certain to encounter in the realms of goals, means, standards, ideology, and other matters of basic policy. But after all the beautiful rhetoric has been uttered concerning the ideology and the idealism of the black university, it will be largely the fashion in which the black university is financed that will determine the form, structure, and flavor of the institution that emerges. The fact is that the blacks who are likely to be most committed to the black university concept are very unlikely to be sufficiently affluent to pay a significant share of the capital costs of such a university, nor are the potential enrollees likely to be able to pay a sum adequate to cover the full operating expenses of the university as well as their own maintenance costs. So the sources of funding the black university are of the first order of importance.

The Howard University Student Association is to be strongly commended for organizing a national conference on this vital topic. In my travels around the country I have had indelibly impressed upon me the fervency with which today's young black college men and women are striving to discover new forms in which they can express their desire to play a meaningful role in building a new future for Afro-Americans. A consensus seems to be emerging that the creation of a black university is perhaps the most promising means for realizing these objectives.

There is no doubt whatsoever that the essential ingredient of this University will be education for the rendering of service to black people. Elitism will probably be taboo, but hopefully not at the expense of qual-

*Delivered at Conference on the Black University, Howard University, Washington, D.C., November 13–17, 1968.

ity. As phrased at the recent conference of the National Association of
Afro-American Educators: "Black is beautiful, but also black is excellence." Excellence in the service of the black community, then, is certain
to be the theme of the black university.

In my visits to various campuses I find that the leading complaint of
the black students at the white universities is that the education which
they are receiving is not relevant to their needs—that they are being
taught from a white perspective, from invalid premises, and in terms of
an inimical value system. The insights, the knowledge, the techniques
which they need for making a contribution to the black community, are,
at least in most areas of study, not being taught to them. It is the desire
to fill these lacunae which lies behind much of the vigorous pressure for
black studies programs to be instituted at colleges having any significant
numbers of black students.

And in a sense it is the realization on the part of many black students
that their needs can never be satisfactorily met within the framework of
basically white-oriented institutions that feeds much of the demand for
a black university. No matter how "liberal" a white-oriented university
wishes to be on this question, no matter how willing it is to bend itself
to comply with the demands of its black students, it is virtually impossible for it to achieve more than an unsatisfactory compromise within the
structure of the university as it exists today. The insistence that certain
courses be taught by black professors and that certain courses be restricted to black students exclusively are reasonable enough in terms of
what the black students hope to obtain from such courses, but such
demands run counter to both the practices and the philosophy of most
universities and are therefore not easily yielded to. They also arouse the
opposition of some of the less nationalistic nonwhite students and thus
become a divisive influence within the black student community itself as
well as between the black and white student bodies. The matter is further
complicated by the limited supply of black instructors competent to
teach the material the students are demanding, especially instructors
who can meet traditional university academic requirements.

This incompatibility between what the black students consider to be
"relevant" education and what the white universities are in a position to
offer nurtures the demand for the emergence of a black university. Real-
ism, however, requires an admission that the birth of the black university
will not mean the disappearance of black students from white universities, for the black university, or even several black universities, will
certainly not be able to accommodate the numbers of black youth seeking
"relevant" higher education.

This raft of circumstances suggests one format and one source of funding for the black university: the black university could well commence as an institution designed to supplement the educational programs of the existing institutions of higher education by providing the black students at these institutions with a fully accredited year of relevant black education. Thus, rather than having a score of inadequate and possibly mishandled black studies programs located on various white campuses, interested black students would be offered a year of study at the black university and receive full credit for their work. There is ample precedent for such an arrangement in the "junior year abroad" programs and in the intercollegiate exchange programs which already exist. (Afro-American studies courses, open to both white and black students, would presumably continue to be encouraged on all campuses so that every student can have an opportunity to broaden his perspective on America and the world.)

Such a cooperative arrangement would relieve some of the pressures on the white universities and these universities should be willing to pay for it by helping to fund the black university without demanding a role in its direction. Such a cooperative arrangement would permit the black university to be launched swiftly by providing it an initial capital fund as well as an assured source of income. With such an arrangement the black university might not feel constrained to offer the more expensive laboratory science courses and some of the other highly technical courses in the physical and biological sciences and in engineering, inasmuch as these courses are the least controversial in terms of racial content and orientation. Unquestionably the black university would wish to move toward a full curriculum as rapidly as possible.

Another variation might be for the black university to begin as a graduate school, offering primarily research and practical experience in the black community, supplemented by some course work of black relevancy.

If a consortium of universities, or a combination of universities and foundations, could be convinced to contribute a capital fund of $3 million to permit the leasing or purchase of an urban building and its remodeling and furnishing plus the nucleus of a library, the black university would be well on its way to operation. If it were to receive two hundred students annually from white universities, at an all-inclusive charge of two thousand dollars per student, the black university could come close enough to covering its operating and administrative expenses (including housing and board) so that the deficit could reasonably be expected to be raised within the black community.

Of course, it would be preferable to create a degree-granting university, and if a cooperative arrangement of the type outlined above could be instituted we would have an adequate base from which to launch a full-scale university from the beginning. In the Appendix to this paper I have included a few typical items of financial data from three small, orthodox-type colleges. How relevant such data will be for the black university remains to be seen.

The degree to which the experiences of existing colleges offer any guide to the needs and resources of a black university obviously depends in large part on the degree to which the black university duplicates the general format of existing institutions. Inasmuch as the concept of a black university is somewhat of an innovation in itself, one might expect that the black university would be novel in many facets of its operation. Thus, discussing the operating budget of the university, or even its capital budget, and how these budgets might be financed, is logically best done *after* the general outline of what the black university is to look like begins to emerge. It may be that the black university should be tuition-free, or a completely cooperative arrangement, or a traveling university; there are any number of other creative possibilities. But pending the determination of such answers we are perhaps best advised to plan in terms of the conventional realities: the black university will wish to be accredited, which means obtaining teachers from the competitive market (although money will presumably not be the factor attracting teachers to the black university); library and laboratory facilities must be available and up to some minimum standard; and a substantial amount of administrative and supervisory service must be rendered to permit a smoothly functioning institution. These resources do not come cheaply, except perhaps on a short-term basis when enthusiasm is high. But if we are talking about laying the foundation for a permanent institution, then free labor and voluntary help of various sorts should not be too heavily relied on. Dedication, brotherhood, racial pride, are ideals which the black university may well cultivate as alternative stimuli to the role which the dollar currently plays, and humanism may well be closer to the nature of the black man than is materialism. But these nonmaterialistic qualities do not spring full-grown from a materialistic society but are developed over time. And even should the selflessness of some of our black youth succeed in setting the tone for the black university, we would not be operating within a vacuum. The local merchants, the public utilities, the publishing houses, the equipment suppliers, would be demanding the market price for every item the university required.

Without, therefore, wishing to predetermine the precise form, size, or location of the black university, one inevitably must make some assumptions with regard to these matters as a precondition for offering figures or budgets. It seems useful to allow these assumptions to be more rather than less traditional. In my mind's eye, I see initially a college of approximately four hundred students, and one which starts from zero rather than one which takes over an existing institution. I also choose to see it as an urban institution located most probably in the North. There is no strong rationale for any but the first of these assumptions. The small enrollment is favored because it is so much more manageable in every way, and because the black university will certainly be an experimental organization and therefore should be small enough to permit maximum flexibility.

I assume a school which starts from scratch only because I perceive none of the existing institutions to be promising imminent conversion to a black image. (From a practical point of view it would probably be preferable to attempt to achieve black control over one or more of the existing Negro colleges. However, the long tradition of dependency on white funding and of conformity to the initative role which they adopted at birth renders these institutions relatively unpromising as candidates for conversion without a bitter struggle which is likely to sap the energies of all parties involved.) I choose to place the assumed black university in the North simply because the South does enjoy, in the Negro colleges, at least a modest degree of black influence over higher education, and it would seem that if the black university proves to be a success some of these Southern institutions will pay it the flattery of imitation and refashion themselves in a black image, either gradually or suddenly. But even partially black controlled higher education does not exist in the North, so maximum returns are likely to be derived from locating the black university in either a Northern or a Western city. In the North the black university almost inevitably becomes an urban university because in the cities is where the black folk are. This in no way minimizes the need for a black university designed to speak to the needs of black pupils in the rural South, but both of these areas cannot be most effectively dealt with by the same institution, at least not at this early stage.

For maximum effectiveness as a community resource as well as in its role as a national focus of pride and center of intellectual creativity, there is a great advantage in having the bulk of the student body housed together. The centralized housing preserves and reinforces the spirit of community among the student body and between students and faculty, some of whom would hopefully share the students' residence quarters.

The carrying out of joint projects is immeasurably eased when the students eat and live together, and there is less likelihood of irrelevant distractions from the main objective. Finally, the centralized housing is supportive of one of my funding proposals (see below).

The simplest facility in which to launch a university such as I envisage would be an existing hotel building of moderate size. Such buildings are usually available within or on the periphery of most black central cities such as Chicago, Newark, Philadelphia. Often they are in advanced stages of deterioration but could be renovated to meet the university's minimal requirements. Several floors could be transformed into dormitory facilities easily enough, with the dining room serving as the cafeteria. Other floors could be converted into classrooms, laboratories, administrative offices, conference rooms, and library facilities. A ballroom could serve as the main auditorium. In some cities such old hotels represent a substantial underutilized investment and could perhaps be obtained for University use at a reasonable price.

Of a student body of four hundred, perhaps 10 percent might be local residents who commuted; the balance would live and board at the hotel/campus. They would be taught by a faculty of approximately twenty full-time persons, supplemented by a few part-time black scholars who might work at other institutions in the area. Liberal use will also be made of blacks who have a contribution to make but lack the credentials which are traditionally used to "qualify" persons to teach. A portion of the students would be graduate students.

Such an institution could be operated for approximately $900,000 per year on a nine-month basis. (It would, however, be desirable to utilize the physical plant on a twelve-month basis.) The breakdown would be somewhat as follows:

EXPENSES
Instructional salaries	$350,000
Other instructional expenses	100,000
Library operation expenses	25,000
Administrative expenses	200,000
Total	$675,000
Dormitory and cafeteria expenses	170,000
Maintenance expenses	35,000
Utilities	10,000
Miscellaneous building operation expenses	10,000
Total	$900,000

This sum would be funded as follows:

INCOME

Tuition	$210,000
Room and board	140,000
University earnings	250,000
Raised for scholarships	300,000
Total	$900,000

Tuition would be $1,200 per year and board would be $800. One hundred students would pay this full amount. One hundred students would pay half. One hundred would pay a quarter, and one hundred would pay nothing.

All students would be expected to give twenty hours per week to university-organized employment. At any one time, a portion of the students would be engaged in traditional student-aid employment such as assisting in offices, library, laboratories, cafeteria, and dormitories. A few, mainly graduate students, might be engaged in research which would be acceptable in lieu of employment. The bulk of the students, however, would work collectively (without pay) on contracts obtained by the university ("university earnings" in table above). Preferably, these contracts would involve the students in the black community, for example, engaging in a massive tutoring program for ghetto children under a contract paid for from federal, state, or local funds. A floor of the hotel/campus might become a virtual elementary or high school, offering supplementary daily instruction to needy youth of the community. Other students, especially those studying advanced business subjects, might be made available to staff university-organized business services (accounting, management practices) and to staff newly organized business ventures in the black community. These ventures might be owned by the university or by the local community. If the mass-tutoring type of contract could not be obtained, efforts would be made to obtain contracts to provide mass clerical services for the general business community. For example, the nightly processing of checks for commercial banks might be done at the university under contract with the major banks of the city. In the New York area, the university might discover a way to contract to do the paper work which has caused the New York Stock Exchange to close down every Wednesday. A pool of two to three hundred college students located under one roof and committed to twenty hours of work per week should prove to be a readily salable resource.

The operating deficit of $300,000 presents a major problem in that the oft-expressed wish of the black students is that the black university must be independent of white funding, with its inevitable controls. Whether $300,000 of operating funds can in fact be raised annually from the black community remains to be seen. Certainly it can be once the university has proved itself, but it is more questionable that such a sum can be raised during the university's first year or two. A portion of this deficit can perhaps be covered from various federal educational programs, such as the Educational Opportunities Program and National Defense Scholarships.

Realistically, it seems to me, white funding will definitely be necessary for the initial capital funds of the black university. The objection to white sources should not be so great with respect to capital funds, for their one-time nature permits of less opportunity for the exercise of unwanted controls. The minimum necessary capital requirements would be for purchase (or lease) of the hotel, for necessary remodeling of the hotel to make it usable, for furnishing and equipping it, and for provision of a library. The sums involved here can vary a great deal, depending on the city in which the university is located and on the availability and price of suitable real estate. Conceivably, adequate quarters could be purchased for $2 million or leased (five years) for less than $1 million. Renovation might require $200,000; equipment and furnishings $250,-000; and a modest library could be launched for $150,000. So for somewhere between $1.6 million and $2.6 million of capital gifts and a prospect of $300,000-per-year operating subsidy, the black university can be on its way. Money of this magnitude is undoubtedly available, despite the reluctance of white foundations and individuals to support projects which are all-black in their conception, orientation, and execution. But this stubbornness is beginning to crumble and the question is increasingly one of black resistance to the accepting of white funds. As I see it, the legacy of political and economic enslavement is still with us, my brothers, and we can ill afford the luxury of false pride. We must be cautious in accepting money from others, to be sure, but money we must have if we are going to make notable improvements in our position. My recommendation would be to admit this unpalatable truth and to accept financing from selected white sources, at least for our capital plant (and for endowment purposes if any is offered). We should, however, make a concerted effort to find our annual operating funds within the black community insofar as it is possible to do so. (Of course, a $4 million endowment would relieve the fledgling university of this recurring headache.)

The need for a black university exists. The human resources to staff it are available. There remains only the will for us to find the funds and to launch the program.

If this conference succeeds in catalyzing such action, it will have rendered an invaluable service to black people everywhere in the world, and to humanity in general.

APPENDIX

Actual recent figures from three United States colleges offering the B.A. and B.S. degrees

	College A Predominantly white, Catholic 433 full-time students	College B Predominantly black, church-supported 950 full-time students	College C Predominantly black, state-supported 1,542 full-time students
INCOME			
Total academic income (from student fees)	$1,200,000 (325,000)	$1,075,000 (702,515)	$1,905,000 (466,275)
Cafeteria income	168,000	266,000	Not available
Dormitory income	138,000	175,000	Not available
EXPENSES			
Instructional salaries	$ 464,000	$ 412,000	$1,026,535
Library expenses	42,000	43,000	57,400
Administrative expenses	350,000	391,000	232,000
Plant operation & maintenance	124,000	168,000	495,000
Other	97,000	Not available	400,000
Total academic expenses	$1,077,000	$1,014,000	$2,210,935
Cafeteria expenses	146,000	207,000	Not available
Dormitory expenses	65,000	280,000	Not available

THE AFRO-AMERICAN COLLEGE

IN AMERICAN HIGHER EDUCATION*

by Darwin T. Turner

DESPITE THE SENTENCES of execution pronounced by David Riesman, Christopher Jencks, Nathan Hare, and others, the Afro-American
college has a role and a responsibility in the educational structure of
America. Nevertheless, many Afro-American colleges are failing to assume the proper role and responsibility required of them in the second
half of the twentieth century.

I do not need to retell the history of Afro-American colleges at length;
it is well known. They were established originally to provide for the
minimal educational needs of the free and the newly freed black people.
Administered and staffed primarily by white professors, they helped train
Negro teachers and administrators, who eventually assumed leadership
of most of these colleges. Almost from the date of their conception, their
purpose was questioned. Some educators argued for curricula concentrated upon the industrial and agricultural arts to provide students with
skills in the occupations to which black Americans were restricted. Other
educators, however, insisted that institutions of higher education must
develop black teachers, doctors, lawyers, scientists—in short, individuals
who would assume positions of leadership in America. Although many
criticisms by current educational sociologists and historians imply only
historical failures, these institutions have answered a need.

Many of the ablest leaders of the "older" generation of Afro-Americans were educated at Negro insitutions. If the doors of the Negro
colleges had been closed, many of these individuals would have been
denied education; for the white colleges were reluctant to accept black
students. Even today, when increasing numbers of predominantly white
institutions are recruiting black students, especially the athletically talented, most future leaders continue to develop at Negro institutions.

*Delivered at Faculty Conference, Benedict College, South Carolina, August,
1968.

But I do not propose to defend the historical validity of Negro colleges; nor do I propose to consider the question of whether they should exist. The fact is that for the foreseeable future they will exist. Therefore, I wish to consider their present possibilities. Even though they have fulfilled their responsibilities miraculously despite serious limitations of money, personnel, equipment, and facilities, the present world has little concern or respect for achievements of the past. The black student, with considerable justification, says to the Afro-American college, "Don't tell me what you did for my old man. Like what are you gonna do for me?" This is the eternal question which higher education must answer for each new generation; unfortunately, some aging Afro-American institutions would not have heard the question if students were not shouting it into their deafened ears.

The newly attentive institutions may be forgiven if they seem bewildered. Riesman, Jencks, and the like argue for closing the colleges because of incompetence and uselessness. Equally eminent educators advise the necessity of supporting all colleges which can possibly help teach the ever-increasing numbers of American youths who recognize that a college education—or a diploma at least—is a prerequisite for most jobs which will provide the conditions which America has defined as the good life. Still other educators, legislators, and philanthropists suggest that indigent Negro institutions be reduced to two-year community colleges or be amalgamated with institutions whose financial benefactors are more generous. Completing the ring are the students, who demand that colleges provide the kind of education which they want. Amid this bedlam, the Afro-American college must re-evaluate itself to define clearly the responsibilities which it must assume in the present and the methods for attaining these goals.

In years past, the Afro-American college frequently has resembled the neighborhood grocery store. Like the neighborhood grocery, it could not match the supermarket's rich variety, but it offered the staples and hoped to prosper merely because it was the only shop in the neighborhood. That hope no longer suffices, for today's consumers have the mobility to reach the large institution a few miles away. For this reason, the Afro-American college must not appeal solely to the immature who seek lollipops or the lazy who refuse to travel the extra miles; instead, it must find a way of attracting consumers from both inside and outside the ghetto.

The old advertisements no longer suffice. Formerly, Negro students attended small Afro-American colleges because family tradition required them to, because Negro counselors in segregated schools advised them to, because these institutions offered financial inducements, because larger universities—especially in the South—denied them admission, or because some private institutions had acquired prestige as a result of surviving for many years. Today, these appeals will attract only a few, and often these will be the less competent students. Family tradition may still coerce some, but black counselors in the high schools derive their academic pride—apparently—from the numbers whom they send to predominantly white institutions. Larger universities have not only opened the doors: they now offer scholarship assistance that talented athletes and students cannot refuse and Afro-American colleges cannot match. And the prestige of small, private colleges in general has suffered as better financial support has attracted teachers and students to the state-supported insitutions.

Despite the waning popularity of the old appeals, the Afro-American institution, like the clever shop owner, can retain old customers and attract new ones if it recognizes its limitations honestly and seeks to minimize them while it examines itself to discover possible attractions which cannot be matched by the larger institutions.

Let me consider some of these ways, not necessarily in the order of their importance but in the order of their significance to me. First, an Afro-American college should be an Afro-American college. That is, it should offer subjects and materials of interest to students of Afro-American ancestry and to those non-Afro-Americans interested in learning more about Afro-Americans.

I have been fortunate in working at institutions which had a course or two focused on Afro-American studies. Nevertheless, this is not sufficient. The curriculum—in social studies and humanities—must be revitalized so that it becomes a meaningful experience for Afro-American students. As I stated in "The Black University: A Practical Approach" *(Negro Digest,* March 1968), aside from the history of the Negro in America, a course in literature by American Negro writers, and possibly a sociology course or two on problems of minority groups, few black educators have proposed courses studying the achievements of black men. There is need for courses in the history of art, literature, and music of Africans and Afro-Americans, for history of education courses which include a study of predominantly Negro segregated public schools and colleges, for linguistics courses which analyze the so-called Negro dialect. There is a need to initiate sociological studies of the problems of people in minority groups and to train individuals to work specifically with those problems. There is a need for business courses describing methods of organizing cooperative community businesses and for more courses concentrated on practices in small businesses. Current curricula frequently include the philosophical ideas of Descartes, Berkeley, Rousseau, Voltaire, Locke, Paine, and Kant. These should be retained, but room should be made for the philosophical ideas of Thoreau, King, and Malcolm X. Psychology courses should direct attention to the psychological effects of the black experience in America.

The list is endless. For example, students at one institution have proposed seventy-two courses. Such courses are desirable and are academically sound despite the absence of those consoling crutches called textbooks. These courses can be established and must be established. The irony is that they may be established first, and condescendingly, at predominantly white institutions.

But I must re-emphasize an idea which I have stated in "The Black University":

> The new information . . . cannot be substituted for other, more traditional knowledge. . . . If the Negro student is provided only with knowledge about Negroes, then his education will be as restricted as it has been in the past. His vision, true, will be black instead of white. But the revisers of the curriculum will be guilty of the same color blindness and narrow vision for which they condemn the planners of the present curriculum.

A second necessity for the Afro-American college is that it must assume and maintain its identity as a small college rather than imitate the manner of a large university. In many large universities, students complain bitterly about the impersonality of their teachers. Students protest that they are made to feel that they are merely faceless figures in a lecture hall, or even worse, series of digits imprisoned in the belly of a gigantic computer. Many of these multiversities now are recognizing the students' needs by establishing small colleges on their campuses. But the Afro-American college has an advantage. It is already sufficiently small to permit the close interchange that students have requested. Yet, despite the mouth-honor frequently paid to the concept of the college as a family, I have rarely seen the creed practiced as I believe it should be.

Too many instructors frequently make the mistake of talking to students as though they were small children. Certainly, the students are young—seventeen, eighteen, nineteen, twenty; consequently, most are somewhat immature and somewhat inexperienced. But they have reached a critical age at which they must learn to think and act for themselves. Both in their homes and in their schools, they are asking— and have a right to demand—the right to make their own mistakes.

Although I regret and criticize this tendency to baby the young, I recognize that it frequently arises from the best of motives. As we teachers age and, year after year, suffer vicariously through students the traumas of the troubled trip from childhood into adulthood, we inevitably regard the young as younger than they actually are. We want to protect them from the pains which we suffered. We try to talk with them, but we recognize the generation gap. Perhaps the only solution is to keep our faculties well staffed with young teachers who can talk as brothers and sisters rather than as parents.

Other disruptive attitudes disturb me much more. Let me cite three illustrations. When I joined the faculty of one college, I considered attending the weekly movies, but I was warned that I would not enjoy them because the students were too rowdy. These charges, made by Negro teachers, reeked of racism in their implication that Negro students were too primitive and uncultured for respectable teachers to associate with them. I have frequently wondered what attitude these same teachers would take towards the truly rowdy white audiences whom F. Scott Fitzgerald describes in recollections of his undergraduate years at Princeton University. Similarly, I once heard a Negro administrator say that the only way to control students is to use guns. I must add that the students were justifiably upset by a situation for which the administrator was to blame. I recall another teacher who proudly stated that she would never dream of having a drink with a student. That teacher was not affirming her impeccable morality. She was merely arguing that she was no longer in the social class of her students. Yet, only a few years earlier, she had come to the same institution with a social and educational background identical with that of the students whom she now rejected.

If these three ideas had been voiced by white teachers, the Negro students would feel justifiably that they had been subjected to white racism. What name can be given to such behavior and such attitudes when they are practiced by Negroes on the campus of an Afro-American college?

I choose not to believe that these Negro faculty members actually scorn students as students. Instead, they are victims of self-contempt. Subconsciously believing the frequently repeated allegation that their colleges are inferior, they are forced to consider whether they themselves are inferior as long as they continue to work at such colleges. Rather than condemning themselves in this manner, they redirect their hostility toward their students.

Such hostility, however masked, inevitably destroys the close, personal faculty-student relationship which is one of the main justifications for the continuing existence of smaller institutions. Please do not misunderstand my ideas. I am not preaching the sermon that every black man must love his black brother. Nor am I suggesting that each teacher station himself in a classroom or dormitory lounge one evening per week for a "Meet the Teacher" night. Such efforts too often reveal all the worst aspects of charity missions. They are uncomfortable sessions, both for the teacher, who self-consciously applauds his fulfillment of his duty, and for the student, who is painfully aware that he has been lured into a class meeting outside the regularly scheduled time. Instead, I do insist that each teacher at a small insitution should assume the responsibility to make himself available to his students, to talk with them, and, more important, to listen to them—after class, on the campus walkways, in the office. And the conversation should not be restricted to the teacher's discipline or even to problems related to the school itself. It should range into any subject of concern to the student.

The student will benefit, for what a person wants at age eighteen is to know that at least one person will actually listen to what he says. (Maybe that is all that a person wants at age thirty-eight or fifty-eight.) The teacher will also benefit, as I discovered recently. During a year's leave for research, I talked primarily with other scholars in the program, with faculty members, and with members of various educational associations. When I returned to North Carolina Agricultural and Technical State University, my new position as dean of the graduate school continued to channel my activities into groups which were primarily adult. Within another six months, I realized that my academic isolation was robbing me of my sensitivity to the reactions of the young. I could write about literature and composition, and perhaps earn the plaudits of peers in my own age group; but, isolated from freshmen and sophomores, I could no longer be certain that I was estimating correctly their possible reaction to these literary matters.

A small college must be a community in which faculty and students can and do talk with each other and listen to each other.

Third, an Afro-American college should be a community college in the most complete understanding of the term. In Ralph Ellison's novel *Invisible Man*, Jim Trueblood, a black farmer, describes to a white college trustee the chasm which separates the black community from the black college on the hill. The posture has been traditional for colleges generally, not just for Negro colleges. Often, the humanities-oriented atmosphere of a liberal-arts college contrasts with the practical, materialistic drives of the surrounding community; or philosophically liberal attitudes of a large university will thrust it into conflict with the small and conservative community in which it is housed. Many faculty members are unwilling or unable to assume responsibility beyond the campus: some have selected college teaching as a quiet retreat from the world's turbulence; others, despite proverbially poor pay, regard themselves as an elite group capable of being sullied by too close contact with the world beyond Academe.

Despite these collective and individual attitudes, the Afro-American college must identify itself with the Afro-American community and seek ways to help solve their common problems. Even though land-grant colleges frequently have assisted groups within communities, the idea is a relatively new one with exciting possibilities which may be more practicable at private institutions than at state-supported institutions, where, conceivably, too rapid innovation may be restrained by disapproving budgets from conservative legislatures. This new contact with communities may take the form of courses for businessmen, seminars for housewives, institutes to retrain those whose skills have been outdated by new technology, close research and instructional relationships with local and regional schools, or a cultural center for the community. Each college, of course, must discover the ways to provide for the unique needs of the community in which it is located. It must discover these by meeting formally and informally with citizens who represent the diverse interests of the Afro-American community.

This relationship with the community is not proposed solely from altruistic motives. Unless it can establish such a relationship, the Afro-American college seems condemned to one of two equally unpleasant alternatives: junior-college status in a community where the major education is available only at the local white college, or existence as a stunted, gray, miniature replica of a multiversity.

Fourth, because its funds are limited, the Afro-American college must attempt to pool its resources with small and large institutions within the region. In Depression days, education was occasionally described as satisfactory if a brilliant teacher could be placed in proximity to a willing student. This attitude no longer prevails. Competent faculty members expect ample salaries, time for research and thought, and adequate materials for instruction. Students demand competent instructors and adequate supplies of the necessary books and equipment. To satisfy these needs, impoverished colleges must have assistance, which cannot be anticipated indefinitely from increasingly cautious state and federal legislatures or from increasingly skeptical private donors. As the one-room public grammar school has been replaced by the consolidated school, so the small Afro-American college must become part of a unit which is consolidated in spirit and concept although not in physical plant. Only disaster can result from the present arrogance which inspires neighboring institutions of seven or eight hundred students each to insist upon absolute independence from each other. It should be possible to devise means by which faculty members and students move with relative freedom from one campus to another, deriving from each the resources which are most affluent at that particular institution. If distance prevents mobility of students, faculty members might move from campus to campus or the institutions may develop videotaped courses which can bring together in a single program the talents of faculty members at different institutions. A model for such cooperation—though not yet a flawless model—is the Atlanta University Center, which permits students to benefit from the resources of four undergraduate schools and a graduate school.

Fifth, Afro-American colleges should be experimental and imaginative in all aspects of their program. Since the future looks bleak if the present methods are continued with the limited resources of the present, Afro-American colleges have little to lose in experimentation which may produce results beneficial to and significant for American education as a whole. Various possibilities suggest themselves:

1. Attempts should be made—especially in the humanities and social sciences—to devise materials which are significant to the needs and relative to the interests of the students. Obviously, materials related to Afro-American history and culture are valuable. But the search need not be limited to these. Literature classes should help students form judgments about the television dramas and motion pictures which they see. Introductory courses in art and music should consider and analyze the art and music with which the student is familiar. Science courses should not neglect the commonplace, which may be elementary to scientists but unknown to students. For instance, after a year-long college course in botany, I was disappointed that I had been taught to identify a jack-in-the-pulpit flower but still had difficulty distinguishing between a rose and a tulip—flowers so familiar that the instructor never bothered to mention them.

2. There should be experiments with new ways to present the materials. Because of limited funds, Afro-American colleges cannot hire as many teachers as are needed to offer the number of courses required. Such a handicap suggests the advisability of greater use of programmed texts in courses where they have been developed. Carefully planned and supervised experiments with team teaching might overcome some of the limitations in the training of faculty members. The institution might draw

upon the ability of students to relate to each other by using students more frequently in tutorial programs for freshmen.

3. A college should experiment with grading practices. For example, since many students come from segregated high schools where they have not acquired the background traditionally expected of freshmen, a college might propose a trial run in freshman courses. That is, the first time a freshman would take a course, he would not receive a grade penalty for unsatisfactory performance. He would be required to repeat the course if his performance fell below "C," but the grade for his performance would be represented by "X" or "U" or some other stigma-free symbol, which would not be averaged with his other grades. Thus, allowance would be made for his impoverished background by giving him two opportunities to succeed.

4. Similarly, because of the weaknesses in educational background of many students, attempts should be made to provide rudimentary remedial assistance in prefreshman summer programs. The use of programmed texts and advanced students may offer a means of providing the individualized instruction necessary in such remedial or enrichment programs.

5. More attention should be given to the development of interdisciplinary courses, not merely in Afro-American studies, but also in humanities, the natural sciences, and the social sciences. This is not a need unique to black students. Most students need more courses which help them understand the similarities and interrelationships of various aspects of a particular academic area. After a term in a humanities course, for example, a student may see more clearly the relationships among literature, music, and the fine arts than if he is expected to infer those relationships from his exposure to separate courses in literature, music, and the fine arts.

6. Since Afro-American students often perform poorly on standardized tests, college should institute a means of experimenting with the performances of black students on various kinds of tests.

These are only a few suggestions. What is essential is that colleges seek innovative ways of providing rich education to meet the needs of their student population.

Finally, and this is the most important, Afro-American colleges, like all other institutions, should focus their attention on the most effective way to develop students as individuals. It is a truism to state that the purpose of colleges is to provide education for students. Nevertheless, many colleges have forgotten this purpose: administrators have concerned themselves primarily with fund raising, and professors have concerned themselves with research and publication. But the Afro-American college should not neglect this responsibility of helping black youths discover their identities and develop their talents along the lines of paramount interest to them.

As I have stated earlier, Afro-American colleges will survive for many years. But survival is not the important fact: they also must educate. In order to do this, most must change. I have suggested six paths along which that change might take place: (1) expanded use of materials related to Afro-American life, culture, and history; (2) development and maintenance of close personal relationships among faculty and students; (3) orientation to the black community; (4) pooling of resources with other educational institutions in the region; (5) experimentation; (6) increased attention to the development of the individual student. I do not propose these as solutions but as hypotheses to be tested. Ultimately, of course, the success of these or any other suggestions depends upon faculty and administration who are imaginative and concerned. If these individuals fail, the colleges will be no more than hotels leased for four years by young adults paying for a meaningless piece of paper. And black people will have lost an important agency for effecting their psychological, economic, and political liberation.

HIGHER EDUCATION AND THE

AMERICAN NEGRO*

by Benjamin E. Mays

HOWARD UNIVERSITY has never been an institution for Negroes alone. It was founded to serve all races of men, all religious faiths, and all ethnic groups. It was interracial and ecumenical in origin. But it was established for the purpose of providing higher education for Negroes. Since this is true and since a majority of Howard's students and graduates are Negroes, the group General Howard wanted the university to serve, you will understand why I begin this address with a bit of history, lest we forget the thought patterns out of which Howard was molded. When Howard was founded in 1867, virtually all science, religion, and states-manship were declaring that the newly emancipated people were a little less than human.

George Washington, Patrick Henry, and many other fathers of the Constitution owned enslaved persons. A majority of the members of the United States Supreme Court at the time of the Dred Scott decision were owners of enslaved persons. Many college presidents and professors defended the system of enslavement. A Yale professor said, "If Jesus Christ were now on earth, he would under certain circumstances become a slaveholder." Governor McDuffie of South Carolina said in 1835, "No human institution is more manifestly consistent with the will of God than domestic slavery and no one of His ordinances is written in more legible characters than that which consigns the African race to this condition." In 1860, the pastor of the First Presbyterian Church in New Orleans preached a sermon entitled "Slavery, A Divine Trust—The Duty of the South to Preserve and Perpetuate the Institution As It Now Exists." Eleven years before Howard was founded, a Richmond minister said, "The institution of slavery is full of mercy. . . . In their bondage here on earth they have been much better provided for, and great multitudes of

*Centennial Commencement Address, Howard University, Washington, D.C., June, 1967.

them have been made the freemen of the Lord Jesus Christ and left this world rejoicing in the hope of God."

Abraham Lincoln had his misgivings about Negroes. Speaking in Peoria, Illinois, in 1854, he said he would send the enslaved persons back to Africa, but they would perish in ten days. Speaking of social and political equality, Lincoln said, "We cannot make them equal."

The Anthropological Society of America, writing with special reference to the Negro in 1868, said, "The greatest achievement of anthropological science we conceive, will be the speedy convincing of all civilized nations of the utter uselessness of all these old and expensive attempts to civilize uncivilized races of men." Josiah Nott and George Gliddon, in their book *Types of Mankind,* wrote in 1865, "In the broad field and long duration of Negro life, not a single civilization, spontaneous or borrowed, has existed to adorn its gloomy past." Louis Agassiz, professor of zoology and geology at Harvard University, wrote about a century ago, "A peculiar confrontation characteizes the brain of an adult Negro. Its development never gets beyond that observable in the Caucasian in boyhood." Thomas Jefferson, architect of the Declaration of Independence, said, "Never yet could I find that a Black uttered a thought above the level of plain narration; never saw even an elementary trait of painting or sculpture." John C. Calhoun declared that he would be willing to give the Negro citizenship when he mastered the Greek verb. Samuel George Morton, the most eminent craniologist in the United States in the nineteenth century, concluded, "The capacity of the Negro cranium was less than that of the Anglo-Saxon by twelve cubic inches, and that, therefore, the Negro was incapable of intellectual equality with the Anglo-Saxon."

Henry Grady, speaking to the Texas State Fair at Dallas, October 25, 1887, said this: "Standing in the presence of this multitude, sober with the responsibility of the message delivered to the young men of the South, I declare this truth above all others, to be worn unsullied and sacred to your hearts, to be surrendered to no force, sold for no price, compromised in no necessity, but cherished and defended as the covenant of your prosperity, and the pledge of peace to your children, that the white race must dominate forever in the South, because it is the white race and superior to that race by which its supremacy is threatened."

In 1910, writing in his book *Social and Mental Traits of the Negro,* Howard Odum helped to perpetuate the image of Negro inferiority. This is what he wrote: "The Negro has little conscience or love of home, no local attachment of the better sort. . . . He has no pride of ancestry and he is not influenced by the lives of great men. . . . He has little concept of the meaning of virtue, truth, manhood, integrity. He is shiftless, untidy, and indolent." Fortunately, Dr. Odum changed his mind before he died.

This is the matrix out of which Howard University was born and the environment in which it was nurtured for approximately one hundred years. The University was founded on the faith of a few men like General O. O. Howard.

I make bold to assert that no university in America has been as free from religious and racial prejudice, and from ethnic bias, and as democratic in faculty and student operation, as Howard University. Even when the great institutions of the East and West were so narrow in their minds that they had a quota system for Negroes and starved them out socially and dared not hire a Negro professor—even one as brilliant as W. E. B. DuBois—this University was a living demonstration of democracy in education. It has never barred or restricted members of other racial, religious, or ethnic groups. While white institutions of the nation are now being praised and even financed for their "liberal" and "open-door" policies since 1954, do not forget that they are being praised and financed for doing what Howard University has been doing for a hundred years. In this one thing alone Howard University has made a contribution to the nation and to the world.

The leadership of Howard University has been sane but courageous. Although you know it, let us look briefly at the role this university has played on the national and world scene since 1867. If by fiat one could blot out Howard graduates in the colleges, universities, and public schools of the nation, there would be an educational vacuum which could not be filled. If one could blot out the medical services rendered by more than six thousand Howard physicians, dentists, and pharmacists, the health of the nation would be greatly impaired. In the arts, social work, religion, engineering, music, journalism, and architecture, the university has enhanced the greatness of the nation.

The statement could be logically defended that Howard University's greatest contribution to the nation is in the legal field. It cannot be denied that the chains of segregation imprisoned both North and South, Negro and white. Segregation, by law in the South and by custom in the North, had become the nation's god—worshipped on rail and land, in housing and education, in industry and government, in church and state. It was this god, Segregation, that gave the United States of America a black eye among the nations of the earth. In my travels in Europe and Asia in the second quarter of the twentieth century, I was embarrassed again and again by the press of Europe and Asia, and particularly by the Asian press, because they wanted me to explain how a democratic, Christian nation like America could practice segregation.

I shall remember to my dying day when in 1937 I was invited to speak at an untouchable school in India. To be sure that I would have rapport with the students, I was introduced as one of America's untouchables. I was stunned, disgusted, angered. Upon sober reflection, I realized that in 1937 I was an untouchable in my native land.

This god, Segregation, had to be dethroned first in the federal courts. The cases designed to dethrone this god, Segregation, were developed not in the law schools of the University of Chicago, Columbia, Harvard, Yale, but in the law school of Howard University. It is not an accident that a university born with an interracial world view would take the leadership in this field rather than the universities named above, which at that time had no concern in abolishing segregation. It is conceivable that if there had been no Howard University we would not have had the May 17, 1954, decision of the United States Supreme Court, declaring segregation in the public schools unconstitutional. That decision was and is one of the most historic documents in the annals of American law. It is most significant that the decision was argued and won by a Howard University Law School graduate, Thurgood Marshall. It is equally history-making that the District of Columbia case was argued and won by the present president of Howard University, James M. Nabrit.

In abolishing legal segregation in the United States, all America was freed from the curse of segregation, which had made our country the world's biggest hypocrite by calling itself a democratic, Christian nation. No longer can the nations of the earth accuse the United States of perpetuating in law a caste system based on race. If Howard University had done no more in these hundred years, it would have justified the millions the federal government has spent on this university. It is quite likely that the cases against discrimination prior to 1954 and the 1954 decision itself paved the way for Montgomery and the sit-ins and the Freedom Riders, and these led to congressional legislation making the court decisions the law of the land.

How strange, how ironical, that this nation, conceived in liberty and dedicated to the proposition that all men are created equal, had to wait 178 years for the descendants of enslaved persons to help it implement the Declaration of Independence. Surely "God moves in a mysterious way, his wonders to perform." This is proof, as someone has beautifully said:

Fleecy looks and black complexion
Cannot forfeit nature's claim;
Skin may differ but affection
Dwells in black and white the same.

It is a fact, as Isaac Watts has said:

Were I so tall as to reach the pole
Or grasp the ocean with my span,
I must be measured by my soul:
The mind's the standard of the man.

On June 8, 1945, I spoke at the Howard University Commencement, using as a subject "Democratizing and Christianizing America in this Generation." I said in that address that it was all a matter of will. I quote from that speech.

It does not take a thousand years to perfect social change. If Germany, through brutal means, can build a kingdom of evil in one decade and if Russia, through brutal processes, can construct a new order in two decades, we can democratize and Christianize America in one generation. . . . We here in America have never deliberately planned to make our democracy function effectively, as Hitler planned to make his kingdom of evil function effectively. And we have never been as serious about living Christianity as the Russian leaders were about building a new economic and political structure. We have never been excited about a Christianity that was to be lived on the earth and that was to function in every area of life.

Listening to that address, one woman called me a Communist. But look! It was prophetic. In 1945, the Southern United States was tightly segregated and the North condoned it by custom. Although we are not fully democratized and certainly not fully Christianized, in twenty-two years we have come a long way.

If we are further along the road to being the land of the free and the home of the brave, we can thank Negroes for taking the initiative—the Law Department of Howard University, the NAACP, the leaders of the sit-in movements, demonstrations, the will of the federal court judges to interpret the Constitution properly, and the leadership provided in the Truman, Eisenhower, Kennedy, and Johnson administrations which supported the demands of Negro Americans for democratic participation in the affairs of the nation. Howard University has furthered this cause through its judges on the bench, representatives in state governments, and a senator from the state of Massachusetts.

Let us turn briefly to the international scene. One out of every seven students enrolled at Howard comes from a foreign country. In relation to the total Howard Student body, this gives the university the highest percentage of foreign students among American universities. The foreign students represent eighty-two countries, and Howard graduates are making their mark in fifty-nine countries of the world. Among her professors and graduates are to be found ambassadors to three countries.

At the beginning of this address, I quoted great men who branded this people as inferior. What has happened in recent decades proves how finite, how fallible, how wrong the most brilliant mind can be when it plays the role of God and speaks ex cathedra about the future of man.

Although we have done fairly well in desegrating America, the job has not been finished. Segregation in housing is widespread. One Negro can still chase a thousand white persons by moving into a white residential area, and two can put ten thousand to flight. And in opposition to open occupancy, the North and the South speak the same language! They joined hands to defeat an open-occupancy bill. The next difficult hurdle to overcome is that of adequate employment. More Negroes will find good paying jobs, whereas more and more Negroes will find themselves at the bottom of the economic ladder or unemployed altogether—despite a desegregated society. Thirteen years after the May 17, 1954, decision of the United States Supreme Court, the South, and the North for that matter, is dragging its feet on desegregating the public schools. Recently, the conservative Republicans of the North and the conservative Democrats of the South joined hands in a measure to slow up desegregation of the schools and to place more control of federal money for education in the hands of the states, which means more opportunity for discrimination based on race. The South has allies in the North and can now rely upon many Northern Republicans and some Northern Democrats to do for it what in previous years it had to do for itself.

We use the word *desegregation* because it is not integration. When the courts opened public schools and universities, golf courses and swimming pools, abolished segregation on dining cars, in interstate travel, and on buses, and abolished the white primary, they were not integrating the facilities. They were desegregating them; when sit-ins, boycotts, and picketing opened restaurants, hotels and motels, this, too, was desegregation—not integration. This is also true when a church votes to drop the color bar. The church is desegregating, not integrating. Desegregation means the absence of segregation.

To integrate means to unite together to form a "more complete, harmonious, or coordinated entity." It means to organically unify, to form a more perfect entity.

In an integrated society, fellowship, comradeship, and neighborliness have no limits or boundaries based on nationality, race, or color. Association will be formed mainly in the realm of spiritual, mental, and cultural values. There will be no laws against interracial marriages, and custom will recognize the right of every man and every woman to marry whomever he or she pleases. Integration is largely spiritual. It is even possible for a married couple to live in the same house bearing and rearing children, fussing and feuding, without ever becoming thoroughly integrated, without ever being unified in their purposes and outlook on life.

As Howard University closes out her first century and enters the second, the university, in the area of human relations, will be challenged on two fronts: First, to do its part to implement the civil-rights legislation already enacted into law. After passage of the Civil Rights Act of 1875 and its repeal in 1883 and after the Hayes-Tilden Compromise in 1877, the federal government felt that it had done enough for Negroes and retreated from the field of protecting Negro rights. Then followed an era of peonage, complete segregation, and lynching. The climax to the retreat came in 1896, when the Supreme Court made segregation legal. The federal government did not return in full blast to the civil-rights struggle until after the middle of the twentieth century. The North grew weary, felt it had done enough by freeing the enslaved persons and by adding to the Constitution the Thirteenth, Fourteenth, and Fifteenth Amendments. Colored Americans must earn the right to complete citizenship, whereas others get it at birth.

I am most unhappy over what I see going on on Capitol Hill today. There seems to be a feeling now that the Supreme Court has slapped down segregation and the Congress has enacted into law many of the Court's decisions, that the federal government has done enough: let the Negro now make it on his own, sink or swim, live or die. As long as we think in terms of black versus white and not in terms of Americans, regardless of the degree of desegregation, racism is a monster to be feared. A partially desegregated or a wholly desegregated society may, therefore, become normal. Herein lies the danger. After the Hayes-Tilden Compromise and the repeal of the Civil Rights Act of 1875, the North largely withdrew from the field of civil rights. Today, the conservative North and the conservative South are joining hands to slow down the process of desegregating America.

According to the Southern Educational Reporting Service, thirteen years after May 17, 1954, the average number of Negroes attending desegregated schools in the eleven Southern states represents 15.9 percent. At this rate, it will take eighty years to complete the job. Housing could remain largely segregated and the economic gulf between Negroes and other Americans could become wider and wider. The Howard leadership must make itself heavily felt in this new area, just as it provided the leadership to break the back of legal segregation.

The second challenge to Howard University in its second century will be to fight discrimination in the interim between desegregation and integration, and to train students who are so competent in their chosen fields and so skilled in their jobs that discrimination will become increasingly difficult. There is a time to demonstrate, to sit in, and to protest; and the irresponsible may precipitate riots; but there has *never* been and there *never* will be a substitute for academic excellence, and none for possessing skills that the community needs. I know the conditions that produce riots and I know that it often takes riots to arouse the conscience of the community to do something about an intolerable situation; but I also know that demonstrations and riots alone have never produced skills in engineering nor competence in surgery. As John Dewey and James Hayden Tufts say in their book entitled *Ethics:* "The freedom of an agent who is merely released from direct external obstruction is formal and empty. If he is without resources or personal skills, without control of the tools of achievement, he must inevitably lend himself to carrying out the directions and ideas of others." We can be like this in a desegregated society.

Finally, let me warn you that we must not be swept off our feet by the glamour of a desegregated society. By all means, enjoy the swankiest hotels, eat in the finest restaurants, live on the boulevard, ride anywhere, worship anyplace, work anywhere, get high-paying jobs, send more men to Congress, get more judgeships—but remember that we can do all these things and not be a part of the policy-making bodies that shape education, industry, and government. We can do all these things and still be grossly discriminated against when there is no sign of segregation in sight. This kind of discrimination which we will meet in the interim between desegregation and integration will be subtle and will be administered not by the Maddoxes, the Wallaces, and the Barnetts, but by our liberal friends in Congress, in education, and in industry. If we aren't careful, we will live another century dangling between desegregation and integration, with all the discrimination inherent therein.

I am going to assume that Howard University in its second century will become one of America's top universities and that Congress will appropriate sums to enable the university to compete with the best in the nation. I am going to assume that Howard will turn out more and more graduates who will be ambassadors to foreign countries, not only to little countries as now, but ambassadors to the great power nations. I shall assume that Howard will send more men to Congress, train more judges, produce abler men in medicine and religion, turn out men who will be cabinet members and governors, and produce a President of the United States—provided we can break through the interim of discrimination that will exist between desegregation and integration and produce a society where this great nation of ours, born in revolution and blood, conceived in liberty, and dedicated to the proposition that all men are created free and equal, will truly become the lighthouse of freedom where none will be denied because his skin is black and none favored because his eyes are blue; where the nation is militarily strong but at peace; economically secure but just; learned but wise; where the poorest will have a job and bread enough and to spare; and where the richest will understand the meaning of empathy.

But even this will not be enough. Howard University fought against racism in the latter part of its first century mainly in the courts. In the future, Howard will be challenged to create and design programs to close the gap between the college and university men and the dropouts and the unskilled, those who live in the ghettos and slums, poorly housed, ill-clad, living on substandard salaries or no salaries at all. Howard will be challenged to take the gown to the town and the slums, and bring the town and the slums to the university campus. This will take a will, a creativity, and an imagination which we may not now have, but it must be done if Howard University is to serve all classes of people in the decades ahead. Howard in the second century should never forget the words of Eugene Debs, who said in essence: "As long as there is a lower class, I am in it. As long as there is a criminal element, I am of it. And, as long as there is a man in jail, I am not free." Howard in the second century should train its graduates to know that we are all a part of mankind and that no man is good enough, no man is strong enough, and no man is wise enough to think that he is better than another man and thus justified in setting himself apart from the man farthest down; for if one man has more intellect than another, is richer than another, it may be luck or fate. We are all what we are largely by accident or God's grace. No one chooses his parents and no one chooses the circumstance under which he is born. I have seen a brilliant mind and a dull mind born into the same family. I have seen beauty and ugliness in the same family. The boy born in the slums has no choice, and the man born in the midst of splendor and wealth has no choice. The man in splendor and wealth has no right to look down on the one from the slums or the ghetto because he too might have been born in the slums. This is what John Donne is trying to tell us when he says: "No man is an island, entire of itself; every man is a piece of the continent; a part of the main; if a clod be washed away by the sea, Europe is the less, as well as if a promontory were . . . ; any man's death diminishes me, because I am involved in mankind; and therefore never send to know for whom the bell tolls; it tolls for thee."

As Howard University becomes more famous in the decades ahead and as her graduates reach for the stars and grasp after the moon in politics, economics, education, and industry, may they also reach down and use their skills to bring a better life to the poor and justice to all mankind. It is my prayer and my prophecy that Howard's second century will be more glorious than the first.

CAN WE LOOK TO HARVARD?*

by Nathan Wright, Jr.

OF ALL THE signs of mounting campus unrest throughout the nation, the 1969 student turmoil at Harvard probably goes the furthest in underscoring the need for college reform. Harvard's apparently perpetual, rationally rooted tranquillity was broken in mid-April of 1969 by one of the most chaotic, brief, and shamefully bloody campus confrontations in recent years.

As an alumnus of Harvard (although one who has always loyally questioned its somewhat sophisticated presumptuousness), I was dumbfounded.

The questions "Just how?" and "Why?" came to my mind, as to the minds of many others.

The "Just how?" question for me was raised primarily neither in terms of the arbitrary student take-over of University Hall nor in regard to the administration's hasty response.

My greatest sense of revulsion sprang from the altogether easy overlooking of the unseemly behavior of the officers who were called to enforce the law. The essential odium within the university community for this deeply unfortunate behavior falls inevitably upon the able president of the university and the normally cool-headed administration at whose behest the police were called.

Those present on the campus report viewing with utter horror and amazement the ugly sight of policemen beating and kicking almost like madmen. The fact that numbers of policemen were reported to have gone even further—in what is the clearest contempt for their public trust—by covering their badges, can only underscore the intent to turn law enforcement into license. The badge-covering could lessen the fear either of being detected or of paying a price for maliciousness under the banner of law and order.

*From Newark *Star-Ledger*, April 27, 1969.

Such behavior by agents purportedly representing public peacekeeping is reminiscent of what was officially adjudged to be police rioting against the public in Chicago. It brings to mind, also, the illegally covered badges and the brutal police behavior witnessed—and publicly condoned—in the 1967 disturbances in Newark, in Detroit, Michigan, and elsewhere.

The Harvard administration's reasonable assertion that arbitrary pressure has no place within its life and its thoughtful and necessary plea for orderly debate and decision-making are shrouded by Harvard's own quiet accepance of the fruits of illicit "justice."

Yet the superficially "responsible" but effectively sinister Harvardian attitude in this regard is scarcely different from that of the nation as a whole. Nearly two years have now passed in Newark since the massacre in cold blood of twenty-six black children and adults by white policemen. To this day, there have been no public marches or any other displays of mourning by a white community which should have been deeply mortified by the glaring inhumanity of the instruments which represent its will for the maintenance of "law and order."

The ease with which official violence is being accepted by our society is one of the most critical signs of a mounting assault upon human worth throughout America today. We cannot hope to continue long as a free nation when the agents of law are implicitly encouraged to turn law into caprice.

Now that Harvard has joined the curbstone crowd which views sadism-in-the-name-of-justice with aloof reserve, what hope can we have that in the forces which allegedly represent reason at its best we can look for a greater measure of sanity and civility among us?

Even as the question "Just how?" was raised in regard to circumstances surrounding the police behavior, so also was the question "Why?"

Just why has not the nation as a whole—and perhaps especially the rational forces at such traditionally responsible institutions as Harvard—not seen the urgent necessity for a vastly different kind of training from what we now have for our officers of the peace?

Our nation's conscientious and dedicated policemen and policewomen are among the most compromised people in America today. Inadequately trained and also grossly underpaid for many of the technical tasks they are called upon to perform, they become as well the "fall guys" for the growing tensions of our nation's accelerating social and technological change.

Our officers of the peace should be thoughtfully pleading and protesting for more professionally oriented training—at the public's expense—

for themselves as well as for far more extensive and appropriate adult college-type education for our general public.

The Nixon administration could do no better thing—both for our national security and for our nation's internal peace—than to become the initiator of a long overdue extension of continuing higher education for all adults. With our increasingly mobile adult population, no states could or should invest heavily in such a task. We must renew in our time the spirit which led, more than a century ago, to the then radical departure of developing land-grant colleges for training our citizens in the evolving agricultural and mechanical pursuits.

The relief budgets need to be cut back and the same resources should be utilized for human habitation. Only in this way can we hope to meet the ever-changing social, political, and technological demands which for now—and for the foreseeable future—will continue to confront us.

The question "Why?" was raised in my mind in a pointed way about Harvard and other institutions to which we have looked for responsible planning and advice for meeting our country's rapidly changing educational needs.

Harvard, however, like most of our educational establishment, has tended to view education as a private domain serving the interests of a few rather than as a public responsibility for meeting the needs of all in the democratic society from the cradle to the grave. This is true—in the most gross way—with Rutgers, the State University of New Jersey, in its present blatant failure to address itself realistically to the crying needs of Newark.

What has happened at Harvard—and is evident across the country in the turmoil at public and private institutions of secondary as well as collegiate learning—should be a compelling reminder that the nation's present approaches to education must undergo substantial reassessment.

To look to such illustrious, traditional institutions as Harvard, in spite of their obvious imperfections, for continued excellence in the disciplining of the mind may be entirely appropriate. This leaves to our citizenry as a whole, however, a far larger and indeed more vital task.

As citizens, we must face the necessity for devising means for continuously challenging and re-forming the nation's questionable or archaic values and for developing in every American—from birth to death—the fullest possible capacity for self-governance, self-sufficiency, and social responsibility. This is the most essential single task facing our nation today.

The major public and private resources and the best imagination of us all should be focused on this humane and self-interested concern.

THE CAMPUS CONFRONTATION*

by Nathan Wright, Jr.

THE MAJOR DISRUPTIVE events which are occurring throughout our nation today are not associated in any way with our black urban ghettos. They are largely unrelated to the poor. Nor can it be claimed that they are grounded in ignorance of our nation's traditions or that they stem from a culture of irresponsibility. The most explosive confrontations which we must anticipate increasingly are those on our once staid college campuses. Those who are moved to the alternative of revolt are, in large measure, the haves rather than the have-nots. They are the sons and daughters from our most substantial middle-class homes.

Our colleges formerly were seen to be among the most solid rocks America's stability was founded upon. They have enshrined what we have thought of as the best of our nation's past. For generations our colleges have shaped those we have considered the elite of our youth into the mold we have seen as that of a model American.

Yet today on the college campuses I have visited from San Francisco and Chicago to Madison and Miami there is increasing disquiet.

As one who is particularly annoyed at any semblance of precipitous or disruptive change, I have winced at what I have seen. My natural sympathies tend to be with those who view the confrontations with sadness and dismay.

As one, however, who values survival more than stability and who prizes more greatly our nation's fulfillment than the preservation of a seeming peace, I must, nonetheless, look to our campuses with some measure of hope.

So must we all. We must probe as deeply as we can to see the issues for what they are, and then we must meet them as squarely as we can. The talents, the insights, and the concern of all of us are needed, for the

*From Newark *Star-Ledger*, March 23, 1969.

issues involved go to the heart of our nation's way of life.

Systems must always have stability. Humane systems have order, however, only for the purpose of providing a secure framework for orderly change and for progress toward human fulfillment.

Our educational and other systems all too easily forget that their essential purpose is not to simply maintain themselves. Systems, rightly structured and properly used, are instruments or vehicles for necessary ongoing change.

That our schools have not facilitated change is an evident fact of life. Indeed, in some respects our nation has needed the skids educational and other institutions have provided, as we have gone topsy-turvy into our present stature of world greatness.

A major need before us at this moment in history, however, is for America to serve as a leader among the nations of the world in facilitating human growth and in developing the full potential of all our citizens. Our schools, like the nation as a whole, have a skewed vision of what America is.

Who are those we see as truly American, and therefore as deserving of the fullest consideration of our schools and other institutions?

They are the conformists. Our schools and other institutions serve best those who conform to society's expectations.

1. Those whom the schools serve best are white.

Our very use of the term *nonwhite* in our schools and in other institutions in the land defines, in a thoroughly arbitrary way, who are fullfledged "Americans" and who are not.

"Nonwhites" are shunted out of college preparatory courses by our teachers in the junior and senior high schools, and so black boys and girls by the twelfth grade generally do not meet the "standards" for college admission.

The vicious use of the track system and its equivalents in such progressive places as Englewood, New Jersey, and in practically every major city throughout the nation, has effectively eliminated black youngsters from any possibility of equitable treatment in higher education.

While higher-educational opportunity has greatly expanded for white youth throughout the nation, black youth—as a 12 percent minority—is represented even in our publicly supported colleges by a national average of somewhat less than 3 percent.

Small wonder that our black youth is saying, "Up the quotas—or else!" Responsible and mature men who are also just and wish for this nation's fulfillment would easily supply positive substance to the issues behind the "or else." They would know that unless the evils we have all perpetrated —or are a complicitous part of—are erased, then inevitably we become ourselves increasingly evil men in the process.

Our black young people are holding before us, then, the mandate for integrity. Those who equivocate, and who dwell on the methodology of the young black students rather than upon their crucial and potentially saving message, simply expose themselves for what they are. They are clearly un-American and effectively serve as subversives who would deny or destroy our nation's promise of fulfillment for all.

2. Those whom our schools serve best are the unimaginative.

Throughout most of the world's history, adult or higher education has been characterized by having students hire the professors or "doctors" who taught or indoctrinated them. Teachers were the servants of the students' own perceived needs for professional preparation and for personal growth.

Teachers were engaged if they had the ability to incite the imagination of the students and to prepare them to make critical judgments. It was thus with ancient learning, which provided the philosophical foundations for our modern world, and some of the oldest European schools, still surviving to the present day, were founded upon this basis.

Today, we are faced with a historic aberration in which the servants have become the masters of those whom they should serve. Our protesting youth today are restaking their ancient and rightful claim to be the center and end of the higher and continuing education process.

For a teacher, whether in our lower grades in our public schools or in our colleges, to feel that our schools are "their" schools reflects an empty arrogance unworthy of lettered and cultivated men. They clearly demonstrate that they are ignorant both of the facts of history and of the human purpose for facilitating each individual's personal growth into the best self he or she may be.

Those who rebel against the primacy of the teachers in the learning process are, thus, essentially on the side of those who are truly conservative. They recognize, as we all must, that our continuing educational enterprises must meet far more widespread needs for growth into imaginative and critical judgments.

They know also that in a society that hopes to be democratic, continuing or higher education must not be for the few who have been considered the elite in the past. In a truly democratic society we must see the term elite as representing the possibility of excellence in every man.

It cannot be emphasized too greatly that we must always have both order and orderly progress. The two go hand in hand. The major responsibility in this regard rests upon those of our honorable men, who would be flexible enough to adjust aggressively to every impetus toward equity, fair play, and good sense in the interests of the common good.

Let us all begin to think more deeply, letting our judgments in every instance be informed both by our national purpose and by the wisdom and insights of the ages.

*WHERE DO WE GO FROM HERE?**

by Elizabeth Duncan Koontz

IN THE NOT too distant past, commencement speeches were used by the older generation to warn the college or university graduate that he was about to make the transition from academic to real life, that he must stop theorizing and become involved in the issues of the day.

How quaint and old-fashioned you have made those speeches seem; for you have not only been involved in the real issues for some time, you have helped propel the colleges and universities into the thick of things.

To many Americans, the university campus looks like a microcosm of our whole society, representing all that is wrong with it or our best hope —depending on the point of view. In effect, this generation has put its finger on many of the evils and inadequacies of the times and has served notice that it does not intend to submit to them any longer. This is the generation that is demanding that its education be relevant—that requires, for example, that its sociology instructors not only know about the poverty of the community but show leadership and participate in plans for remedial action; that wants not only to learn math but also to have the opportunity to use that learning to help the poor, those who are almost daily fleeced because they cannot read, write, or perform numerical gymnastics in purchasing. Indeed, this generation of students is questioning not only our whole educational system, but the very foundations of our society, and questioning it with some justification.

There have been mistakes, of course, as might have been expected. The most crucial mistake has been that dissenting students have sometimes lost control of their own cause. Sometimes others, with only a desire for power and showmanship, have taken away the students' protest, forced them to set aside their legitimate, justified plans of action against archaic structures, and left the students with a manner and methods which they

*Commencement Address, Coppin State College, Baltimore, Maryland, June 12, 1969.

cannot support, but are unprepared to oppose. This, I believe, has been the real tragedy of student protest—a protest which could have been and still could become the orderly means of bringing about the changes that educators, students, and parents alike are hoping for.

Students today at the university, college, and even high-school level are questioning the value system of our society; our entire societal framework is on trial. Indeed, the generation gap, I believe, has been one not so much of age, but of communication. These are uneasy, turbulent, difficult times: Uneasy for those who have never known a day of peace during their lifetime; uneasy for those who face the uncertainty of a draft and of fighting in a country for the freedom of another people, while they themselves do not have that freedom at home; uneasy for those who wonder if they will ever know the joy of love, marriage, family, career; uneasy for an entire generation that wonders if it has a future.

Similarly, they are uneasy times for that generation which earlier fought the battles for freedom, a freedom which now permits this generation to protest; uneasy for those who recall similar times and similar days of anxiety and doubt, of questioning and frustration, even of fear of death because of what they believed.

But no matter what the age or the generation, we all share one thing in common: the desire to be free and to enjoy a life of respect, dignity, and equality, to be accepted for ourselves as individuals. So there is dissent, as there has always been dissent since this republic was founded.

What, though, is the nature of dissent? To be effective, dissent must be carried out within a framework that will enable it to accomplish its goal. Otherwise it is only wasted effort, fruitless activity, a denigrating experience of chasing oneself around in circles. Thus, we who admit that our people do not have freedom in its fullest sense must take stock and ask ourselves, "Where do we go from here?" The answer depends on all of us. Those who would use dissent to serve justified ends must take into account several factors: Who is the dissenter? Does he truly know himself and his people? What do they feel? Are they knowledgeable and aware of their heritage as a result of having searched the annals of the past? Can they understand the people and the principles of that heritage, or do they merely reiterate isolated facts? Are the accomplishments of the past understood in their true historical perspective? Is there a quality of rationality leading the dissent, or is it led by immature emotion? Is there confusion of the symbols of race and origin with the pride of man? Is there belief that God created all men, and although they did not make the design, what He made is good and deserves respect for being His creation?

Who are we? Who are the dissenters? Are we a people who know the discrimination and injustice of our land, while knowing also that the democratic system permits even those discriminated against to protest and to bring about change? Surely, we must admit that the disorders have attracted attention and have gained some results; but we must also take a look at what may happen in the face of continued disorders.

The dissenter must know himself. Is he an advocate of permanent, meaningful change, or a thoughtless disrupter who expects no punishment, even though he may break the very system of law that protects his right to protest? If he does not know himself, then he cannot lead and, indeed, can do no good in the quest for justice and equality for all men. He becomes like a riderless horse or one of the six blind men as they perceived the elephant or the drowning man who does not see the shore within reach.

If he knows who he is, he must also know where he is going. He must pursue his goals with strategies which will enable him to reach those goals —no matter how small each step forward may be. He must never lose sight of his purpose, for that purpose determines the difference between foolhardy and worthwhile action and determines the pace forward. He must expect ultimately to succeed and plan his course of action to synchronize with the action of others. He must not only know who he is and what his goals are, but he should always know why he has acted. He should never answer, "I don't know," to a query of, "What do you expect to accomplish?" And when he has achieved his goal, he should know what he will do with his accomplishment.

What does this mean to us here today? A recent event gives us a dramatic example of what dissent can accomplish. That event was the election of Charles Evers to the office of mayor in the little town of Fayette, in Jefferson County, Mississippi—in the heart of prejudice, racism, bigotry, and hatred. Charles Evers—who was linked with many people who lost their lives as victims of a pervading sickness in our society, such as Medgar Evers, Martin Luther King, the Kennedys, Schwerner, Chaney, Lee, Violet Liuzzo—in spite of personal intimidation, threats of reprisal, numerous indignities, discomfort, and illness kept his eye on the goal: to gain the power to produce change. With the help of many people and many organizations—black and white—he gained this power. He knew where he was going. He knew that he did not have the education that many men had earned, but he knew that he was intelligent and had the capacity for loving his fellow man even though he himself had been mistreated, abused, scorned, and thwarted.

He knew that the answer lay in the power of the ballot. He set his strategies and planned the action that would get people to use the ballot to gain the ends they desired. He knew that changing the system required looking beyond the frustration and hatred that whites had exercised toward him, otherwise he would not achieve his goal and would only dissipate the strength so badly needed for systematic progress. He gave the people hope and, in their extreme fear, someone to walk beside. He opposed violence as the means to the end, for he knew that the violence he and his family had experienced had not stopped him nor deterred him from his goal. He had no time for hate; he was too busy mapping the strategies that would give him power within the existing system.

Those days when he sat with the Drew Pearsons, the Stokely Carmichaels, the Dick Gregorys, the Whitney Youngs, the Roy Wilkinses, the Robert Kennedys, and many more, he knew that it would take white and black together to repair the system so that all men could enjoy freedom and equality. And so he has started, this new mayor, and he has decreed that no man will be intimidated in Fayette and that no person will be falsely accused or prosecuted or persecuted because of the color of his skin. His council has outlawed the carrying of firearms in Fayette; the new mayor will not seek vengeance. He has the power, and he will get the help he needs. Help will come to Fayette because there are people of all races who want to make this democratic form of government work for the good of all.

The new mayor will be paid seventy-five dollars a month—twenty-five dollars more than is given to welfare recipients. But he will make it. Charles Evers, who has every reason to hate, will not make the mistake of so many. He will not become what for so long he has detested in others. He knows that hate makes animals of human beings; and he is not willing to swap one oppression for another. He is a dissenter who knows what could be accomplished if every black man and woman of voting age would just learn how to use that weapon—the vote—for which so many have died. We must realize that destroying our institutions only cuts off our opportunities for effectiveness. Change, yes; destruction, no.

You who graduate must share in this decision. You will affect future action by the advice you give and by the principles for which you stand. In entering the job market and competing for jobs, you will sometimes feel frustrated, anxious, restless, or inadequate. In coping with these feelings, you will need all your self-confidence and common sense, all your ability to think things through. You will be able to influence the structure of our society by working within its framework, by participating where decisions are being made, by speaking out articulately, and by proposing strategies to achieve goals.

Your privilege of education will enable you to see beyond single acts and to penetrate to the core of problems. You must use that enthusiasm, zeal, and desire for change in the academic process to become yourself one of the changers—one who plans with students and teachers, instead of for them; one who works with the needy, not for them; one who helps those who have no marketable skills to develop attitudes for work as you help open up jobs for them. You will, because you are of the generation under thirty and because you are college graduates who use words to express ideas and plans but who know that words are no substitute for the constructive action so vitally needed. Where do we go from here? We go not like sheep being led by those whose way ends in folly; but, we determine the course because we know who we are, where we are going, and what it takes to get there and, finally, because we know how to walk in and use the success we will find.

THE BLACK PRESENCE IN AMERICAN

HIGHER EDUCATION*

by Andrew Billingsley

AS THE DECADE of the 1960's draws rapidly and anxiously to a close, no issue in American life has caused greater agony, or held greater promise for the simultaneous liberation of black people and the healing of the historical wounds of the whole society, than the issue of black studies. For in its very essence, the movement for black studies goes to the heart of the predicament of the black man in America and strikes at the core of the intellectual, emotional, and cultural underpinnings of white racism, which is predicated upon the "Anglo-conformity doctrine" (i.e., the belief that there is a "natural" superiority of European culture) with very deep roots in white Anglo-Saxon Western civilization.

None of the specific aspects of the black liberation movement to date challenges the rightness of this basic doctrine as do the demands on the part of black youth for black studies. For at their best these demands go considerably beyond a request that black people be let into certain aspects of higher education from which we have been excluded. They move beyond the urgent and legitimate demand that certain courses be added, certain numbers of black students admitted, and certain numbers of black teachers be hired. In its most radical sense, the movement for black studies demands a rather substantial overturn in the present conception, structure, and operation of the system of higher education, by challenging the very ideological basis on which it is founded. The demand, then, is for a black presence in higher education that would reflect accurately and adequately the existence of black people in the world and in this country.

That this existence is largely denied in the conception of higher education in America is itself undeniable. Black studies so conceived, then, is the radical assertion of black peoplehood. It is the notion, considered

*Originally prepared for a conference on blacks in higher education, Berkeley, California, July, 1969.

arrogant fiction by some of our best friends of the white liberal persuasion, that we black people are an important people in our own right with an important anchor in history, and with a historical stream of culture and humanity which stretches far back into the early history of the modern world beginning in Africa and reaching far into the future of every major aspect of contemporary world civilization. We are, the new demands insist, a complex, varied, long-suffering, resilient, proud, angry, beautiful people. And we intend to tell this to our children, ourselves, and the world. Furthermore, we intend to use this cultural heritage to push our way into the modern world in order to reform it and perhaps even redeem it. And we intend to use all the means at our disposal to do that —including the mechanisms of higher education.

Not since the tremendous social ferment which followed the 1954 Supreme Court decision in *Brown* vs. *Board of Education* has the presence of black people and our movement for liberation been so widely considered and discussed. A wise old man predicted a generation of litigation before the principles underlying that decision would be accepted. He was wrong, of course. After a generation and a half of half-hearted litigation, the American white people have demonstrated conclusively that they are not about to accept the concept of racial equality. No substantial interracialism has been allowed to develop in public schools anywhere in the country, with the particular and only partial exception of Berkeley, California. For even in Berkeley, where interracialism applies to students, it does not yet apply to teachers, principals, janitors, curriculum, or the school budget.

The movement for black studies in higher education seems to be gaining very rapidly. In all likelihood, it will take at least a generation of agitation before any substantial and permanent changes in higher education are wrought that would adequately reflect the black presence. This is true in part because the task is so new, so monumental, and the course is so uncharted. It is true mainly, however, because the forces of resistance to meaningful black studies are massive and the forces of reaction have already set in. But if the battle for black studies is far from won, and if it will yet take a great deal of agony, hard work, and suffering on the part of black people and others in order to achieve it, the black youth of today and tomorrow are determined that the movement should proceed with all deliberate speed. They, at least, if not their older brothers, are increasingly willing to insist that it should be done by all means necessary. This is a new element in modern higher education. It is a most agonizing element. It may be the element that provides the greatest promise of success.

What, then, are some of the major sources out of which the demands for black studies come? What are the sources of resistance? What patterns are taking shape in the development of this movement? What are some of the inherent dangers in this movement? And what are its promises? These are the questions on which the rest of this essay will focus.

SOURCES OF BLACK-STUDIES DEMANDS

From where spring these new, angry demands, for a black presence in higher education? Was it from some foreign ideology, Marxism, Maoism, or Castroism? There are people, very wise and highly respected people in American higher education, who are firmly convinced that each of these ideologies is the major source of these new demands. I know. I have spent hours in long and earnest discussion with faculty members who are convinced that American black people could not have possibly thought up all by themselves so searching a set of demands that seem so contrary to the traditions of Western civilization.

Nor did these demands come from some giant conspiracy hatched in the head of Stokely Carmichael, H. Rap Brown, or Eldridge Cleaver. Surely many college administrators are convinced that these demands come from outside agitators, most generally from out of the state, and always from off the campus. "They're trying to bring politics and civil rights into higher education, where it has no place," more than one irate, harassed, white liberal college administrator has been heard to say. "They are attacking us for the problems created by other people." It is true, of course, that black studies are part of the more general movement of black people for liberation, and that that in turn is an aspect of the worldwide struggle on the part of subject peoples to throw off the yoke of colonialism, and that to some extent that movement is given impetus by ideologies of a variety of types, some of which are in their essence contradictory. And it is also true that there is a generalized feeling on the part of black people that we must increasingly take over the initiative for our own liberation without depending on the good will, intelligence, or abilities of well-meaning white people to integrate us into their hearts, their culture, and their institutions on their own initiative and in their own good time. This spirit of defiance and revolt is infesting every aspect of black life from the ghetto to the financial houses on Wall Street, from the churches to the police departments. And black people are organizing to protect their humanity, and their people. It is a new kind of faith in the democratic process. And each incident in one institutional or geographic location gives impetus to the general spirit of revolt. And so maybe Stokely, Rap, and all the others who have challenged racism in any quarter and in any manner, do bear some responsibility, and may take some credit for the new demands for black studies. But the sad and hopeful fact is that the movement for black studies is home-grown. The most important source is the racism which is so endemic to American institutions. The next most important source is the external hunger for freedom, recognition, and opportunity which black people have nurtured since the dawn of civilization, and which was not crushed by slavery even though it was the most cruel form of human bondage known to man. And the even sadder and more hopeful fact is that in every aspect of institutional life in this country, black people are expressing in a variety of ways their disillusionment with the status quo, including traditional ways of attacking the injustices we suffer.

Only a quarter of all black people queried in a 1969 national study expressed the view that the federal government is helpful in protecting the rights of black people. More than half expressed the view that black people should oppose the war in Vietnam specifically because black people are denied freedom in this country. At the same time two-thirds of them expressed the view that there will be more riots in the near future, and three-fourths believe that black is beautiful. All these trends are interrelated. They reflect the inner turmoil in the black community, as we grope for a sense of our essence while simultaneously demanding with decreasing faith and increasing determination that this essence be accepted by others. It is an explosive mixture which provides only part —but a meaningful part—of the context out of which the demands for black studies stem.

Yet, more specifically, the sources of the major demands for black studies can be localized within the institutions of higher education themselves. For these institutions—all of them—cry out for reform. They have become as encrusted, rigid, insensitive, as the worst features of our national institutional life. They have certainly not provided the leadership that the society deserves from the investment made in higher education. And in none of the many ways in which higher education has failed is this failure more conspicuous than its dual failure to effectively educate black people, and to effectively educate white people about black people. They have failed, as the other major institutions of our society have failed, to incorporate black people and the black perspective into their conception of their function, their structure, or their operation. The University of California alone graduates more than a thousand Ph.D.'s every year. In any just system of higher education, in a state which is 25 percent black, Mexican, and Indian, and in a community whose population is one third of these minorities, one to two hundred of those Ph.D.'s would be black, brown, or red. But instead, in the years from the founding of the University of California one hundred years ago until 1969, there have never been as many as ten persons from these three minority groups receiving Ph.D. degrees. Actually in most of the annual graduating ceremonies, there was not even one black, brown, or red person being awarded a Ph.D. degree. And on the Berkeley campus alone over one hundred new faculty members are hired each fall. Certainly one would think that in a reasonably open institution at least ten of these would be black, brown, or red. Again most years, not one black, Mexican-American, or Indian is hired.

Out of a regular faculty of more than thirteen hundred, the university's Berkeley campus boasts six blacks, two Mexican-Americans, and one American Indian. This is not only rampant racism out of all proportion to the interests or qualifications or availability of black scholars, but it is a situation which I report with a great deal of personal agony. For it has been my responsibility in part to do something to correct the situation. And this situation is only symptomatic of the rampant racism which exists in every aspect of the university, including the curriculum, the student body, the administrative officers, the blue-collar work forces, and the university budget. Of the hundreds of millions of dollars the university brings into and spends in the economy of the community, no conscious effort at all is made to spend some of those funds building up the economic fabric of the black community. Virtually all of it is sent to white firms. When a black architect recently asked to bid on a contract to renovate a major building he was treated with the utmost discourtesy. The university can find money to defend the status quo, as in the recent People's Park controversy, but it can find only a minimum amount of money to build a third-world college or to channel into the black community. It would not take a great deal of wild-eyed radicalism on the part of the university to allow black businessmen to bid on some of the vast numbers of contracts the university handles. What could be more American? Yet not even the paper clips the university uses are purchased through economic enterprises owned, managed, or controlled in any way by black people. It is a situation which could be easily corrected by a bit of farsighted planning on the part of the Regents, the purchasing agents, or even the student government.

The situation at Berkeley is, of course, no worse, though perhaps no better, than at all the other major institutions of higher education, which have made no substantial effort to rid themselves of racism, or the systematic exclusion of black people from all aspects of their structure, daily operation, and utilization of resources. So higher education is in dire need of reform. And this is a basic cause of the black student revolt and the demands for black studies.

But while racism is as rampant as it is invidious in American higher education, it does not bear the total responsibility, not even ideologically for the absence of the black presence in higher education, and consequently does not bear total responsibility for generating the black student revolt. Other forces in the academic milieu conspire with racism to produce this effect. Chief among these other forces are traditionalism, political conservatism, political liberalism, bureaucracy, and intellectual arrogance. Nothing can unite the political liberals and political conservatives on the faculty more quickly than a demand or set of acts on the part of students, particularly black students, which threatens the sanctity of the bureaucratic procedures which have enabled these faculty members to prosper and which protects their academic and intellectual domain. In this respect the liberals outdo the conservatives in resorting to the traditions of the university, to the correct procedures, to the need to protect academic excellence, and the like. I have sometimes felt during our struggle for black studies at Berkeley that we would be better off if all the liberals could have been muzzled during our great debates, and let the black student militants and the conservative faculty members engage in debate. They had a bit more respect for each other. But I hasten to add that I do not mean to pit the white conservatives against the white liberals. I mean instead to suggest that the complex pattern of resistance to black studies and other meaningful innovations cannot be expected to follow these ideological lines or to benefit from these ideological labels. The opposition to black studies has come from both camps, just as has the support.

Nevertheless, these labels and philosophies are not as relevant as they might seem to the kinds of innovations represented by black studies. For black studies challenge them both. Both are essentially white. Neither grew out of or is indeed very responsive to the black perspective. And perhaps because many of the white liberal intellectuals have been considered friends of black people in the past and have been personal friends of mine, it rankles a bit more to listen even now to the ringing raves of racism, couched ever so correctly in the king's rhetoric, which have been dropping from their lips and their hearts during the past year of agonizing reappraisal of black people in higher education. I have visited more than a dozen major white universities, and examined the arguments for and against black studies which have emanated from at least two dozen more campuses; and I have found that this phenomenon, this liberal nightmare, this crisis in the liberal imagination, is so pervasive as to constitute a crisis of major proportions not only in the universities, where white liberals are so prominent, but also in the government, the church, and other institutions which depend on intellectual leadership from the universities and which have been served fairly well at other times and on other issues by these men of intellect and scholarly and critical persuasion. Thus one of the unanticipated consequences of the demands for black studies has been to expose the bankruptcy of white liberal intellectual scholarship and action. This is due in no small measure to the fact that the demands for black studies go to the heart of the Anglo-conformity doctrine, which in turn is at the heart of the cultural basis of much of what has come to be described as Western civilization, of which these white liberal intellectuals have been among the major definers and benefactors.

Nevertheless, although the racism, traditionalism, conservatism, liberalism, bureaucracy, or academic arrogance on the part of these universities provided the basis for the black student revolt, they did not in themselves produce the revolt, or the demands for black studies. The demands for black studies did not come from the managers of the great universities, deciding to rescue their institutions from decadence through their foresight and leadership, suggesting to their faculties and governing bodies that they strive to embrace the black presence, incorporate it, study it, develop it.

Nor did the black studies come from university faculties, not even the most radical, the most socially conscious, or activist elements, not even the faculty members most identified with the civil-rights movement, and certainly not from the faculty members most identified with the study of black life as a career.

One of the saddest features of this whole movement for black studies is that Caucasian experts on black history, and culture, and social life have been prominent among the opponents of black studies. They have often given the impression that they are more interested in their own personal careers, theories, academic domains, and expertise than in the liberation of the people who provided the raw material for their studies and their success. The notion that black people have something special to contribute to the study of black people has been denounced more than once in angry tones to me by several white experts on black people. Race, they have argued, is, or ought to be, irrelevant. What this has always meant is that the black race was irrelevant. Obviously it has not meant the white race. "We take no account of a man's race except as an object of study," has been said by white people, who are in such an overwhelming numerical majority in the country that they don't have to think of themselves as a race. This has the effect of denying the legitimacy of blackness while protecting the domain of white people. It is one of the more subtle aspects of racism.

But if we must point with derision to white governing boards, administrations, and faculties of whatever persuasion, for their failure to anticipate, or demand black studies, we must not overlook a smaller band of culprits. These are the black educators within the white and black universities who have also failed to assert the black presence in higher education.

They have equated black studies somehow with the evils of segregation. I remember distinctly a few years ago when some black students approached me to ask for leadership in the struggle for black studies. I was not prepared to give it. It did not seem right. In the last two years, as I have had more and more dealings with black students both in my classes and outside, I have been less impressed by what I have taught them than by what they have taught me. For example, they taught me that the major difference between segregation and self-determination is who makes the decision. Segregation is a situation in which white people say to black people, "You must stay over there, in those inferior facilities, and you are free to decide to leave; and we, the white people, will control and manage the institutional aspects of your lives." That is segregation. That is an example of the type of colonialism, international or domestic, against which black people are increasingly rebelling.

Self-determination, on the other hand, is the situation in which black people decide among ourselves that we want to recognize our heritage and common interest and culture and live and work together to build something superior, of which we can be proud, and in which we exercise control over the institutions which affect our lives most intimately.

Thus, if white people were to decide that there should be a black-studies department, and all black students and faculty must work in that department and would not be encouraged to study and work in other departments of the university, and if the facilities and resources of the black-studies department were inferior to those of other departments, and if the major policies governing the black-studies department were made by the white people outside the black-studies department, that would be segregation American style. That is the only kind of segregation we have ever had in this country. There are no major institutional aspects of our national life in which black people force white people into inferior facilities, refuse to let them out, and control the policy decisions affecting the lives of white people. It does not exist. This is not recommended by any of the advocates of black studies, and so to denounce black studies as segregation is mischievous and misguided at best.

The difference is who decides. The difference is self-determination. The difference is whether one group of people are robbing another group of people of their rightful heritage and the resources of their society. Black people have not done this to white people in this country and are not proposing to do it now.

In black studies as in other aspects of life, what we are proposing—in fact, demanding—is to have enough breathing room, without the ever-presence of white domination, to create and develop our own thing, in our own way, and then to spread that thing around to others who are able and willing to share it. For it must be observed that white people, even in small numbers, have a very stifling effect on the creativity of black people. The reasons for that are partly historical. But the fact is that the most creative innovations of black culture, have been created within a black context, within the black community, while white people were not there, looking over their shoulder, controlling, and dominating even while not intending to do so. These creations, in music, art, literature, dance, theology, and even scholarship, have then been shared with the wider society. One of the reasons white people have such a difficult time imagining that black people wish to or should be allowed to do anything among themselves without the ever-presence of white people is that they can not imagine how oppressive their presence is to black people. Not always, of course, and not invariably, but generally. And of course this oppressiveness varies tremendously, depending on time, place, and people. But it is too general a phenomenon to be dismissed under the guise of "integration" or fighting "segregation in reverse"—whatever that might mean.

But all this is a fairly new reality for many of us who are black intellectuals, administrators, and scholars in higher education. We too have been victimized by the Anglo-conformity doctrine. We have benefited to a limited degree from the exclusion of other black people. We have gloried in our culture, our status, our representation as the talented tenth, and as leaders and exemplars for our race, all the while helping to perpetuate and legitimatize systems which oppressed our people. And so we have been blinded and incapacitated by the forces of racism and by our own self-interest. Little wonder, then, that it was not black scholars and intellectuals who demanded black studies. This, perhaps for the same reasons that black scholars and intellectuals have seldom been in the vanguard of any revolutionary innovation. This is not to depreciate either the role of black intellectuals or their contribution to the black revolution in general or black studies in particular.

Furthermore, if the black revolution is to succeed at all, and if black studies are to succeed it will be because black intellectuals play an increasingly dominant role in their formulation, administration, and operation. It is important, however, to emphasize the crippling nature of our racist society, which prevents the most privileged and articulate members of the oppressed people from taking leadership in advocating new forms of attack on the oppression of our people. It is at a later stage, a stage which is now upon us, that black intellectuals will be called upon to do our thing.

As for the more than one hundred black colleges and universities—most of them in the South—two things must be said in passing. First, they have been the intellectual salvation of black people in America. There would be no substantial group of college-educated men and women in the black communty today, were their education left to the white or integrated institutions. Over half of all black college graduates in the country today, including the overwhelming majority of those who have gone on for advanced degrees and occupy significant places in the educational leadership of the country, were educated in black colleges, and would not have been accepted in the white colleges. It is still true today that roughly half of all black college students are enrolled in these colleges. Their functions in the past, present, and future can not be minimized. As a product of a black college, I yield no quarter to those in the white or the black communities who call for the dismantling or destruction of these centers of learning, and socialization. These have been islands of culture in the truest sense in a sea of hostile white racism, oppression, and indifference to the minds and spirits of black people.

At the same time, it must also be observed, in passing, that not one of these more than a hundred colleges has done an adequate job of reflecting, representing, honoring, or developing the black presence in higher education. For all their contribution to the education of black people, they have been essentially white-oriented colleges. In this respect they have been a product, victim, and perpetrator of the Anglo-conformity aspect of white racism, while at the same time one of the most effective means of coping with racism, and perhaps even one of the most effective agents of its destruction. It must be remembered that some of the most effective movements against racism have emanated from and been sustained by the black church and the black colleges; and some of the most effective revolutionaries have been the young black students who started the black student revolt out of the black colleges in the South. And every civil-rights cause—from the NAACP to the Black Panthers—has relied heavily on the leadership of youth trained in these black colleges.

The fault of this blind search after European ways, this effort to do nothing or teach nothing that was not done or taught in white colleges, has not been the fault completely of the administrators of these colleges, or the black community generally. For these institutions, like all institutions, are creatures of the larger white society. They are dependent on that society for sanction and support. It is very clear that until recently any black college president or faculty which wanted to strive for excellence was told in a variety of ways more effective than words that the white way was the right way. And any substantial deviations, or innovations, in the direction of the black experience would have resulted in the college's losing its accreditation, its budget, and a substantial portion of its faculty and student body. This is not to deny a certain amount of pigheadedness, authoritarianism, backwardness, timidity, or even anti-intellectualism on the part of some of the administrators of these colleges. But even this behavior is socially and culturally determined. And we are aware, with Nathan Hare, not only of the varieties of Uncle Tomism, but of the functions which these roles serve in the struggle of a people to survive. But more than that, we are aware that many of these administrators and faculty members of black colleges have given more of themselves, their talent and energy, than have white men and women, of half their worth, who have received twice the financial and social rewards from our society. Not only are the black colleges of today controlled largely by white people whether they are public or private, many of them are still staffed too largely by white faculty members. One of the ironies of the black student revolt is that some black students at one of these black colleges set forth as one of their "nonnegotiable" demands that at least half the faculty in one department should be black. More than one department in more than one of these colleges have no black faculty members whatever. However, the whiteness of these institutions is reflected mainly in their educational mission and in their curricula. It is sad that with the exception of black-history courses, very few of these institutions have developed any comprehensive curriculum on the history, culture, problems, or progress of black people in the world. Nor has any one of the black universities given an honorary degree to Duke Ellington, or offered to make him chairman of its music department. Furthermore, many of the music departments of these colleges have abandoned black music altogether in their search of the holy European grail of "classical" music. Unfortunately, many of these institutions have succeeded in teaching their students to be ashamed of their black heritage, and to seek to overcome it and submerge themselves into the European culture rather than use their considerable intellect and talent in the creative development of the Afro-American presence in the world. Not only the black community but the whole society has been deprived of rich cultural, scientific, and economic potential by this development.

Fortunately the situation is changing in the black colleges. They are discovering the black experience along with the rest of the country. This is due mainly to the efforts of black people in the ghettos of America who have not seen the inside of any college. It is also due to the efforts of the civil-rights movement.

And finally, the turn toward blackness in the black colleges is awakened by those same black students in the South and the North who, building on their heritage of protest, are making life so painful for certain administrators. The contributions of these black colleges to black studies will be different from that of the white colleges if they are authentic. They will be better if allowed to develop organically and utilize the considerable talent among the faculty, student body, and the black community in the South. But this will happen only if the administrators of these colleges are wise enough to listen to their most radical students, and at the same time fortunate enough, or perhaps wise enough, to garner the considerable financial resources they need from the conservative boards of trustees, legislatures, and foundations, and the federal government. It is no easy task. The agony is apparent. The promise is no less inherent, though it is perhaps like the shore dimly seen.

In this respect the Martin Luther King, Jr., Memorial Center in Atlanta under the inspired leadership of Professor Vincent Harding, working in collaboration with the Atlanta University system, has tremendous potential for honoring the spirit of the man it memorializes by developing, enhancing, and sharing with the rest of the world some of the basic essentials of the history, culture, and the potential of black people in the world, and their contributions to world civilization.

A sober consideration of the sources of the demands for black studies must reflect on the fact that the major thrust of these demands has been the black students, not the black students who have been already established in the universities, but those newly admitted thereto. It has been a terrible burden on these young people. Imagine for a moment those people in the system most vulnerable—newly entered freshmen, admitted on scholarship, and admitted by the grace of a white administration newly aware of black students, eager to provide opportunities for culturally deprived youth, and expecting conformity and gratitude for their efforts. But the essential correctness of the cause of these new students has brought quick acquiescence or collaboration from other black students, black faculty, and indeed other nonblack people as well, especially white activist students. But consider the plight of these new black students who have been faced with the responsibility of demanding black studies, striking, picketing, and denouncing the racist administrations and faculties in order to get an audience, and then being saddled with the responsibility of designing curriculum, hiring faculties, and administering new programs, all the while having to attend their classes and pass their courses. No students in the recent history of higher education have assumed so faithfully such a heavy burden. The rest of us should be ashamed of ourselves. Yet many of these students have become the casualties of their own efforts to reform the universities. It was perhaps inevitable. And in a sense it is another accolade due these young people that they have suffered voluntarily for something in which they believe. Still it is sad to see such talent and optimism wasted or deflected by the insensitive and inhumane punishment meted out to them by racist administrations and faculties, courts, and governors.

IN THE NAME OF MALCOLM, MEDGAR, AND MARTIN

In a sense, these black youths were the most appropriate ones to start this phase of the revolution. They have been freer to see its necessity than the rest of us. They have also been freer to demand the kind of sweeping reforms inherent in this new conception. The rest of us compromise too easily with a bit of progress and a lot of injustice. But they have not raised this new battle cry in isolation or out of their own limited experience. They are a product of the black resurgence. Their demands for black studies grew out of the general struggle for self-definition and self-determination most strongly voiced by Malcolm X back in the early 1960's. They are indebted to all the special efforts which have come before.

At the opening of a recent jazz festival at the University of California sponsored by the black students and the student government, the invocation was given by a young black minister identified with the black struggle. He implored the performers, and the audience, to "do your thing, in the name of Malcolm, Medgar, and Martin." It is a new trinity: Malcolm X, the first man of modern times to challenge so radically the foundations of the white racist society; Medgar Evers, who, we should be reminded, represented the historic efforts of that movement for first-class citizenship of black people under the auspices of the NAACP, however limited is its perspective for today; and Martin Luther King, Jr., surely a modern incarnation of Jesus of Nazareth, who was crucified by a society too wicked to understand and accept and follow him.

It was said, not at all in disrespect for the old trinity but in perceptive admiration of the function of these men in symbolizing the black man's struggle for peoplehood in his own land. It was as appropriate and right as was the later urging by Charlie Brown, the black student leader, and the master of ceremonies that the audience should "free Huey." Black people are more and more determined that our cultural heritage should no longer be separated from our political struggle for freedom, but should be used as a means of our own liberation, which, as Harold Cruse has urged, must be won on the political, economic, and cultural fronts simultaneously. For people are certainly not free if they are free only to express and develop their cultural forms for the benefit and entertainment of white people, while being denied the economic and political control of their communities or the control of their own institutions, or a fair share of the control of those larger institutions which serve the total community.

It is out of the converging strains of this black resurgence that the students have fashioned their conception of black studies. They have brought the black revolution to the intellectual heart of our society.

If the ideas of Malcolm X are the dominant intellectual theme of the demands for black studies, the spirit of Martin Luther King, Jr., provides a more recent stimulus.

When Martin Luther King was assassinated on April 4, 1968, it was a tragedy for the whole world. It was a tragedy and a crisis of special proportions for black people in this country. Three reactions ran in rapid succession through all of the black communities of the country. The first was a heightened sense of aloneness, hopelessness, and alienation. The feeling was quite generally expressed that if the American white racist society would not respond to the eloquent, moral, and scholarly work represented in the life of Martin Luther King, Jr., and his special pleadings on behalf of his people and all humanity, then certainly life would be grim without him. The second type of reaction was rage expressed overtly by only a small proportion of the people who actually felt it, but still in sufficient proportions to cause a major crisis in many communities in the country. The statistics reflect only part of this reaction. Thus over two hundred cities in thirty-five states experienced major disorders following Dr. King's assassination. Altogether forty-three persons were killed, 3,500 injured, and 27,000 arrested. It has been estimated that over 56,000 National Guardsmen and federal troops were utilized on twenty-five different occasions during those few fateful days in April. Following this sense and expression of rage was a third response, which was perhaps more constructive. Black people in every community, and every social status, and almost every type of organization, group, or institution began to express the view that if white people could not take the initiative to incorporate black people in the society as equals under the leadership of Martin Luther King, Jr., they were not likely to take this initiative now: black people must band together in spirit and action in order to take the initiative on their own behalf. The view grew rapidly and is still expanding throughout black communities—that no one black or white leader or group of leaders will be able to deliver the black people from their subordinate position in the social structure. The sense of common status, condition, and future on the part of black people was heightened.

The educational institutions were among the targets of this concerted action and these intensified demands. They were perhaps more vehemently attacked than some other institutions in society, partly because educational institutions have been more intransigent than economic and political institutions, but chiefly because black people have come to view education as the major source of their achievement as a people. Thus, the universities, colleges, high schools, and grade schools were approached with demands by black students often in cooperation with black faculties and community people, and often with large numbers of white students.

These demands have been amazingly uniform across the country and at every level of education. Black people demanded a measure of influence or control over the operation of these educational institutions commensurate with their needs and their representation in the institution or in the community. Second, they demanded that black people be hired to help govern, administer, and execute the functions of these institutions in significant numbers and at all levels. Third, they demanded that larger numbers of black students be admitted into these institutions of higher education. Fourth, they demanded that black people be more adequately represented in the course offerings and scholarly content of the curriculum. More courses on black history, culture, and contemporary conditions, and more content of this type in existing courses, were demanded. Fifth, they demanded that these educational institutions implement their own philosophic commitments to equality of opportunity and hire larger numbers of nonacademic personnel in some fair proportion. Finally, these black students and citizens, with considerable support among white students, demanded that these educational institutions use their economic power and funds, their investment portfolios and purchasing power, to enhance economic viability of the black community.

This sense of racial and ethnic identity, solidarity, pride, and concerted action was not new. It has been seen before and is still current among other ethnic groups. It was not new even for black people in this country. But it was more widespread and more stridently expressed, perhaps more desperate, perhaps more hopeful than during previous periods of black protest and assertion.

It must be observed that up to now black students have not demanded that these educational establishments be destroyed. And they have not played any major role in destructive acts. Nor did they demand of themselves that they abandon these institutions. They want to be inside. They want to be educated. They have a certain faith that these institutions can and will change in order to make their education more relevant. They think this can best be done by giving extra special consideration to ways of incorporating black people and the varieties and complexities of the black experience into the structure of these educational institutions at every level. They insist that the patterns of excluding black people from these institutions, whether deliberate or inadvertent, must be reversed. They want these institutions to serve them and their educational needs at least as well as they now serve the needs of other students. And they want to have considerable voice in the manner in which this is done. And they want these changes to take place either next week or at the beginning of next quarter.

These demands, which are highly consistent with the American tradition, are both legitimate and urgent. The response of the educational institutions has been varied. One very common response has been primarily to the form and language of the demands: finding these repugnant, they resist the legitimacy and urgency of the proposals. Another response has been acceptance of the the proposals' legitimacy but rejection of their urgency. Even when the students' proposals have been perceived as legitimate, the pattern of response has been varied. Some universities have done nothing, but that response, is rare. For all over the country major and minor universities, colleges, junior colleges, and private and public lower schools, particularly those in urban areas in the North and West, have responded with positive action. Even when positive action has been taken, stimulated by the general students' demands, these responses are highly varied. One response pattern, for example, has been to do as little as possible in order to allay a threatened crisis or period of student unrest. A favorite act has been to hire one or a few black people in advisory positions, without authority. Black students at Berkeley call these "assistant niggerships." More meaningful acts have been stepped-up efforts to recruit more black students. Sometimes one new course on black history has been introduced.

One tendency which is the greatest danger has been for white university administrators and faculties to take over with token integration the development of black studies and fashion them in their own image, which is at best self-defeating and at worst a giant conspiracy to perpetuate white control over black people and the black experience in every area of life—even in the black-studies department. This is a reassertion of colonialism in the guise of innovation and responding to black demands.

WHAT PATTERNS ARE TAKING SHAPE IN BLACK STUDIES

Some of the country's major universities have made substantial commitments to meet the needs pointed up by the student demands. In order to consider the various patterns the development of black studies are taking, it seems well to consider the question, Just what is meant by black studies? For some, any course about black people is called black studies. For others the course must be taught by a black lecturer and from a black perspective in order to qualify. For still others one course alone does not constitute black studies any more than one swallow makes a summer. A series of interrelated courses is required. And for still others the series of course offerings must lead to a degree in order to be considered black studies in higher education. In announcing a new postgraduate fellowship program to train teachers of black studies "without regard to their race, creed, or sex" the Danforth Foundation took special note of the ambiguity of black studies conceptions to date. "For some, any topic related to the Negro is included in 'black studies.' For others 'black studies' must pass the test of being geared to the urban United States in the 1960's. For a few, the test is structural: 'Black Studies' are courses taught in a specific departmental framework." Recognizing that black studies will be taught before they are defined, the foundation has set out to train persons who already hold teaching positions in the social sciences and history for special work in this new undefined field.

In its essence, however, black studies, or the black presence in higher education, requires the incorporation of black people and the black experience in the world into every appropriate aspect of the structure of higher education in proportions which reflect adequately and accurately the experience of the people of African origin in the world today. Anything short of that is tokenism. Most of the programs being set up called black studies today are examples of tokenism.

A second question, which follows closely the one about what is black studies, is, For whom should black studies be developed? At its best the black presence in higher education is designed for several audiences or student bodies.

These are: (1) the black students in the universities and those who will be entering; (2) the white students, who are even more ignorant about the black experience than the black students and in many instances just as eager to correct this ignorance; (3) the white faculty, which is by and large even more ignorant of the black experience than their students, but not as willing to admit or correct it; (4) the black faculty, which though small in number is a powerful source of potential enlightenment; (5) the black community, which stands to benefit from this new activity on behalf of black peoplehood; and (6) the white community, which needs enlightenment perhaps more than any of these other student bodies but which resists it more. In short, the black presence in higher education, or the development, enhancement, and honoring of the black experience in the world will benefit the whole society. These programs should take into consideration the specific audience for which they are designed. They may not be able to meet all these needs with any one or two standard approaches. At the present time there is no sophisticated conception of these different audiences and the appropriate kinds of black studies which will be addressed to their somewhat different needs, levels of awareness, and potential for learning.

But to say that black studies are for everybody is not to say that they should all sit in the same classes and take part in the development and control of these programs in equal manner. Clearly, if black studies are to be developed to any degree authentically, they must be developed by black people with a maximum sensitivity to and experience in the black community with other people providing supportive roles. Otherwise black studies will not only be corrupted by the ignorance and arrogance of white people, but will become still another tool in the hands of the white establishment for the misuse of black people.

The black students have been clearer than the rest of us about the major audience and purposes for which they would like to see black studies designed. For them, they and the black community are the primary targets. The black students at Berkeley, in their manifesto of April 1968 made the point very clearly:

> As students on the white college and university campuses of America, we have learned something which we choose never to forget.
> WE ARE NOT WHITE. WE DO NOT WISH TO BE WHITE. WHAT IS GOOD FOR THE WHITE PEOPLE IS OFTENTIMES WORSE THAN BAD FOR US.
> The young black people of America are the inheritors of what is undoubtedly one of the most challenging, gravest, and [most] threatening sets of social circumstances that [have] ever fallen upon a generation of young people anywhere in history. We have been

born into a hostile and alien society which loathes us on condition of our skin color. . . . Sentenced to inaneness, subservience, and death, from our beginning, many of us came to regard our beautiful pigmentation as a plague. . . . We act now because we realize, beyond any doubt, that our "souls," i.e., that which is all and the end of us, has been stifled to the point that we can no longer bear it. We have been forced to the point where we must (and will) insist on those changes that are necessary to our survival. There is nothing less to settle for and nothing less will do. . . . We have found a kind of self-discovery which has snatched our minds from the rank of a historically insignificant, persecuted minority and placed us among the world's majority populace, which is crying from one end of the earth to the other that "we are." We are decided that we alone can define ourselves, that we are beautiful despite the white negative concept of us, that we have a history, an art, and a culture that no race or nation can stamp out our "souls" no matter the intensity of this foolish effort.

We must therefore ask with unrelenting insistence that our future education be radically reformed. We demand a program of "BLACK STUDIES," a program which will be of, by, and for black people. We demand that we be educated realistically; and that no form of education which attempts to lie to us, or otherwise miseducate us, will be accepted.

The black students at Cornell were somewhat more general.

Many have argued that there is no place within the university structure for an Afro-American studies program. After all, there is no Jewish-American studies program; and in any case, the Negro experience and culture are only one variant of the more general culture and experience of mankind, and thus can be understood by way of studying mankind's experience and African and American culture. It is our conviction, however, that the black experience is a sufficiently unique aspect of human history and social relations that its study will contribute mightily to our understanding of general human culture and experience; and that, if this were not the case, the problems associated with race in this country are so pressing and so little understood either by academics or by the general public that to perpetuate the subordination of the study and instruction of Afro-Americans to the classical university structure would constitute the perpetuation of the classical academic inattention to the race problem and unwittingly academic compromise with prevailing social norms.

The University Ad Hoc Committee continued its rationale for a black-oriented subculture for the black-studies program as follows:

> Neither a white assimilationist ethic nor the "universalism" ascribed to Anglo-American particularism in many of our institutions of higher education should be allowed to prohibit black scholars from establishing valid criteria for their own educational programs and finding critical answers to meet the problems of their own communities. Thus, black particularism as an academic bias will supplement and not replace white particularism. This type of pluralism will permit an appreciation of the black experience as something which is more than a reflection of the dominant white society or ideology and which, thus, is worthy of study in its own right.

Black students have been in the forefront but not alone in their demands that universities educate black students better than they have in the past by tying their education positively to their experience as black people. Black educators have been quick to join them in the articulation of this imperative.

Perhaps the most eloquent statement of the underlying philosophy of this program has been stated by Dr. Edward W. Crosby, a black scholar and the director of education in the program at Southern Illinois University:

> For absolutely too long the educational establishment has listened to those professed experts of the "Negro problem" who speak to the breakdown of the Negro family, the pathology of the fatherless child, the lack of self-concept or the identity crisis, the inability of black children to deal with abstractions, the language barrier, and, ironically, how well discrimination has worked.
>
> These experts have exaggerated the myth attesting to the uneducability of black youth. It is high time we shut our ears to them, stopped debating about how difficult or impossible it is to educate these students, and get the damned job done.

A group of black instructors in a course entitled Black Ideals offered at Antioch College have also placed black studies in context of the black movement more generally.

> The time has come to make black more than a slogan. The time has come to make black a way of life, a philosophy for action. As Malcolm said, whatever you think you are, the white man sees us, all of us, as niggers. Whatever you do, whatever job you aspire to, wherever you are going, YOU face one crushing humiliating reality: the absolute supremacy of the white man. A white man can cut off

your water; a white man can slap a curfew on your section of town; a white man *has* got the power, plenty of power. But the greatest power the white man has is control over our minds. The white man has been able fo define our thinking (even when it ran counter to what we felt in our hearts) both about ourselves and about him. By defining our thinking, he has successfully defined our actions. For instance, he has got us thinking that the only time to get down is in long hot summers. More than that, he has got us fighting for TV sets, knots, and gators. He has successfully defined the fields of battle and we lose every time we let that happen. As Malcolm said, the white man is both wolf (beastly crude) and fox (beastly clever) but always a rotten dog in his relations to black people.

The time, Brothers and Sisters, is the midnight hour. The night is ours if we can get our minds (hearts) together. If this world is going to be ours, if everything is going to be all right when the morning comes, all right for all the babies on the way, *we got to start thinking black!* Black thought is total! It is concept. It is emotion. It is spirit. It is ethic. And most important it is the basis of action.

Clearly, then, for some purposes both the instructors and the students in black-studies classes should be black. For others, even if the students are mixed or all white, the instruction should be by black people. And for almost all purposes, if black studies are to be taught and learned meaningfully they must take place within a black context. If the black community can not be incorporated into the university fast enough for this kind of relevant instruction to take place, then the instruction, whatever the color of the teacher or the students, must move off the campus into the black community and be surrounded by it. Otherwise the specter of white instructors teaching white students with a few token blacks in the class about black studies in the splendid isolation of the racist white university, though too grotesque to contemplate, will be the ever-present reality. It is even now an ever present danger. To do black studies right will obviously require radical changes in the current standards and conceptions about who is qualified to teach what. The black experience must be taught by people who have lived it. Few white people can make that claim.

The structure of black-studies programs are less important than the basic conception and design of them. For the basic conception should be very similar from one place to another. Structurally, however, a great deal of variation will be both necessary and desirable. Programs may be structured differently in white colleges and in black colleges. They may be structured differently in large public institutions and in small private ones. Five structures are emerging which seem to have considerable viability. First, the large comprehensive course in Afro-American history and civilization.

Harvard University introduced for the first time, beginning in the fall of 1968, a year-long, two-semester, comprehensive course in the history and contemporary conditions of Afro-Americans. The course was chaired by a major Harvard professor with two junior faculty members, one of whom was black, as participants. The course was designed to accommodate one hundred undergraduates. Black students were given preference. This course did not work out too well at Harvard and has been abandoned in favor of a more comprehensive and black-oriented program of studies leading to a degree and requiring the hiring of ten black scholars as instructors, with black students having a major voice in both the curriculum and the selection of faculty. The first comprehensive course did not work too well because it was not sufficiently black-oriented. It was essentially a white man's version of black studies controlled completely by white and white-oriented faculty, with no major voice for the students.

Yet for many campuses such a comprehensive course, if done properly, will be not only appropriate but sufficient. There is no reason to suppose that all the small colleges in the country should have new comprehensive programs or departments of Afro-American studies. It would be undesirable if all of them did. They could not possibly be staffed properly. But all of those who teach anything about Western civilization or the American experience should do something to include black perspective in their courses. And since their regular instructors will not be very well prepared to make the necessary innovations in their own course offerings, a comprehensive course such as the one envisioned by Harvard may be an effective instrument for the study of the black experience. That it requires almost no structural changes in the college is both a strength and a weakness. It is a strength, for it may be quickly and easily installed. It is a weakness, because it may be peripheral to the major and "more important" course offerings of the college.

A second manner of structuring black studies is to offer a series of closely related courses from several different departments in a loosely coordinated program.

Yale and Cornell have designed black studies along program rather than departmental lines.

Professor Robert A. Dahl, professor of political science at Yale, has described their new program as an interdisciplinary approach to studying the experience and conditions of people of African ancestry in Africa and in the New World. The program would permit a student to examine these topics from a broad view and at the same time it would require him to concentrate in one of the relevant disciplines in Yale College. Students would receive a grounding in the history of black people in Africa and in the United States. On this foundation it will be possible for the student to build knowledge of the cultural, economic, political, social, artistic, and historical experiences of Africans and Afro-Americans.

The Yale program will be administered by a special faculty committee. The majors in Afro-American studies will devote the major portion of their junior year to a divisional seminar on Afro-American studies, and the major part of their senior year to a senior colloquium and prepare a major paper under the guidance of a faculty member.

In most large urban campuses in the country, however, the limitation of this arrangement is that since "programs" as distinct from departments do not generally have the power to appoint their own faculty and authorize their own courses, they must be sanctioned by existing departments. The limitations this approach places on innovation and relevance to the black experience are as apparent as they are pervasive. The insistence of the faculty at Berkeley in the College of Letters and Science on a program rather than a department, with all the controls this implies for the established departments, was the central cause of the strike of the Third World Liberation Front at Berkeley during January, February, and March 1969, which resulted in the establishment of an independent department outside the major College of Letters and Science which reports directly to the Chancellor's Office.

A third type of structure is a special institute with the power to design its own courses and employ its own faculty. The Antioch program follows this pattern.

A fourth type of structure is a regular department of the college or university devoted to black studies. This has been a very difficult structure to create. Much of the difficulty at San Francisco, Berkeley, Cornell, and Harvard was occasioned by the reluctance of the universities to establish such "autonomous" departments. In each of these universities such departments were authorized, but only after prolonged agony and disruption.

A fifth type of structure for black studies is particularly appropriate for the large public universities such as California, Wisconsin, Michigan, and Illinois. This is a special college on the university campus devoted expressly to black studies. One of the best conceptions and designs for such a college within the university has been developed at Washington State University.

The College of Third World Studies, which has been proposed at Berkeley, and the proposed Zapata-Lumumba College at the University of California at San Diego are examples of colleges designed to encompass not only black studies but studies of other nonwhite minority groups which have been left out of American higher education.

A sixth type of structure is a whole campus, a university expressly conceived, designed, administered, staffed, and operated to provide maximum development of the black experience in higher education. The new Community College in Bedford-Stuyvesant is an example. The new college at the University of California at Santa Cruz comes close. There is no good reason, however, why large state legislatures should not establish whole universities devoted to black studies. Private foundations and even private universities might also consider endowing such new institutions.

In short, when we consider the structure of black studies as when we consider the conception and the curriculum, a great deal of variety and experimentation are required. We have only begun to explore the marvelous potential of this new concept for the invigoration of the whole of higher education in this country.

But whatever the variety of its curriculum, or its structure, or its student body, three essentials of black studies seem clear even at this early stage of their development: (1) that they embrace the black experience as a special area of study in its own right without insisting that it be subservient to some other field of study; (2) that they involve black students and black faculty in the major roles of conceiving, defining, governing, and administering these programs; (3) that they reach out into the contemporary black community; and (4) that they maintain a somewhat loose, flexible, perhaps experimental format without hasty and premature rigidity. For the spirit of innovation and improvisation are as much a part of the black experience as anything else. It would be a tragedy for black studies to become fixed and rigid in content and form before they have had sufficient time and practice to develop.

THE BLACK CRISIS ON CAMPUS*

by Franklin H. Williams

I WELCOME THE opportunity to be here at Smith College this afternoon, although I must say that I find the view from here somewhat awesome! Another black man in an earlier time was not intimidated by women, however. In fact, Frederick Douglass was one of the first men to fight for women's suffrage, and in so doing gave innumerable speeches to women's-rights conventions and groups. In one such, delivered a few years before his death, he said:

> There are few facts in my humble history to which I look back with more satisfaction than to the fact . . . that I was sufficiently enlightened at the early day, when only a few years from slavery, to support your resolution for women's suffrage. I have done very little in this world in which to glory, except this one act—and I certainly glory in that. When I ran away from slavery, it was for myself; when I advocated emancipation, it was for my people; but when I stood up for the rights of women, self was out of the question, and I found a little nobility in the act.

Douglass, clearly, was an individual with the capacity not only to see beyond his own immediate problems, great as they were, but to *do* something about what he saw. Unfortunately, as we look around us today, we do not find many comparable individuals. People are drowning in statistics on war and human misery, and the word "crisis," like "diapers," has become a household cliché. Americans are deluged with the facts of the human condition, but they don't *feel* them, or think they can *do* anything about them.

Reaction to the flood of material on racial problems is similarly diffuse. A year ago the Kerner report described America as "racist" and increasingly polarized into two societies, one white and one black. Several weeks

*Jacob Ziskind Lecture, Smith College, Massachusetts, April 18, 1969.

ago, a follow-up report came out with an even more chilling conclusion. It said: "We are a year closer to being two societies, black and white, increasingly separate and scarcely less unequal."

Many of the reports and statistics on our "crises" today, of course, were spawned by the racial disorders that have hit American cities over the last five years. According to a Kerner Commission Supplemental Study published last July, they "left hundreds dead, thousands injured, and tens of thousands arrested." Property damage ran into the millions of dollars.

The reaction of much of white America and some moderate Negro leaders to these riots has been somewhat unenlightened. In their attempts to "explain away" what happened, they have come up with the "riffraff" theory of riot participation. According to this theory, only an infinitesimal minority of black people—1 or 2 percent depending on your source —participates in the riots. Secondly, the rioters in no way represent the black community, but are composed of the "riffraff hair": the criminal, juvenile, unskilled, unemployed, and uprooted—together with outside agitators. Many public figures rely heavily on the shibboleth of "outside agitators" to explain virtually all unrest in America, be it in black communities or on white campuses. Thirdly, the theory insists that the vast majority of black people—the remaining 98 or 99 percent—are actively opposed to rioting and unequivocally condemn the rioters.

The theory is a comforting one, which perhaps explains its popularity. By assuming that a tiny group of agitators and riffraff are responsible, it presupposes that future riots can be prevented by crash programs to elevate the riffraff, and by identifying and silencing the outside agitators. Furthermore, if the bulk of the black community was not engaged in or sympathetic to the riots, there is no need to radically restructure either the black ghetto or the white community which created it.

However, the theory rests on very flimsy evidence. New studies have found that a substantial portion of the black community—10 to 20 percent according to the commission—actively participated, and that a sizable number of people in the black community sympathized with the rioters even though they did not participate. The commission concluded, and I quote, that "the 1966 riots were a manifestation of race and racism in the United States, a reflection of the social problems of modern black ghettos, a protest against the essential conditions of life there, and an indicator of the necessity for fundamental changes in American society. And if the riffraff theory has not been accurate in the past, its accuracy in the future is seriously questioned. The riots appear to be gaining recruits from all segments of the Negro community. . . ." It also found that fully 39 percent of the Negroes polled by Louis Harris in 1966 either would join a riot or were uncertain what they would do. The lower-middle, middle-, and upper-middle-income Negroes were more likely to respond affirmatively than the lower-income Negroes. And of the Negroes thirty-four years and younger, the current generation, fully 19 percent said that they would join a riot, 24 percent that they were uncertain.

A recent study of over a thousand Manhattan children—black, white, and Puerto Rican—found that 12 percent are suffering from serious mental illness, 34 percent are "moderately" impaired, and only 12 percent mentally healthy or slightly impaired. A central finding of the study, reported at the annual convention of the American Orthopsychiatric Association, was that susceptibility to mental disorders is a function of poverty and the life style that goes with it: lack of schooling, low-income work, and constant tension over lack of money. It revealed that *28 percent* of the children whose families are on welfare—over twice the average—are seriously disturbed.

These are appalling statistics, yet the really chilling finding of the study was that although the risk of mental illness among whites and Puerto Ricans was found to decrease as the family's income and educational level rose, this did *not* hold true for black children. As Dr. Langer said, "I think this is where discrimination takes hold. Even with money and education, the Negro is still a marked man." Black children start on about an equal footing with white children in regard to impairment. But the statistics change dramatically in the early teens, when the proportion of markedly impaired black children starts to exceed that of whites. The hardest-hit group of all is that of black girls: by late adolescence, the percentage suffering from serious mental illness is 28 percent.

My concern is that not enough Americans can truly empathize with the reality these statistics represent. Because of the history of black people in this country, it is difficult, if not impossible, for a white person to understand what it means to be black, and live on a day-to-day, year-to-year basis in a white society. People have flashes of insight, especially when sudden catastrophes, like the assassination of Martin Luther King, momentarily shock them into awareness and activity. But the awareness and the activity both quickly fade. Unfortunately for us, far more Americans are hung up on law and order than they are on the poverty and degradation that produce crime and violence.

One group in America has seen the nature and dimension of the problem perhaps better than any other. I speak of most students, black and white alike. They have come a long way from the beatnik passivity of the late 1950's. The uprisings which have struck universities and to an increasing extent high schools as well, present to me some extraordinarily hopeful signs for the future.

I cannot sympathize with some of the more destructive expressions of this dissatisfaction and anger, but I agree with many of their goals. What they are saying to us, in effect, is that the traditional, hidebound white establishment has gone off the track. It has abandoned the essence of its democratic ideals, and bogged down in the sterile, technocratic forms.

A Mamaroneck High School girl, in her valedictory address last June, put it this way: "General Motors wants crewcuts, punctuality, and respectful conformity. Uncle Sam wants patriotic cannon fodder. A world like this deserves contempt." She and other high-school students, like college students, are demanding that today's problems be brought right into the classroom. They are no longer willing to wait until they are "responsible," adult members of society. A typical sign of their concern was their response to the annual financial forum sponsored by Chase Manhattan Bank. Usually the students who attend simply listen politely. But last year they posed some tough questions, such as Why do banks lend so little money in slum neighborhoods, where it is needed most? and Why does Chase invest so many millions in apartheid South Africa?

Students today—of all ages and colors—want an education, and a life, that is intimately related and responsive to what's going on around them. They have a wide range of interests that reach far beyond the purely academic—interests that embrace the whole spectrum of human and urban problems. They are genuinely concerned about the quality of their lives and the lives around them, and just as genuinely want to do something to improve that quality.

The great cry on campuses, as you well know, is for relevance. For example, many students at Columbia and elsewhere are advocating a marking system where faculty simply give credit—or no credit—for courses. The students feel, and I think rightly, that the grade system has reduced college to a frantic competitive scramble. As a Harvard Law student put it, "The idea of every man for himself, clawing his way to the top over someone else, can't be allowed to dominate legal education any more."

In the past year, the student movement has undergone a significant shift. We are hearing less about Vietnam, and more from black students on racial issues. Several years ago, for example, tutorial programs—in which white students went into black communities to teach—became very popular on all the major university campuses. The Smith-Amherst Tutorial Program seems to delve deeper than most such programs, and reach black Springfield students on a continuing, year-round basis. But many tutoring programs have been tainted, in the eyes of black people, by do-goodism. The Association of Black Collegians took a stand against such attitudes last year: they felt that white students should concentrate on the institutional racism in their own back yards, and drop the patronizing paternalism of the past.

Many white students took the cue quickly. The National Student Association is currently preparing a comprehensive survey of institutional racism on college campuses across the country, and I recommend for careful reading the material they are collecting.

An NSA leader phrased the problem this way at their November meeting: "If tomorrow every American were to awaken with all racial feeling wiped from his heart and mind, racism would continue almost unchanged in America. It is not the occasional and explicit acts of individuals that threaten to split the nation on the question of race, but the anonymous, unintentional forms of behavior that ensure continued white supremacy. Clearly this means tackling a much broader and deeper problem than we have addressed to date."

Let me say a word here about the term "institutional racism." To every black person in America racism is a fact of life, that he lives with and adjusts to as best he can. Responsible groups like the Kerner Commission have discussed and documented its pervasiveness in America. Yet I find that whenever I use the term to a predominantly white audience, it evokes a defensive, if not angry, response from some people. The fact is that unless you are black, or an extraordinarily sensitive white person, you simply do not stop to think of the effect these "anonymous forms of behavior" have on a black person, on or off the campus. Few people realize how alienated most black students feel on the average white campus, for example.

Many of the black students interviewed in the NSA study felt that tokenism runs rampant in classrooms, dorms and administrations. Black students are expected to behave in a preset, stereotyped pattern, or experience general ostracism. They all spoke of the constant chain of minor incidents that were part of the "larger thing." One student wrote, "They can keep you bugged so much you can't work." At one college, a black student was asked to start the dancing at a party "because you dance so well." It so happened that the girl who asked him didn't know him well enough to know he didn't dance at all well. At Barnard, the black students are constantly asked for their identification cards by the guards—the white girls never are.

These are perhaps small incidents. But how many administrators are aware of them, and aware of what their effect is on their students? Let me cite one more excerpt from the NSA files, which perhaps best conveys the problems which face a black student on a white campus. This quote comes from a student at a college not too dissimilar from Smith—Connecticut College for Women.

A white liberal Eastern women's college such as Connecticut is subtly racist in nature. The racism is hidden in intellectual platitudes and rationalizations . . . a strong effort is being made by the administration to recruit "disadvantaged" students and to integrate them into the mainstream of college. Despite the fact that this mainstream has a negative, inhibiting effect on the creativity and responsibility of every student, the more frightening fact is that the black student is expected to assume the role of teacher, counselor and priest to the white majority. She is continually expected to educate the white community in techniques for overcoming their own biases and changing their marshmallow minds. This is a task which almost transcends human possibility.

Her criticism of the "mainstream" of university life, I believe, is directed at the fact that there is no integration of *emotional* with intellectual understanding, in either the education itself, or as regards black students. Students want universities to combine free intellectual inquiry with the relevant issues of the day. Yet I am afraid that too many college administrators still agree with Jacques Barzun's rather low opinion of relevance, as expressed in his book *The American University:* "If a university is not to become an educational weathervane, a sort of weekly journal published orally by aging Ph.D.'s, it must avoid all relevance of the obvious sort." I wonder what he means by "the obvious sort"? Because nowhere in the book does he mention the problems of race, of black people, or of Columbia's suffering neighbor—Harlem. Would these, perhaps fall under the rubric of "relevance of the obvious sort"? I think not.

What Mr. Barzun has not yet grasped—and what most college administrators have not grasped—is that it is no longer enough for a college to adopt a positive, liberal stance. It must take active steps to end discrimination and to identify and root out institutional racism, because simply by doing nothing it perpetuates the system.

For the simple facts are that the system, for whatever reason, *has* kept black students out of colleges. The disparity between white and black enrollment is enormous. Fifty percent of college-age whites attend college, but only 4.5 percent of black college-age students. On the graduate level, .72 percent of total enrollment is black, and a mere .8 percent of all doctorates granted between 1964 and 1968 were given to black students. They number only an estimated 2 percent at most New England universities, and at Smith the percentage is even lower, I am sorry to say, although 126 black students have applied for admission for next year, so the percentage may jump significantly.

Phil Hutchins, the director of SNCC, is often characterized in the press as aggressively militant. But his views on these young potential black students are eminently sane. As he phrased it, "In our society a college education can no longer be a privilege. It must be a right. A man can no longer succeed on just a high-school education. That's why we must revise our thinking about what it means to keep a man out of college." The handful of black students who *have* made it to college has a difficult but challenging role to play. Every student, black or white, must sooner or later grapple with the question of identity: Who am I, where did I come from, and where am I going? But the process is infinitely more complex for black students. They are in the storm center of the black-consciousness movement, and the questions, answers, and definitions are flying around thick and fast. When they ask "Who am I and what is this world I am in?" they are delving a lot deeper than the hero of *The Graduate*, for until recently a black man in America was nobody. According to all the books and the prevailing white definitions of him, he had no past, no roots, and little future. He was, in effect, invisible, as Ralph Ellison put it in this moving passage from his brilliant book:

> I am an invisible man. No, I am not a spook like those who haunted Edgar Allan Poe; nor am I one of your Hollywood movie ecto-plasms. I am a man of substance, of flesh and bone, fiber and liquids —and I might even be said to possess a mind. I am invisible, understand, simply because people refuse to see me. Like the bodi-less heads you see sometimes in circus sideshows, it is as though I have been surrounded by mirrors of hard, distorting glass. When they approach me they see only my surroundings, themselves, or figments of their imagination—indeed, everything and anything except me . . . you ache with the need to convince yourself that you do exist in the real world, that you're a part of all the sound and anguish and you strike out with your fists, you curse and you swear to make them recognize you. And, alas, it's seldom successful.

Black students today may not be invisible, but they have to eradicate the deeply ingrained images and definitions of black people that perme-ate our culture. No one can even begin to enumerate the ways in which Anglo-Saxon culture elevates white over black, for example. "I am black *but* beautiful," says the Shulamite maiden to the daughters of Jerusalem. That "but" is an eloquent one. Images abound in Shakespeare and the

Bible which exalt white as pure and beautiful, and equate black with ugly and evil. Pauli Murray, in her 1956 novel *Proud Shoes*, expressed the anguish experienced by virtually every black child until recently—and still felt by some:

> The world revolved on color and variations in color. It pervaded the air I breathed. . . . Always the same tune, played like a broken record, robbing one of personal identity. . . . It was color, color, color, all the time color, features and hair. . . . Brush your hair, child, don't let it get kinky. Coldcream your face, child, don't let it get sunburned! Don't suck your lips, child, you'll make them too niggerish! Black is evil, don't mix with mean niggers!

You may think that such concerns are a dead issue now, and that the "black is beautiful" concept has taken hold and all black people have a strong, positive image of themselves. But if you talk to any black person in an inner-city community you will find that centuries of oppression are not so easily sloughed off. The black students you are likely to meet are the most sophisticated and best educated—but they represent the elite, the 4 percent who made it to college—and the majority of them feel a definite sense of "mission" toward the other 96 percent. Most of them are not trying, like many of their middle-class elders, to "make it" in the white world, on white terms. They want to make it on their own terms, and it is not always easy.

A pivotal element in "making it" is the attempt to recapture, to recreate if you will, their past. The black-studies issue has by now become a political football on many campuses—yet people are wondering where the sudden upsurge of black student protest—and black student anger—has come from. The sound, rational bases for their anger and bitterness tend to get clouded in the morass of politics. Yet they simply want the opportunity to study, from an objective, unbiased viewpoint, their past and their history.

This history has never been presented except from a distorted viewpoint. They want a right to learn, for example, that as early as 1789, a black man wrote a bitter denunciation of slavery entitled: *Negro Slavery, by Othello: a Free Negro*. It is a biting, courageous piece. Let me quote from it:

> When the united colonies revolted from Great Britain, they did it on this principle, "that all men are by nature and of right ought to be free." Can Americans, after the noble contempt they expressed for tyrants, meanly descend to take up the scourge? . . . The importation of slaves into America ought to be a subject of the deepest

regret to every benevolent and thinking mind. And one of the great defects in the federal system is the liberty it allows on this head. Venerable in everything else, it is injudicious here; and it is much to be deplored that a system of so much political perfection should be stained with anything that does an outrage to human nature. ... The members of the late Constitutional Convention should have seized the opportunity of prohibiting forever this cruel species of reprobated villainy. That they did not do so will forever diminish the luster of their other proceedings, so highly extolled and so justly distinguished for their intrinsic value.

If you think back over your own education, you will realize how little you were taught about the black experience in America. Mental images of toiling slaves or "happy darkies" spring to mind. Until very recently, Africans were always depicted as savage, cannibalistic peoples in grade-school geography texts. Harold Isaacs, in the *New World of Negro Americans*, interviewed a significant number of black leaders in America. Virtually every one of them recalled, with startling clarity, the textbook picture of a naked, ignorant African. One of them told him that "the picture in the book—a savage, a cannibal, the tail end of the human race —was the picture of where and what I came from. I carried that idea along with me for years." Isaacs describes a typical geography book:

Alongside the Emersonian white man in his study, the Japanese aristocrat, the Malay nobleman, and the Indian chief—all obviously selected to depict the highest social rank in each case—a comparable figure might have been an African chief in *his* best clothes. Instead, the "African" appears as a prehistoric figure of a man, naked, stepping out of primeval ooze, carrying an antedeluvian club and shield.

Think how you would have felt, as a young black child, reading such books. How could you relate to a white Anglo-Saxon world, except as a second-class citizen, if that was truly your past? Many Negroes, unfortunately, accepted the debased image and status forced on them; many more did not. Claude McKay, one of the greatest poets of the Harlem Renaissance of the twenties, certainly did not when he penned these lines:

If we must die—let it not be like hogs
Hunted and penned in an inglorious spot,
While round us bark the mad and hungry dogs,
Making their mock at our accursed lot.
If we must die—oh, let us nobly die,
So that our precious blood may not be shed

In vain; then even the monsters we defy
Shall be constrained to honor us though dead!
Oh, Kinsmen! We must meet the common foe;
Though far outnumbered, let us show us brave,
And for their thousand blows deal one death blow!
What though before us lies the open grave?
Like men we'll face the murderous, cowardly pack,
Pressed to the wall, dying, but fighting back!

It may surprise you to learn that this poem was read by Winston
Churchill to the Joint Houses of Congress when he was trying to per-
suade the United States to enter World War II. Unfortunately, for whatever reason, he didn't bother to name the author.

This kind of oversight is seen by today's black students as but one
example of the conscious or unconscious obliteration of their heritage
from the general American consciousness. Only recently have we been
told of the innumerable slave revolts, and only recently have psychologists begun to make us aware that what has been called "typical Negro
laziness" was in fact an intelligent response to an intolerable situation.
Black people had to learn to dissemble in order to survive. Lawrence
Dunbar, writing just before the First World War, described the process
this way:

We wear the mask that grins and lies,
It hides our cheeks and shades our eyes.—
This debt we pay to human guile;
With torn and bleeding hearts we smile,
And mouth with myriad subtleties.

Countee Cullen's famous sonnet "Yet Do I Marvel" captures some of
the agony experienced by the black artist in trying to live, let alone
create:

I doubt not God is good, well-meaning, kind,
And did he stoop to quibble could tell why
The little buried mole continues blind,
Why flesh that mirrors Him must someday die,
Make plain the reason tortured Tantalus
Is baited by the fickle fruit, declare
If merely brute caprice dooms Sisyphus
To struggle up a never-ending stair.
Inscrutable His ways are, and immune
To catechism by a mind too strewn
With petty cares to slightly understand
What awful brain compels His awful hand.

Yet do I marvel at this curious thing:
To make a poet black, and bid him sing!

No one can be a whole man in a society which shuts him out, treats him as an invisible man, or denies him a past. Until recently, therefore, black writers have had to address America from outside, as it were. They were seeking to free black people from the imagery and symbolism of the white world, but they were alienated from the majority psyche. Listen to Claude McKay again:

Your door is shut against my tightened face,
And I am sharp as steel with discontent.
But I possess the courage and the grace
To bear my anger proudly and unbent.

Black students today are determined to open that door. They *are* thinking about what it means to keep a man out of college, as Phil Hutchins said—and what it means when a college continues to transmit only a common homogeneous culture. Black writers like John Oliver Killens and Lerone Bennet, Jr., are challenging the idea of such a culture. As Killens wrote,

[black Americans] even have a different historical perspective. Most white Americans, even today, look upon the Reconstruction period as a horrible time of "carpet-bagging," and "black politicians," and "black corruption," the absolutely lowest ebb in the Great American Story. . . . We black folk, however, look upon Reconstruction as the most democratic period in the history of this nation; a time when the dream the founders dreamed was almost within reach and right there for the taking; a time of democratic fervor the like of which was never seen before and never since. . . . For us, Reconstruction was the time when two black men served in the legislatures of all the states in Dixie; and when those (corrupt) legislatures gave to the South its first public school education. . . . Even our white hero symbols are different from yours. You give us moody Abe Lincoln, but many of us prefer John Brown, whom most of you hold in contempt as a fanatic; meaning, of course, that the firm dedication of any white man to the freedom of the black man is *prima facie* evidence of perversion or insanity.

Black students, along with a growing number of other black Americans, are demanding that school and college curricula reflect these new perspectives, that all American students, black and white, be given significant exposure to Afro-American culture and history.

Many colleges and universities, either from a genuine desire for change or from a desire to keep up with Yale and Harvard, are in the process of setting up black-studies programs, seeking more black students and faculty, and initiating community programs. I hope they realize that massive concerted action is needed to deal effectively with the problems. Because halfhearted recruitment schemes, token courses on "the black experience," and public-relations gestures directed to black communities are clearly not going to solve anything. What is needed now is an emotional, as well as an intellectual, commitment to change, from college trustees and presidents on down. But many colleges, like Barnard, are discovering that one or two courses taught by whites are not going to fill the bill. Furthermore, black students are demanding a decisive role in shaping these new black-studies programs. As Tom Wicker pointed out in *The New York Times*, they are no longer satisfied with the kind of "patronizing courses that one black scholar called 'Chitlins 101.'"

Harvard was not the first major university to launch a degree in Afro-American studies—Yale and Stanford offered majors in the subject this winter, and many others are moving in this direction. But the prestige of Harvard has stimulated interest throughout the country, and others have been quick to agree that, as the report stated, "We are dealing with 25 million of our own people with a special history, culture, and range of problems. It can hardly be doubted that the study of black men in America is a legitimate and urgent academic endeavor."

Fine. Right. But the question on many campuses now is not *whether* to set up a new discipline, but how. And the answer is likely to have a far-reaching impact on all of higher education.

For what the students are demanding is full or partial control of these black-studies programs. At Brandeis University, for example, sixty-four black students held a key administration building for eleven days until they were given veto power over the selection of a chairman for the proposed black-studies department.

The reason black students are demanding control of these black-studies departments is simply that American universities have failed resoundingly in this area. As the Students' Afro-American Society at Columbia phrased it in their statement to the president, "The university has systematically excluded the history and culture and political theories of black Americans from its curriculum. The university has also systematically ignored the intellectual capabilities of blacks and their desire to learn: therefore the number of blacks in the university is extremely low. Since the university is also devoid of 'experts' on the black experience, a black-studies program must rely on knowledgeable members of the black community."

Black student groups at Columbia and throughout the country are therefore forcing new methods of evaluating faculty members. Instead of seeking professors with traditional academic backgrounds, students—and some administrations—are looking for teaching ability and "classroom charisma," as James Gibbs, head of the program at Stanford, put it. There simply aren't enough "qualified" teachers to fill the demands, and black students are not satisfied with white professors who have thrown together a course outline over the summer. Like Cicero Wilson, president of the Students' Afro-American Society at Columbia, they feel that though many white faculty members admit their ignorance of black studies, they still want to set up and control the program. Frequently, prospective black faculty are rejected on the grounds that they aren't qualified. "Our standards are higher than theirs," Wilson has said. "They yell quality and then they give you instructors who don't know the course material."

Students like Wilson distrust the bureaucratic mechanism through which professors traditionally are located, approved, and hired. The lily-white complexion of most universities today indicates that these mechanisms don't work. He and others argue that black students today may be better judges of who does or does not know black history than the history departments that ignored black history for so long or the professors whose very prominence as historians condemns them as participants in the conspiracy to distort American history insofar as the black man's role is concerned. I think he has an extremely valid point.

The point is that the present conflicts—and scrambles—over black studies are the result of the inexcusable neglect of this subject over the decades. However, a black-studies program will be fully effective only if it has, in addition to its educational purposes, the broadly social function of helping black students toward what Charles Hamilton called a "firm base of self-awareness and identity." Acquiring such a "base" is never an easy process, for black or white.

It may, and indeed often does, involve a certain amount of friction with university administrations used to unilateral, paternalistic, or disciplinarian methods of dealing with student demands. A great deal of sensitivity and tact will be needed, both to avoid open confrontations and to create truly meaningful programs of which both students and presidents can be justly proud.

One of the reasons for the alienation of black students on campuses is simply that there are not enough of them there, as I pointed out. Institutions have been falling all over themselves in the last few years in a race to enroll black students—but they want "qualified" black students.

The catch here, of course, is that ghetto life and schools are not likely to churn up vast quantities of "qualified" students in the traditional sense of the term. Schools in black communities, as Jonathan Kozol's *Death at an Early Age* and other accounts testify, are not only unspeakably poor; they are damaging our children. Not unnaturally, many drop out, and their chances of a high-school, let alone a college education, are remote.

College entrance requirements and grading systems, based as they are on white middle-class standards and testing mechanisms, have done their not inconsiderable bit to keep black and other minority children in the ghettos. When faced with the problem of recruiting so-called "disadvantaged" students, many admissions officers retreat and say, "We can't possibly lower our standards." They are missing the point. What's called for are not "lower," but "different" standards. Some colleges, like Smith, are beginning to recognize this, and are relaxing their traditional requirements.

For clearly, the black student who comes to college from a second-rate school in a black neighborhood *will* face problems. Let me give you an example. An eighteen-year-old black freshman at the University of Illinois was "delighted," as she put it, when she was admitted last fall under a special program for students from so-called "disadvantaged" backgrounds. Now she's far less enthusiastic. "People here make you feel different," she says. "We're treated like the dumb group."

Students recruited under such programs are not always the grateful, diligent students some college administrators expect. Often they form the vanguard of protest groups that are tearing campuses apart from San Francisco State to Queens College. Colleges are finding it rough going to adjust their curriculums and methods to accommodate the new arrivals, whose backgrounds differ markedly from those of the predominant white middle-class group.

Every college will have problems unless it displays an extraordinary —and unprecedented—sensitivity in this whole area. If you encourage students from inner-city areas to attend a college you cannot expect them —and should not want them—to behave like nice white middle-class kids. Their background, and their life style, is their own, and must be respected. This is why it is fundamental that colleges actively recruiting in this area have extensive guidance services on campus, and allow black students to set up and run black student centers. The more inner strength and group solidarity that any minority student has on campus, the greater the chances not just that he will *make* it at the university, but that his experience there will be a positive and meaningful one, both for him and the university.

Scholarships, on a vast, unprecedented scale, will have to go hand in hand with stepped-up recruitment drives. Lewis Mayhew, now president of the American Association of Higher Education, discussed this problem last spring at their annual meeting. "what is called for," he said, "is a major revision of what is proper for higher education. The states must be prepared to offer massive scholarships of from $2,000 to $3,000 a year for Negro youth regardless of past academic achievement and regardless of whether or not the students appreciate it." He went on to recommend that American higher education expand its capacity to handle from seventy thousand to a million additional students, the number required to make enrollment proportional. He will believe the desire for reform is serious, he said, if white institutions make it their policy to recruit 10 percent of their student bodies from black and other minority groups without respect to formal admission requirements.

The job to be done is staggering—but it has to be done. Colleges must take it upon themselves to recruit and fund significant numbers of non-whites in order to close the gap, and begin to meet the enormous dimensions of the manpower shortage in the black, Puerto Rican and Mexican-American communities of the United States. Making vague commitments about "getting more" nonwhite students won't be enough. Colleges must set specific minimum goals, hire black recruitment officers, find the money required for scholarships, and establish precollege and college-level training and guidance programs. The commitment must not only be specific, but must be made publicly and formally by the president and trustees of the college if it is to be fully effective, and if it is to receive the necessary funding.

None of these things can be done overnight. But they *should be done the day after tomorrow.* The key elements are commitment to change and a certain amount of humility, not a commodity always in evidence in college administrations. Where black students, black professors, and black communities are concerned, the time is already very late. There *is* a balance to be redressed, and America cannot expect gratitude, even if it offers a scholarship to every black youth who applies to college. Black people don't want to be guinea pigs and teach all the white kids how terrible it's been to be black. When a black student finally gets a good education, he learns just how bad the oppression of black people has been, and his reaction is not likely to be one of undying gratitude. Black people have never achieved respect by trying to be white. They are finally achieving it by being black, like Thee Smith, a junior at Exeter School last spring. As he put it then:

I am the New Black. Last year I felt that an investment had been made in me—not merely by this school but by your whole society —to prove a "safe," well-balanced, and responsible leadership for the black revolution. . . . The fact that I once accepted your definition of my role as a black nauseates me.

I see in your definition, and in my agreement, a continuation of the efforts to teach blacks how to act "white," and at the same time teach them to deny the legitimacy of their own culture. . . . I feel that we, as human beings, have much more to gain by remaining true to ourselves, true to our culture, and true to our blackness. . . . When we become leaders, we will derive our strength not from your friendship, or your brains, or your money, but from ourselves. I am a black first, and an American when I can afford to be.

I return to the point I have made again and again. It is America's emotional, *intuitive* response to what Thee Smith is talking about that will decide the future of American race relations. Those who react to it negatively haven't really "dug" what it's all about. They may have read the statistics, and made the intellectual decision that yes, things are indeed bad and we must do something—but they haven't scratched the surface of what it's like to be a black American. Until they do, the Thee Smiths will remain black first, and Americans when they can afford to be. And America cannot afford to let that go on much longer.

PART IV

EDUCATIONAL REDEFINITION

THE RELEVANCE OF EDUCATION

FOR BLACKAMERICANS*

by C. Eric Lincoln

IN 1903, one G. F. Richings published a volume entitled *Evidences of Progress Among Colored People.*[1] He was moved to undertake the effort, he explained, because:

> To my mind the last generation has been characterized by greater conflicts and has been freighted with more thrilling events than any generation through which the history of this country has brought us. . . . It is therefore important that some close observer of events constantly keep before the people in whose interest these factors have been set in operation, full accounts of all the developments, that the young may be inspired to noble aims and lofty endeavors.[2]

Richings achieves importance because he appointed himself the task of observation and investigation. By his own account, he spent sixteen years cataloguing and visiting hundreds of schools, seminaries, colleges, and businesses and professional offices operated by or for Blackamericans, and documenting at first hand the "evidences of progress" he noted. Richings' book is not a scholarly compendium, but it does provide an interesting and useful account of the Blackamerican's unprecedented struggle to educate himself and to challenge the crippling stereotypes with which he was bound then and now by a frequently hostile society. The fledgling efforts of our historic institutions are noted and appraised. Some of them are no longer in existence: Walden,[3] Roger Williams,[4] Leland,[5] Straight,[6] Dorchester Academy,[7] Avery Institute,[8] Western University,[9] Monticello Seminary,[10] Eckstein Norton University.[11]

Richings, who was white, expressed the opinion (remarkable for his time) that "the color of the skin, the texture of the hair, and the formation of the head have nothing whatever to do with the development and the expansion of the mind.[12] That some Americans are less confident now,

*From *Journal of Negro Education*, Summer, 1969.

almost seventy years later, is indicative of the persistence of the racial myth which contaminated our history and our science so long ago. Finally, I cannot refrain from one further quote from Professor Richings, whose remarkable clairvoyance relating to issues which are the inevitable corollaries of education must certainly establish his relevance:

> I only hope that the white friends may be made to feel that the colored people are entitled to more consideration and ought to be given a better opportunity to fill the places for which they are being fitted, in the commercial and business life of this country.[13]

For most of the sixty-six years since Richings completed his informal study, the "better opportunity" to make full, logical use of the education they won at such a dear cost has not generally been available. That is in part what the contemporary black revolution is about—the relevance of the Blackamerican's education to the prevailing socioeconomic structure —the logical end of the struggle to know.

Observations like Richings' are important because, however challenging it may be, we cannot speak with profit about the contemporary educational experience of the black minority except against a background of history. Terms such as "compensatory education," "desegregation," "community control," "black studies," "cultural deprivation," and the like have no meaning except within the context of the peculiar development of segregated education in the South (where more than 75 percent of all blacks lived prior to World War II). The poor quality of public schools for Negroes in all of our history is of course well documented, but the extended effect of the miseducation of blacks as recently as a generation ago suggests the usefulness of citing some comparative statistics to illustrate the morbidity of the infrastructure on which past educational experiences were built. The effects of the past ramify in the problems of the present and produce the terminology (and the unresolved racial dilemmas) which characterize contemporary education. In 1900 the white school population of the South (thirteen states) was 4,069,175. The black school population for that year was 2,349,968. In 1940, the white school population for the South was 6,614,734, an increase of 62.6 percent. But the black school population remained practically constant at 2,454,198—an increase of only 4.4 percent in forty years![14] Even in a truly open "democratic" society, the implications for competitive socioeconomic development would be astounding. How much more so for a society in which educational preparation is qualified severely by racial identification! The school-age mortality rate in the black population was matched (possibly encouraged) by the per-pupil expenditure differential. As late as 1952 the South was still spending $132.28 on white pupils for each $90.20 spent on blacks. This was a vast improvement over the arrangement in 1940, when the ratio was $41.99 to $16.29.[15] After the Supreme Court decisions of 1954 (*Brown* vs. *Board of Education*), some Southern states instituted crash programs to bring per-pupil expenditures into alignment in order to stave off integration. They would seem to have met with extraordinary success (although credit for that success is certainly not limited to the equalization of expenditures on white and black pupils). Fourteen years after the court order to desegregate (with "deliberate speed"), the U. S. Office of Education could report that only 18 percent of America's black children *at most* were attending school with whites in the South. Even this unspectacular estimate is probably inflated, perhaps by 100 percent, because it considers a "predominantly black" school as being "desegregated" if it has one white pupil.[16]

Since "desegregation" implies the previous existence of "segregation," we confront now the crucial implications of minority-group status, or more specifically, being black in a white-oriented society. Before 1954, segregation in education was the rule throughout the South, being required by law in all Southern and some border states. Black recognition of the accrued disability incident to segregated education antedated *Brown* vs. *Board of Education*, however, by more than a hundred years when Charles Sumner argued the case of *Roberts* vs. *The City of Boston* in 1849. During the brief period of the Reconstruction, when Blackamericans held some decision-making power in public education for the only time in history, they underscored their vital concern for participation in shaping educational policy by the avidity with which they sought the office of superintendent of education.[17] Five states—Arkansas, Florida, Louisiana, Mississippi, and South Carolina—elected black superintendents.[18] Some of them, like Dartmouth- and Princeton-educated Jonathan G. Gibbs of Florida, and J. C. Corbin of Arkansas, who graduated from Ohio State in 1853, were distinctly superior in education and administration to most of their white counterparts in the South. Their unfortunately brief tenure in office was not sufficient to effect lasting policies of educational accessibility and parity which might have anticipated—and obviated—the problems which confront the black minority today. The power of black men in Reconstruction offices was not unlimited. In spite of the brilliant work of Gibbs in Florida, perhaps the administration of Superintendent James Brown of Louisiana was more typical and more realistic in terms of the times. Brown was described by a contemporary as " 'a quiet inoffensive man' who did not 'obtrude himself' into white schools where he was not wanted."[19]

At any rate, the education of Blackamericans had a rather singular development in segregated public schools and (for the most part) private or church-related black colleges in the South; and in increasingly *de facto* segregated public schools in the North with occasional blacks in the Northern colleges and universities. Nowhere were curricula and ancillary programs designed with the peculiar, fundamental needs of Blackamericans in mind; and nowhere did the academic credentials acquired by blacks carry with them the logical consequences of academic investiture. The period between the World Wars saw dramatic gains in the *numbers* of blacks who were engaged in the educational process:

> From 1940 to 1960, the percentage of Negroes who had attended college more than doubled; from 1950 to 1960 the percentage of Negroes who had completed high school rose from 14 to 22 percent, a faster rate than that of whites; and from 1950 to 1960, the median school years completed by all adult Negroes increased over a grade, 6.9 to 8.2 years.[20]

But the increased *numbers* of blacks who improved themselves educationally was not reflected in the *numbers* of those who achieved reasonable levels of participation in the socioeconomic process of affluent America. The Negro college graduate carrying mail, waiting tables, or redcapping was a familiar phenomenon of the 1940's and the 1950's.

The Supreme Court decision of 1954 has not produced "integrated" education; nor has it effected through the educational process the more generalized racial assimilation so optimistically predicted fifteen years ago. Indeed, outside the South we are more segregated than before.[21] Professor Thomas Pettigrew of Harvard University attributes continuing segregated education to the following causes:

> (1) The basic cause is structural: the way we organize our school districts, especially the way we organize in the main metropolitan areas. . . .
> (2) The existence of private schools—parochial schools in particular. . . .
> (3) The careful misplacement of schools, the zone drawing. . . .[22]

"Our problems," Dr. Pettigrew avers, "are less the machinations of evil men . . . than structural problems." Perhaps so, but "structural problems" are structured by men, evil or otherwise, and the net results for black children seem to be the same. *Men* organize school districts, build, endow, make exclusive, and send their kids to private or parochial schools, and "misplace" public schools. However, the old argument that the future of black America hinges on physical juxtaposition in "integrated" classrooms is no longer convincing to a substantial number of Blackamericans. Integrated schools may be desirable from many points of view —the provision of extratribal experiences for white children among them, but the latest data seem to show that factors other than the integration of children in the classroom are more critical to the learning process. The Coleman Report suggests that social class is the more crucial variable. If that is in fact the case, perhaps our educational strategies are being crippled by misplaced emphases. While education is a prime determinant of middle-class status, other avenues of mobility, such as employment equivalence, suggest the perspicacity of G. F. Richings' remarks when he was studying black educational institutions at the turn of the century: "The colored people are entitled to more consideration and ought to be given a better opportunity to fill the places for which they are being fitted. . . ." It is patent that classroom integration without corollary behavior in other aspects of our human relations is not a panacea for what is wrong with America.

There are perhaps as many as 25 million Blackamericans in this country, most of them involved at some level in striving to escape the disabilities or the symbols of caste. The tenuous involvement of black people in the educational process has been both a symbol of powerlessness and social degradation and an effective means of disablement. As a result, the contemporary educational crisis is so intertwined with other factors only peripherally related to it as to obscure and confuse the central issue at times, and make it difficult to bring about orderly change. What I am saying, of course, is that the Blackamerican has a compelling stake and an unprecedented interest in changing his *whole condition*. Education is but one aspect, albeit a vital one, of a much larger social construct which has operated to the Blackamerican's disadvantage—or to a disproportionately lesser advantage than for others in the society. "Education" is the formal instrument by means of which a society socializes developing members and prepares them for meaningful and satisfying participation in that society. Our socialization process has prepared white children to continue the privileged traditions of the established white hegemony, while black children have been programmed for social and economic oblivion. The black insistence upon meaningful involvement in decision making, curriculum offerings, administration, instruction, and every other aspect of the academic enterprise denotes the more basic intention of destroying the racial caste structure, and cannot be seen in isolation from that interest. Similarly, the extraordinary resistance to the burgeoning programmatic demands of black students, black instructors, and black parents is not totally a resistance to changing the configuration of traditional patterns of *education*, but a resistance to changing larger patterns of relationships which are touched by educational procedures.

If the education available to Blackamericans and their rate of involvement have improved steadily since the 1940's, why should there be a "crisis" in 1969? First of all, the improvement of the black's educational position in contrast to that of the white man has been only relative. When seen in perspective, it is not impressive. Dr. Thomas Pettigrew, who is committed to the necessity for integration[23] and is not impressed greatly by black gains in education outside an integrated system, suggests why:

> Negro education has yet to approach that generally available to whites. It remains in general less accessible, and especially less adequate. In 1960, Negro college attendance was . . . only about half that of whites; the percentage of adult Negroes who had completed college was considerably less than half that of whites; and the percentage who had completed high school was precisely half that of whites. . . . Negro hopes for the future are so centered upon education that training of poor quality at this stage could well undercut the determined thrust toward group uplift.[24]

Furthermore, the devaluation of the black man's academic credentials will keep him at a competitive disadvantage vis-à-vis the white man. Christopher Jencks and David Riesman, interpreting the data of the Coleman Report, find that when black men are compared with white men with three-fourths as much formal education, the better-educated blacks earn 10 to 20 percent less then white men with only 75 percent as much training.[25] Jencks and Riesman support the contention that the factors determining the continuing differentials which operate to the disadvantage of Blackamericans now derive from segregation by "class" rather than by "race," thus implying a relatively unrestricted mobility and acceptance across class lines for "those Negroes who acquire white middle-class habits and attitudes."[26] One does not need to argue whether this is true or to what degree, or whether the "new" segregation is substantively different from the more familiar kind, so long as Negroes, who are *racially* identified, remain at the bottom of the class structure, and their *visibility* operates to keep them there.

The "improved" circumstances of contemporary blacks is precisely the key variable in their present commitment to the renovation of our educational structure. The black middle class, as measured by conventional criteria, is five times as big as it was in 1940. Two important by-products of an increased middle-class base are (1) relative economic security, and

(2) leisure. For the first hundred years out of enslavement, the black man's all-consuming interest was expressed in terms of visceral needs— to provide food and shelter for the family; and to keep out of the way of the Man,i.e., to stay alive. Education, formal or informal, functioned almost entirely in these interests. Now that the visceral needs of an important minority of the black community have been met substantially, there is *time* and a *psychological readiness* to examine the systems of strictures which function to perpetuate black subordination. Education represents and reflects one of those strictures. The "radicalization" of black students demanding a wide assortment of institutional and pro- grammatic changes in the universities is a by-product of the security and leisure ("introspection") now available to a small minority of black peo- ple. So is "community involvement" in school issues, even when that involvement may utilize the physical pressure of parents who are them- selves from the less emancipated black masses.

Blackamericans are more acutely aware now of the critical importance of education to the general improvement of their conditions of living in and participating in our kind of society. They know that "our kind of society" is geographically indifferent. It extends North and South. East and West. For decades they have fought through the NAACP and other agencies for better schools, better-paid teachers, integrated classrooms and faculties, and the like. There have been some successes; but, as has always been the case, "the development of schools and programs of education for Negroes has represented largely the influences of social forces outside the Negro community and over which he had little or no control."[27] To the extent that this remains true, to that extent will the larger spectrum comprising the life circumstances of Blackamericans remain inaccessible to their control or moderation. In a truly democratic society, the issue would be less crucial, for the socialization of children, and the preparation of youth to be meaningful participants in the ongoing life of the society, would be indifferently conceived and executed. In a society where racial preference is itself one of the institutions which modify and shape all others, decisive involvement at every level of the educational enterprise is critical. The democratic process will be strengthened by the new commitment of Blackamericans to help make education relevant and responsible.

NOTES

1. G. F. Richings, *Evidences of Progress Among Colored People.* Phila- delphia: George S. Ferguson Co. (1902).

2. *Ibid.*, pp. 17–18.
3. Nashville, Tennessee.
4. Nashville, Tennessee.
5. New Orleans.
6. New Orleans.
7. McIntosh, Georgia.
8. Charleston, South Carolina.
9. Kansas City, Kansas.
10. Montecello, Arkansas.
11. Cane Spring, Kentucky.
12. *Op. cit.*, p. xii.
13. *Ibid.*
14. Truman M. Pierce *et al.*, *White and Negro Schools in the South*. Englewood Cliffs, N.J.: Prentice Hall, Inc., 1955.
15. *Op. cit.*, p. 165.
16. See Thomas F. Pettigrew, "School Integration in Current Perspective," *The Urban Review*, January 1969.
17. E. Franklin Frazier, *The Negro in the United States*. New York: Macmillan Co., 1949, p. 142.
18. Horace Mann Bond. *The Education of the Negro in the American Social Order*. Englewood Cliffs, N.J.: Prentice-Hall, Inc., 1934, p. 49.
19. *Ibid.*
20. Thomas F. Pettigrew. *A Profile of the Negro American*. Princeton: Princeton University Press, 1964, p. 184.
21. Cf. Pettigrew, *op. cit.*, p. 4.
22. *Ibid.*, pp. 5, 6.
23. *Ibid.*, p. 4.
24. *A Profile of the Negro American*, p. 190.
25. Christopher Jencks and David Riesman, *The Academic Revolution*, Garden City: Doubleday, 1968, p. 412 n.
26. *Ibid.*, p. 411.
27. Virgil A. Clift, *The American Negro Reference Book*, John P. Davis, ed., Englewood Cliffs, N.J.: Prentice-Hall, Inc., 1966, p. 360. See also Jencks and Riesman, *op. cit.*, p. 418.

ON CORRECT BLACK EDUCATION*

by John E. Churchville

SOME PRELIMINARY IDEOLOGICAL AND PHILOSOPHICAL CONSIDERATIONS

WITH THE INCREASED black nationalist consciousness which has developed over the past two or three years among a broad cross section of our people, a new surge of black activity has erupted. This activity has serious political-directional implications which necessitate definition and analysis in order that we might clearly see what path we must take toward a correct struggle for freedom.

Let us begin with some definitions. Nationalism is the advocacy of making one's own nation, race, or people distinct, and separate from others in social, cultural, and political matters. Within this loose definition, there are many forms black nationalism may take; however, for the sake of simplicity, we will treat briefly the four basic forms: regressive, bourgeois or reactionary, progressive, and revolutionary.

Regressive nationalism is culture-cult oriented: its premise is rooted in worshipping the past and discovering one's identity by returning to African costume and culture. This form of nationalism is apolitical, and maintains that the oppression of black people is solely cultural—i.e., white people have stripped us of our culture; hence, our deprived and degraded position. Regressive nationalists contend that all we need do is rediscover our true identity and return to the ancient tradition of our forefathers, and our oppression will end. They reject certain of the minor values of the present system, but do not take any position which might antagonize the ruling class. Their focus is to parallel the system in every area. Inherent in this position is the maintenance of the present system and ruling class. Their built-in self-interest in maintaining the present

---

*Prepared for Freedom Library Day School, Philadelphia, Pennsylvania, June 24, 1969.

system—which coincides with that of the ruling class—makes the regres-
sives very unreliable, in that they can be expected to fall away to the
reactionary nationalists in the time of acute crisis which will soon come
to black communities all over this country.

Bourgeois or reactionary nationalism is the vehicle by which disgrun-
tled black opportunists attempt to extort certain concessions and personal advantages from the ruling class. They use black slogans, natural
hair styles, and Afro-oriented dress to gain an intermediary position
between certain white sub-power structures and the masses of black
people, to the end that they might develop a measure of personal power
and prestige while they work to confuse and subvert their own flesh and
blood in the interests of the oppressor. Most so-called black militants are
of this group.

The reactionary nationalist calls for self-determination in the black
community—owning the businesses, controlling the schools, manipulat-
ing the resources—coexistent with the present system and in total agreement with its decadent and evil principles of greed, exploitation, and
dehumanization. These nationalists work in complete collaboration with
the ruling class. Their position has a certain emotional appeal to a people
whose only experience has been that of the ruled since their abduction
to this country. However, the reactionary line is incorrect and inimical
to the interests of black people, because its aim is the establishment of
a black sub-sub-ruling class, which would function as warden and direct
repressive agent against the masses of black people. When the crises of
direction arise in the black community, this same group will openly turn
against the masses and—with white-ruling-class backing—attempt
repression of all progressive and revolutionary elements which oppose it.

Progressive nationalism sees some of the inherent fallacies in both
regressive and reactionary nationalism. It tends toward a political perspective which recognizes that the black struggle must be waged against
the present system, and hence the ruling class. The progressive nationalists raise fundamental questions about the nature of this society, but have
no clear analysis or direction. They are at present unable to see the
revolutionary position, because their attempt is to get the system over-
hauled, revamped, and liberalized. Some progressive nationalists classify
themselves as revolutionists, and maintain that they are struggling to
overthrow the present system. Though their rhetoric rings, on occasion,
with "down with the pigs and the pigs' system," they inevitably show
forth either no concrete action at all, or that kind of foolish, ego-oriented,
individualist phenomenon which is best described as leftist adventurism
—daring, dramatic, but nonetheless stupid moves which could bring

martyrdom to the individual, and which in no way advance—in fact actually retard—the struggle of black people.

For all practical purposes, progressive nationalists have been disillusioned by the present system, and are consequently lost in a vacuum of identitylessness, meaninglessness, and complete internal personal confusion. This state is generally not admitted; they cover it over by pretending to be involved in some deep and complicated revolutionary intrigue. At best, these nationalists play a distorted and glorified version of the dangerous game of cops and robbers.

Revolutionary nationalism recognizes the need for total and complete revolution, both here and everywhere in the world. The revolutionary nationalist understands clearly that black people in this country suffer from a twofold problem: external and internal.

The external problem facing black people is the oppression, exploitation, and attempt at dehumanization instituted and perpetuated by the white ruling class. The internal problem facing black people has two facets: intragroup and intraindividual.

The internal problem of black people as a group is our slave mentality brought about by our acceptance of the values, goals, and ideology of the oppressor. This manifests itself in the way we treat one another, and in the way we strive—with all our blackness—to emulate the oppressing group in all its ways. The internal problem of black people as individuals is that we are totally corrupt and need to be purged from our own incorrect desires, motives, thinking, and actions.

The revolutionary nationalist understands that revolution must take place in him before he can correctly struggle externally toward a new world order. The revolutionary understands that by himself he is powerless to become a new man. The revolutionary finds out through constant seeking and searching that someone outside himself must make him a true revolutionary. He knows that only Jesus, the Son of the Almighty God, can cope with the corruption and confusion which is his, and make him what he must be.

The born-again revolutionary nationalist learns that correct struggle is not based on strategy and tactics, but on Truth. It is from Truth and Truth alone that the revolutionary operates. Truth is his base; Truth is his motive for struggle; Truth is his will to remain uncompromising and strong.

The revolutionary nationalist wages a daily struggle against the forces of the present order by being a personal example of the New Man who is renewed in spirit, mind, and body. His being a true revolutionist inspires the people. His actions show forth a glimpse of what lies ahead in the new order. He gives clear direction in word, deed, and in his very being. He is patient, considerate, helpful, compassionate, strong, and uncompromising.

The revolutionary nationalist understands that the real enemy is the force which controls the visible adversary; so he shuns hatred, malice, envy, and strife, refusing to deal with petty personalities. He makes his moves on the basis of Truth and Principle, realizing that inherent in the means of struggle is the end: and the end of correct struggle is the New World.

THE FUNCTION, BASIS, AND EXTENT OF CORRECT BLACK EDUCATION

Education is, rightfully, a function of a system which has definite goals, values, and interests. It is the prime function of education in any political system to instill in its subjects the values, ideology, and vision of the system; the end of which is the perpetuation of that system. Hence, education is by no means the teaching of reading, writing, and arithmetic; it is the teaching of a particular ideological orientation by means of reading, writing, arithmetic, and other skills.

We must clearly understand the above before we can talk seriously about black education, because black education does not exist in a vacuum, but presupposes a total system or frame of reference which engenders it.

Correct black education, then, is an arm of the revolutionary nationalist position. It is based on Truth, and instills the principles of Truth, Integrity, and Character in its subjects. Its aim is the total overthrow of the present system and ruling class, and their replacement by a system and ruling class totally antithetical to them.

In our approach to correct education, we begin not with curriculum but with ideological orientation. Our next consideration must of necessity be the correct or revolutionary teacher. This follows because our students learn more from what we are than from what we teach.

It is imperative that Truth be the watchword, and criticism and self-criticism the watch-action, of the revolutionary teacher. It is not sufficient for the teacher to recognize his failings, contradictions, and other assorted hangups; he must act immediately and have these obstacles moved.

The revolutionary teacher must understand that his total life—in and out of the classroom—is an object lesson not only for his students but for everyone with whom he comes in contact. In short, he must teach precept and be example.

The test of the truly revolutionary teacher is his living in and by the Truth daily. One cannot live in Truth and continue to be incorrect. He must come daily to the Fount of Truth and refresh himself. It is the overflow of his refreshing that implants itself in the minds and hearts of his students. He must ever be alive in his convictions, and all must be able to see the concrete practice of his theory.

The revolutionary teacher is the bridge between identity and alienation. It is through his instruction and analysis that relevance and priorities are established in the minds of his students. Therefore, the teacher cannot just teach and in so doing justify his existence; he must engage in objective struggle that involves him in a dynamic relationship with his students' families and friends. The revolutionary teacher must be a worker, a helper, an encourager. He must exhort all his students to be teachers in word and deed. The revolutionary teacher may be summed up as the vanguard of correct struggle on the basis of Truth.

The question of curriculum must now be raised and placed in its proper setting. If we were to write down a formula or priorities, we would say the following: Ideology is everything, the teacher is everything, curriculum is everything.

Curriculum must take into account the objective situation and environment of the black people to be affected, and the tools and skills necessary to deal concretely with this reality. In this regard there are two aspects of curriculum that must be examined; its generality and particularity.

The generality of curriculum refers to those fundamental components of learning which apply always and in every circumstance—e.g., reading, writing, arithmetic. The particularity of curriculum refers to those components of learning which are adopted because of the specific environment—e.g., agriculture, plumbing.

The content of the curriculum is always viewed as a vehicle for teaching or demonstrating a revolutionary truth. It is not so much the content as the analysis and application of curriculum which makes it serve a correct function. One plus one will always equal two no matter whether a good or a bad person with a good or a bad perspective teaches it. But the social and political implications of one plus one equals two depend upon the medium used in its teaching, and in that light the person who teaches makes the difference. For any example that a teacher would give to illustrate the fact that one plus one equals two would invariably touch on some social and political reality, or some prevalent value of the social and political system. Hence, the treatment of curriculum must be studied. Examples must reflect the new reality and project correct struggle.

The challenge for revolutionary nationalists is to institutionalize correct education by developing independent schools. A school is any place of regular meeting where there are at least one teacher and one student.

Black children from the age of two up must be reached and taught in revolutionary schools across the country. These concrete establishments will give stability to an ongoing, protracted struggle, and will ensure a new generation of correct thinkers and doers who will carry on the struggle.

It is the task of correct black education to raise up a new generation of young people who know how to live and function on the basis of Truth and Principle—people who, when they are old, will not depart from it.

It is the task of correct black education to turn around the present generation from its course, which will ultimately end in self-destruction, and to point it to a better hope, based on a better life, with better promises and better rewards.

It is the task of correct black education to fit a people to live in the New World; to teach and exemplify correct struggle on the basis of Truth; to show forth its revolutionary effects now in the midst of chaos, corruption, and confusion; and to inspire the masses of black people to seek the newness of life, which can come only from total immersion in revolutionary struggle.

THE QUESTION OF DISCIPLINE*

by John E. Churchville

ANARCHY, CHAOS, and disorder are destructive to the interests of any people, at any time, and in any place. There can be no correct development in a state of utter confusion. And where there is confusion, either there is no standard, law, or guide present, or the laws and standards which do exist are ignored and disobeyed.

At this stage in history, black people in America must understand the forces at work among us which would tend to lead us down an incorrect path to self-destruction. The tendency that would undermine a correct revolutionary struggle on the part of black activists is lawlessness—the total unwillingness to submit to the principles of Truth, Order, and Direction.

We would be making a fatal mistake if we concluded that because the system under which we presently live has abused us and kept us down, therefore all systems will abuse and keep us down. This kind of conclusion would lead us into an incorrect antisystems position. System is order, arrangement, regularity, and consistency, and is absolutely essential. Without a system, utter confusion reigns.

Where does our incorrect thinking come from? What motivates us to move further and further away from the Truth? We ourselves are to blame; our own corruption is responsible.

When most of us talk about freedom, we mean our own individual freedom: freedom to do as we please, unrestricted, uninhibited, unchecked; freedom from the values of morality, goodness and Truth; freedom to indulge ourselves in every lust and vice to our hearts' content; freedom from guilt feelings when we know we are wrong; freedom from such a word or concept as "wrong." Our motives are, for the most part, selfish and opposed to the collective advancement of our people.

*Prepared for Freedom Library Day School, Philadelphia, Pennsylvania, March 19, 1969.

We have accepted the white man's ideas concerning freedom; ideas which are always self-centered, opportunistic, and exploitative. We must define freedom in Truth, not in myth.

True freedom is the total submersion in, and willing subjection to, the TRUTH. Anything short of single-minded obedience to TRUTH is slavery. Hence, freedom and system—order, arrangement, discipline—are inseparable. The question, then, becomes whether we are really interested in struggling toward freedom or whether we are just rebelling against the present system as pawns of those forces that intend to set up a more insidious system of slavery.

The above questions must be answered before any clarity can be brought to the present confused state of affairs. There must be a sincere search for TRUTH first; then discipline will be the natural outgrowth of that quest.

Inherent in discipline is direction. Direction is a specific path of travel. Inherent in correct discipline is a goal. Discipline is the means by which a goal is achieved.

A serious boxer understands that he cannot fight effectively and win if he is overweight or if he does not get proper exercise and rest. A serious runner in a five-mile race does not attempt to break speed records the first mile or two, but paces himself so that he can endure to the last mile —by which time he has his second wind and can push with everything he has to get to that finish line. In short, discipline is doing what is necessary to create the optimum conditions to win.

Correct discipline flows from TRUTH and leads to freedom. It is not easily attained. It requires uncompromising struggle. Correct discipline demands that we look inward so that we can act correctly and decisively in the interests of the masses of black people. Acting on the basis of Truth and Principle is always in the best interests of black people.

Correct discipline is law and system—but law and system based on Truth. It imposes limits, and inflicts penalties for infractions of the limits.

It is especially important that we raise the standard of correct discipline against the decadent cries of "freedom of self-expression," and "freedom of the individual." We must raise our children in an environment which demonstrates the power and purposefulness of the disciplined life of correct revolutionary struggle.

Where there is no discipline, there is no correct revolutionary struggle; but where there is correct revolutionary struggle, there is discipline. The one cannot exist without the other.

Lawlessness on the part of black activists is our most deadly internal enemy. It is the nourishment of the oppressor—he instigates it, encourages it, and actually thrives on it! Lawlessness organizes the oppressor but splinters and disrupts the oppressed. Lawlessness is by nature counterrevolutionary—totally opposed to the establishment of the New World.

Discipline is difficult, lawlessness is easy. Discipline seeks the good, the right, and the True for the group; lawlessness seeks to destroy the group by perpetuating the individual's self-indulgence. Discipline is life; lawlessness is death.

"I call heaven and earth to record this day against you, that I have set before you life and death, blessing and cursing: therefore choose life, that both thou and thy seed may live" (Deuteronomy 30:19).

TOWARD A NEW SYSTEM

OF EDUCATION*

by Grace Lee Boggs

I'm 14 years of age, and have not yet learned
The confusion of life and why it is so stern.
Is it hate that makes one love
or is it love that makes one hate
or is it the heart that overtakes.
Is it curiosity that killed the cat
or the cat killed his curiosity
You see to me this is nothing but philosophy.
Is it peace that starts a war
or is it the war that starts peace
Such crises have already started in the middle east.
Is it money that buys happiness.
or happiness buys money
Does the sun shine cause it's dark
or it shine cause it's sunny.
Is it violence that creates a riot
or riots create violence
Is one statement right? or they both have the same resemblance.
Is it people fills a church
or the church fills the people
Is both right I look up at the steeple.
Is it the law we go by or the law go by us,
Is it right? It must.
I'm 14 years of age and have not yet learned
The confusion of life and why it is so stern.
Will I soon gather bits to pieces

*Keynote Address, Inservice Day, Ann Arbor School District, Ann Arbor,
Michigan, October 8, 1968.

or gather pieces to bits
or will I still ask the same thing is it.

Cornell Norris, eighth grade,
Junior High School 271,
Ocean Hill–Brownsville
District, New York

No one of us, young or old, parent, teacher, or administrator, with academic degrees or without, in the lowest track or the highest, black or white, knows the final answers to the questions that Cornell Norris has asked in this poem—for the simple reason that there are no final or prepackaged answers. These are the questions man has been asking since he became man, questions which, if he survives, he will be asking a thousand years hence. Out of his unending wrestling with these questions have come science, religion, and philosophy, production, poetry, painting, and politics; in other words, all that we lump together under the word "civilization," varying from epoch to epoch, country to country, and continent to continent.

All the compensatory, remedial, or enrichment programs in the world, funded by billion-dollar federal legislation or million-dollar foundations, could not have produced this poem any more than they have been able to produce any significant change in the achievement level of inner-city children. Nor could dedicated teaching alone have inspired its writing, although dedicated teachers in a specific situation played a key role in making it possible.

The specific situation was this. Last May, when the black community in the Ocean Hill–Brownsville district of Brooklyn was struggling to establish its control over schools in the face of opposition from the teachers' union, the Board of Education, the city administration, the press and the police, some 170 teachers defied the strike call of the union. Out of the new learning environment created by these dedicated teachers under these siege conditions, this poem and a number of others were written.

To me it is an example of the creative energies in our children which are being stifled and destroyed by the present system of education. If an increasing number of our kids take pot, speed, and beans, it is because of their mistaken belief that these chemicals will "blow," i.e., liberate or unbox, their minds. If they continue to resort to these desperate devices, it will be because we as educators (by which I mean not only teachers and administrators but also parents and other young people) fail to realize that (1) a new system of education with new objectives and methods is now a question of survival; and (2) that such a new system is already being created out of the living turbulent struggles that are both cause and effect of the crisis in American schools today.

I want to analyze this crisis as scientifically as I can. How scientific this analysis is you will have to judge for yourself as events unfold.

A revolutionary or prerevolutionary situation exists today in education in this country. Not only in the public schools but also in the universities. Not only in cities like New York, Detroit, and Philadelphia where black students are a majority of the school population but in little towns like Kalamazoo where blacks are a small minority. Not only in black universities like Howard and Wilberforce but also in such citadels of white supremacy and authority as Harvard and the University of California.

The main symptoms of a revolutionary situation were defined more than fifty years ago by the leader of the first successful revolution of this century, Vladimir Lenin. *First:* It is impossible for those in power to continue their rule in an unchanged form. So obvious is their failure that divisions and fissures emerge among them, opening up the way for the indignation and discontent of those below to burst forth. *Second:* The conditions and suffering of those oppressed by the system steadily worsen. *Third:* As a result of the first two circumstances, there is a considerable increase in the activity of these oppressed layers.

I don't see how anyone can deny that this is the growing reality in the schools and universities of the United States today. Everywhere you look, school and university administrators and faculty know that the system of education which they represent has failed. Searching for remedies and differing among themselves as to strategy and tactics, they are helpless in the face of growing student and community revolt. The mass struggle over issues in education, which was initiated fourteen years ago by Southern black students and parents, the most obvious victims of the system's failure, has now spread to schools and universities from coast to coast.

Not every revolutionary situation leads to a revolution. But a revolutionary situation demonstrates that a revolution is necessary. Or to phrase it in language more congenial to this officially sponsored occasion, unless or until there is a revolution in education in this country, teacher-student relations will become increasingly inhuman, to the point where police and police dogs in the classroom will become the rule.

I have to define what I mean by "revolution" because the word has by now achieved the status and therefore meaninglessness of a TV commercial. First of all, a revolution involves an escalating struggle for power, culminating in the displacement from power of one social group or stratum by another group or stratum which has been ruled by those in power. Secondly, a revolution replaces one system of production which has obviously failed to meet the needs of a given society with another system of production which purports to meet these needs. In education the production we are talking about is the production of educated people.

Until recently, these formulations might have appeared like phrase-mongering or language from another planet. But now, even here in the no longer peaceful city of Ann Arbor, some of you teachers must have been wondering what significance the teachers' strike in New York has for you.

Briefly stated, the situation in New York is this. Two years ago, in the fall of 1966, black parents in the Harlem I.S. 201 community, abandoning the struggle for integration as the key to better education for black children, began a new struggle for community control of schools. From that point on, the struggle for black power in education has centered around the demand for community control of schools.

In July 1967, acceding to this pressure from the black community, the New York Board of Education established three special districts, including I.S. 201 and the Ocean Hill–Brownsville District, to test community control of schools. The Ford Foundation then granted planning money to each of these three districts to help them set up community governing boards, comprised of parents, teachers, supervisors, and community representatives. Each district then chose a unit administrator and developed a plan of operation for submission to the Board of Education. Among the powers sought by all three local governing boards were the hiring and dismissing of teachers and supervisors, the setting of curriculum and methods of instruction, budget freedom, and the making of supplementary contract agreements with the UFT.

From the moment that Mr. Rhody McCoy, a black man, was elected unit administrator by the Ocean Hill–Brownsville board, both the UFT and the Council of Supervisory Associations began their opposition to the Ocean Hill–Brownsville project. Both groups brought suit against the eight new principals appointed by the board (four Afro-American, two Puerto Rican, one Chinese, and one white, and all with state certification as principals) because they were not off the civil service list. At the beginning of the 1967–68 school year one hundred teachers transferred out, some of them in groups. During March and April, particularly at JHS 271, the majority of union teachers stopped teaching and even supervising.

The local governing board met with the mayor, union officials, the State Commissioner of Education, the entire Board of Education, and the

superintendent of schools, informing them of the desperate crisis resulting from the refusal of personnel to cooperate. Each promised help but
no offer was ever made to transfer out the specific number (nineteen) who
were the main source of agitation against the local Board and the minimum transferees needed to avoid real danger to the children. Finally, on
May 9, amid almost total chaos and for the safety of the children, the
local board transferred out the nineteen. In support of these nineteen,
another 350 of the 550 teachers in the district then stayed away from
classes for the last six weeks of the term, taking with them in many cases
the records and roll books of the children.

Since then, the Board of Education, the city administration and the
State Commissioner of Education have all done everything possible to
appease the union and undermine the local board. A so-called impartial
examiner (predictably Negro) was appointed to review the qualifications
of the nineteen and, predictably, declared them qualified. The 350 teachers who refused to teach for six weeks were paid for those six weeks. The
city administration supplied police to enforce the return of the nineteen
to Ocean Hill–Brownsville against the expressed determination of the
community. The Board of Education suspended the local governing
board, the eight principals appointed by the local board, and Mr. McCoy.

In the face of this unprecedented intimidation and pressure, the Ocean
Hill–Brownsville community has refused to accept these teachers back.
With the opening of the school term, it interviewed and hired other
teachers with whom it has kept the district functioning, while on a
citywide basis the union has kept schools closed. Meanwhile, inspired by
the Ocean Hill–Brownsville example, teachers, parents, and students
have organized district councils in other areas to open and run the
schools.

Two very fundamental conflicts are here involved. First, there is the
conflict between the black community's rights and powers and the teachers' rights and powers. Secondly, because the teachers are overwhelmingly white and the community overwhelmingly black, there is the race
conflict.

Most of you, as teachers and particularly as white teachers (I understand that out of eleven hundred teachers in the Ann Arbor School
District, only about fifty-five are black), probably identify with the teachers and supervisory unions in New York. Understandably, since if the
black community is able to hire and fire teachers and supervisors (particularly supervisors), it can hold them accountable as they have never
been held accountable to any constituency and particularly to the black
community. That means job insecurity, a growing problem with teachers

as automation increases and white parents move to the suburbs.

But looking at this issue not in terms of your personal situation (how much you sacrificed to become a teacher or your house or car note) but in terms of the human rights of our children and the future of this society, how many teachers do you think deserve job rights separate and apart from accountability? In my teaching experience in the Detroit inner city schools, I would estimate that three out of four teachers have already quit psychologically. A Chicago black teacher says she would estimate nine out of ten in her area. Yet the record shows that out of nearly sixty thousand teachers in New York City only twelve have been dismissed in the last five years for incompetence. Meanwhile, year in and year out, millions of black children have been turned off, pushed out, beaten, bored, and embittered by culturally deprived teachers who look upon our children as little animals.

There are two sides to every question, it is true, but only one side is right. And a revolution involves a choice between rights, usually between the hard-won rights of an earlier generation, in this case the workers in the thirties, and the more universal rights of a deeper layer which was not freed by the earlier struggles, in this case, black children.

But a revolution involves not only power and rights. It involves a system and the failure of a system.

The system of education in the United States today is a part of the overall system of American society. It serves the purpose of the system today, just as yesterday's systems of education served yesterday's purposes. During the pre-Civil War stage of American society, the main purpose of education was to produce a political elite to govern the country. It was therefore exclusive, aristocratic, and essentially British-oriented. Then, with the Industrial Revolution precipitated by the Civil War, education was reorganized to give the children of industrial workers, chiefly European immigrants, the minimum literacy needed to man the machines in mills and factories. The question of educating black children didn't even arise because, in their place as field hands and servants, blacks weren't even supposed to need minimum literacy.

But the Industrial Revolution in turn brought about the mechanization of agriculture, forcing the black field hands into the cities, while the technological revolution has continued its advances into automation and cybernation, rendering their unskilled labor obsolete. Meanwhile, with World War II and the decline of the European powers, Russia has begun to emerge as a rival to the United States and the colonial peoples in Africa, Asia, and Latin America have begun to take the revolutionary road to economic development.

As a result of these two developments, technological and social, a third purpose has begun to dominate American education, namely, (1) the production of scientists and technicians to enable the United States to accelerate its economic development, particularly to compete with Russia in inner space and outer space; and (2) the production of social scientists, including sociologists, political scientists, and anthropologists, to enable the United States to contain the mounting social revolution of the colored peoples, at home in the cities and abroad in Asia, Africa, and Latin America.

Once we understand that this is now the fundamental purpose of American education, then we can understand why it operates as it does. The track system and the authoritarian structure of American education are not accidental. The track system enables the schools and universities to concentrate their main energies on those showing aptitude and interest in mathematics, engineering, and administration, and relegates those who do not show these aptitudes and interests to a kind of prison-camp existence in which the teachers are the jailers. The authoritarian structure operates to keep the minds as well as the bodies of students in chains.

The catastrophic effects of this system are all around us. The United States has now reached the point where it is the *technologically* most developed country in the world and *politically* the most backward. *This is the fundamental contradiction of American society.*

That this country is economically and technologically the most advanced in the world is obvious. That it is politically the most undeveloped and backward takes some explanation on my part and some reflection on yours. Just ask yourself who but a politically backward country could have tolerated for so many years the racism which has systematically elevated whites and systematically degraded blacks? Or sanctioned the genocidal war in Vietnam? Or produced the swelling Wallace movement within which are already visible all the barbarism and savagery of the Hitler movement? Wallace isn't responsible for his followers; his followers are responsible for him. And what is coming to the surface in the Wallace movement are all the years of miseducation in the glories of the American way of life, with all its racism, materialism, opportunism, and political irresponsibility. The rise of Wallace challenges us to examine the system of education in this country with the same ruthless objectivity that we demanded of the Germans vis-à-vis their system of education.

It is against this system that there is a revolt now going on at two levels: (1) by those on the lowest track, mainly black, centered around the issue of community control of schools; and (2) by those on the highest track who have been promoted and advanced by this system but who, chiefly because of the war in Vietnam and the black revolt inside the United States of America, have seen through its essential inhumanity, refuse to be integrated into it, and are determined to expose and ultimately overthrow it. These are the revolutionary students in the universities, black and white.

The revolt of these two layers of American society is so firmly rooted in the failure of the present system and has already achieved such momentum that no one of us can ever go home again. In the foreseeable future, not just in terms of months but in terms of years, not just at the beginning of school but throughout the year, every one of us, students, parents, teachers, and administrators, must be ready for the reality of school boycotts, sit-ins, parents ousting teachers or taking over schools during teacher strikes, clashes (usually nonviolent but sometimes violent) between parents and teachers, students and teachers, teachers and teachers, students and students, students and parents, administrators and administrators, often with police and police dogs or armed militants guarding one or the other side of the controversy.

It is not a pretty picture. But it can happen here in Ann Arbor, just as it has been happening in New York and elsewhere. The most important question for us as educators is not whether we like it or don't like it, but (1) which side we will be on as the conflict sharpens and (2) how much we are ready to sacrifice materially and free our minds from psychologically in order to bring a new system of education into being. Are we going to choose the side of the existing educational system, which is obviously bankrupt, in the name of law and order and due process, or are we ready to make the sacrifices and do the pioneering work necessary to develop a new system of education?

I am not so rash as to attempt to give you a blueprint of what must be done, but I can offer some guidelines as an indication of my own thinking.

1. The fundamental contradiction between economic development and political underdevelopment in the United States has reached the stage where this country faces the same fate as Hitler's Germany. A revolution in education is not the only solution to this contradiction by any means, but since it is the arena which best expresses and continues to intensify this contradiction; and since there is already a revolutionary or prerevolutionary situation in this arena, educators can play an important role in resolving this contradiction *if they join forces with those who are in revolt, and work with them to reorganize the system of education from top to bottom.*

This requires, first of all, a new philosophy of education, i.e., defining the goal of education to be the production of masses of people who are capable of political self-government in the last quarter of the twentieth century, instead of the production of technical and administrative elites. The technical problems of mass production of goods have been essentially solved. The critical problem of this society is how to develop the means and methods for the mass production of a politically developed people, i.e., people who are able to make an objective analysis of the revolutionary and counterrevolutionary forces in their society and ready to do the thinking and activity necessary to defeat the counter revolutionary and strengthen the revolutionary forces. *Politically* responsible activity, not *economically* responsible activity (i.e., labor), is the socially necessary activity of our day. Revolution, with all that it implies in conflict, turbulence, rapid change, is necessary because it is only through revolution that this country can accelerate its political development to correspond to its economic development—just as it is only through revolution that the countries which have been systematically deprived of economic development by colonialism can accelerate their economic development. The most useful members of society are those who can recognize this need for a social revolution in this country and help to bring it about; not those who are the most willing to work in order to produce more goods and earn more money to buy these goods.

The first prerequisite of political development in the United States is deeply felt understanding of the role racism has played in this country's development, the degrading effects it has had on whites and blacks, and the role it has played in making American democracy a system of political irresponsibility and the American way of life a nationwide track system in which each ethnic grouping successively tries to climb the social, economic, and political ladder on the backs of the groups below it, and all groups on the backs of the blacks. This means much, much more than the study of Negro history or the so-called contributions to American history of such distinguished individuals as George Washington Carver, Jackie Robinson, or even Frederick Douglass, Martin Luther King, and Malcolm X. It means giving Americans of all ages such an insight into the barbaric role that racism has played in creating the American way of life that at the very minimum they will welcome the black revolution and even hopefully wish to join it as so many young white university students would like to do.

2. Simultaneous with a redefinition of the purpose of modern education must be a fundamental reorganization in methods, based upon the revolutionary developments taking place *outside* the classroom and impressed upon young people by the mass media. As Margaret Mead has put it, children today are understanding things out of their continuous

experience that adults have to learn. Or, as many children in black community obviously think, "Why should we go to school to interrupt our education?"

a. First there must be a change in the teacher-student relationship from the present authoritarian relationship in which the teacher presumes to know and hand down truths. Instead the relationship must become a dialogue in which each is learning from the other. It is obvious that our children are not learning from the present method and that it is stifling the curiosity and learning energies which they show outside the classroom. Instead of the objectives being defined and developed in lesson plans by the teacher, they must be developed according to the interests which the children bring with them from outside the classroom. The teacher essentially should act as a guide, confident that in the pursuit of their own interests and concerns, the students will not only master existing skills but themselves develop new ones to obtain information or create new truths in the field of their interests.

Practically speaking, such a reorganization requires a spectacular development in cybernation and computers with which the students can enter into dialogue and find the information or develop the skills they need on an individual basis. Only such a spectacular use of educational technology can relieve the teacher of the impossible task of being a repository of the constantly expanding information or of being a master teacher in every method or every skill adapted to the needs of every student. This means that teachers, instead of feeling threatened by and fighting for their job rights against computers in education, should welcome these for the individualized instruction they can provide.

b. Side by side with the elimination of authoritarianism in the teacher-student relationship must go the elimination of the track system and its replacement by heterogeneous learning situations where youngsters of widely varying backgrounds and aptitudes can carry on genuine, and therefore not just polite, dialogue and interaction with each other.

c. Just as children must feel free to bring with them into the schools their interests outside the schools, so parents and all adults, including teachers, must find in the schools, a place where they can develop the resources to solve the questions that concern them and where there is continuous interaction between different age groups, all learning from one another. The schools will then become a center for the continuing education that is absolutely essential in this age of technological and social revolutions which make the skills and standard of one year irrelevant in the next. Besides, the more we have machines doing the work, the more people will be freed to learn for the sake of learning and not for the sake of making a living.

Some of what I have outlined here is described most appetizingly in *Education and Ecstasy* by George Leonard, *Look* senior editor. Where I differ from Mr. Leonard is in his insistence that such an ecstatic system of education can be brought about without a revolution. Leonard says that to bore a child is as cruel as beating him. The statement should be posted in every classroom. For to bore a child is like boring a hole in his head and taking out his mind. Leonard also points out that the present system is for the purpose of taming, not educating, our children, and that the task of preventing the new generation from changing in any deep or significant way is precisely what most systems require of their educators.

Yet he concludes with an explicit rejection of revolution as the means of reforming education and appeals instead to foundations to fund pilot projects that will develop new alternatives. I am not against pilot projects. But I do not think that any real re-education of ourselves as educators (and again I include in this parents and students as well as teachers) can take place separate and apart from the ongoing revolutionary struggle to replace the existing power structure.

No system has ever yielded to a new one without revolutionary struggles. Any system exists because it has the support of those who have benefitted by it (in this case, the great majority of teachers and supervisors) and are therefore sympathetic to its aims and methods (in this case, the aims and methods of a society centered around labor and economic development). Hence when this system is threatened, as it is at present, by those who recognize its essential inhumanity, those who have benefitted by the existing system take counter revolutionary steps, as they did in Hitler's Germany thirty years ago and as they are doing in the Wallace movement today.

Moreover, as I tried to illustrate by the poem of Cornell Norris, out of these living struggles, with the difficult choices and often costly mistakes that we will all make, we can begin the challenging but enormously difficult task of building a new system of education, a system which will create politically developed people, able to cope with change and to make socially responsible decisions that will benefit the whole human race and not just their own particular segment of it. The best way to develop such political capabilities at this stage is to engage in revolutionary politics, i.e., to support and encourage black power and student power in education. It is also the only way to reverse the present suicidal course of this nation.

On the other hand, any attempt to subvert the revolutionary social forces already in motion by setting up puppet advisory councils will only create more bitterness and conflict with these forces who can only survive by transforming the system from top to bottom. The net result of any such efforts at subversion would therefore in all likelihood be civil war on the scale of the war in Vietnam today.

AN ALTERNATIVE TO MISEDUCATION
FOR THE AFRO-AMERICAN PEOPLE*

by Edwina C. Johnson

POSITION STATEMENT

THE AFRICAN DECENDANTS in America, having passed through three phases of education in America—de-Africanization, dehumanization, and, finally, an inferior caste status—through application of self-determination and the establishment of a voluntary self-separated school system, can educate themselves.

The country as a whole is unable to meet the challenge due to deep-seated racism which permeates the educational system as well as every other institution of the society.

As stated in 1964 by Brother Malcolm X, the case is clear for an alternative: "When I was in the 8th grade, they asked me what I wanted to become. I told them I wanted to study Law. But they told me law was not a suitable profession for a Negro. They suggested I go into something else . . . like carpentry, maybe. . . ."

"Education is a dependent, inter-acting unit of the whole culture."
—Doxey A. Wilkerson, Associate Professor of Education, Yeshiva University

As America developed throughout the centuries, first as small overseas colonies of Europe and eventually into an independent nation, the educational system developed and refined itself in order to meet the needs of the society. Education is, from the anthropological standpoint, one of the several major societal institutions. As Professor Wilkerson states (above), education interacts with the other institutions of a society. For purposes of clarity of focus, some historical setting is necessary at this juncture.

The American colonists copied European schools as much as possible. The schooling of the young was designed throughout the centuries to

*Seminar for teachers, New York City Public Schools, December 13, 1968.

meet the changing needs of the whole society. The society as a whole changed from overseas colonies to a struggling, fledgling "democracy" and finally developed into a technological world power. The Afro-American was and is educated to serve that society (the colonies, the fledgling democracy, the technological world power) as a subordinate without human benefit or dignity.

EDUCATION AS IT WAS DEVELOPED FOR PUPILS

1600's—The colonial government had general authority over schools. The poor children were apprenticed to learn a trade. Latin grammar schools were offered as secondary education to wealthy boys. In 1636, Massachusetts founded Harvard College.

1700's—Practical education developed in the colonies for jobs in business, trade, navigation, etc. Benjamin Franklin helped found an Academy in Philadelphia in 1749. By 1776, there were already nine colleges: Harvard, William and Mary, Yale, Princeton, Columbia, Pennsylvania, Brown, Rutgers and Dartmouth.

1800's—Gradual establishment of state systems of public education. Separation of church and state became a reality. The elementary school curriculum was expanded to include (besides the "three r's") art, bookkeeping, drawing, geography, history, homemaking, science, etc. In the 1820's, teacher training institutions were founded, and later these became four-year colleges and granted degrees. By 1875, free public education was established.

1900's—Technological developments. Thousands of advanced institutions of learning became a reality.

EDUCATION OF THE AFRO-AMERICAN PEOPLE

1600's—Africans, indentured servants, then perpetual enslaved persons, then enslaved persons by law. The colonial government varied colony by colony as regards the eventual "slaves by law" status. The African was, however, set apart almost at once and excluded from the general population of persons to be admitted to the educational program for whites.

1640—Perpetual servitude defined in Virginia.

1662—System of enslavement established by law in Virginia.

1664—System of enslavement established by law in Maryland.

1673—System of enslavement established by law in Carolina.

1684—System of enslavement established by law in New York.

Strict separate social codes for the blacks were developed throughout the colonies to reinforce the subordinated status. The African was forbidden to speak his own language, to practice his own religion, he was, in effect, de-Africanized during the early colonial period.

Learning for the African, then, was to lose his identity as an African, give up his African institutions, even his name. Learning to memorize some bible passages was permitted for the sake of "saving his soul." His education was in the field, in the enslaved persons quarter, where he adjusted or died in the state of servitude to whites.

1700's—Slave or Black Codes: an enslaved person for every white person.

1. No freedom of assembly—except at church or at Christmas time. This meant no more than four or five blacks could assemble normally.

2. Firearms forbidden.

3. No beating of drums or blowing of horns (to prevent signalling for insurrectionary actions).

There was some effort on the part of religious groups to establish "Negro Schools" during the 1700's.

1. A Negro School in New York, 1701.

2. A Negro School in Philadelphia, 1770.

These were most often met with hostility from the white community due to the general feeling that an educated black was a dangerous one and would no longer be of service to a master.

1800's—Professor Benjamin Quarles describes the education of the Afro-American succinctly for this century:

> "The lot of the typical slave, regardless of locale or occupation, was influenced in large measure by the psychological and legal controls brought to bear on him. All slaves were inculcated with the idea that whites ruled from God and that to question this white divine-right theory was to incur the wrath of heaven, if not to call for a more immediate sign of displeasure here below. A slave was told that his condition was the fulfillment of the will of the Master on high, catechisms for the religious instructions of slaves commonly bore such passages as:
>
> Q. Who gave you a master and a mistress?
> A. God gave them to me.
> Q. Who says that you must obey them?
> A. God says that I must.[1]

Freedmen were regularly ostracized, lynched, resold into a system of enslavement, and generally rejected. Attempts to educate themselves were discouraged with threats or acts of violence.

Free mulattoes occasionally were educated abroad. In Georgia and Florida, even when free, an Afro-American was forced to have a white guardian to whom he had to report regularly. Curfews were enforced, and except for churchgoing (which was considered good for the continuance of docility), the right of assembly was denied. Every Southern state had a law forbidding immigration—hence, the Afro-American was "boxed in" by law and denied entrance to schools where whites were enrolled.

Enslaved persons were taught trades as a means to better serving the white master. However, once a freedman, the same man was excluded from the trades.

The Afro-American child learned that his family members were scattered through the auction of enslaved persons, learned to loiter in the fields, to sabotage the progress of field work, to feign illness as a means of escaping a day in the fields, learned to pretend to be "happy" to prevent a whipping, learned to bend his inner pride in order to survive the severity of enslaved life, learned that any posture of dignity on his part could lead to a severe beating or an instant removal to a worse locale. The Afro-American child, enslaved or free, learned that he was not a human being. This was the dehumanization stage of the education of the Afro-American.

1900's—Outcast from participation in American life, relegated to peonage with practically no education in the South and segregated in the North. This is the inferior caste status of the twentieth century. So-called Negro colleges, established with funds in the South by philanthropic whites, educated the Afro-American to accept his subordinated position in America, to be a "good Negro," that is.

The foregoing briefly describes the vast differences between the development of education for the white and for the black in the United States. The white was educated to become a community citizen, to be productive and to earn his living. The black was educated to serve the white community as an enslaved person or as a free man, to accept a role of a subordinate to the white in every facet of his life. "The northern capitalists who were giving their support to Negro education in the South were not interested in making 'men.' The southern whites were opposed for other reasons to the development of a truly educated leadership among Negroes."[2] Industrial education, as proposed by Booker T. Washington, became a tool of white supremacy. Industrial education schools were supposed to instill in their students a spirit of humility and an acceptance of their inferior status. Moreover, no teacher in a school of industrial education could mention the existence of labor unions. The emphasis on this education was supposed to be on the "heart and the hand" rather than the head because southern white people did not want the Negro's head to be educated.[3]

The unevenness of the pattern of "informal" (enslaved person–field) but rigid education given the Afro-American as well as the varied and irregularly attempted patterns to develop "formal" educational institutions for the Afro-American sharpened the controversy within the country over whether or not the Afro-American was educable at all, was "dangerous" if educated formally, or even if he was to receive benefits from the public educational institutions founded by state laws and for which he paid taxes as a freedman. The following may assist in shedding light upon the genesis of the current conflict and the need for an alternative to mis-education for the Afro-American people.

Every early liberal tendency regarding the education of the African was discouraged and finally overwhelmed as the system of enslavement evolved. During the American Revolutionary era, a slight progressive trend developed because of a temporary decline in the economic value of the system of enslavement.

As enslaved persons' power expanded and resurged during the first half of the nineteenth century, negative attitudes toward educating the Afro-American re-emerged. In this light, two periods are deemed important:

1. 1600-1835—Faint affirmation of the prudence in educating people of African descent.

2. 1835 on—As the Industrial Revolution altered the system of enslavement, a negative attitude developed: it was dangerous to educate a black, for he would then possibly no longer serve as a an enslaved person.

Important, too, is a consideration of the types of persons who were interested in educating the Afro-Americans during the period of enslavement:

1. Masters who taught bookkeeping and clerical duties to their enslaved persons in order to increase the economic efficiency of the labor supply.

2. Persons who felt pity for the oppressed and wished earnestly to help them.

3. Missionaries who felt that Africans should learn the English language in order to understand the principles of religion as they espoused it.

The Revolutionary War increased educational opportunities for Afro-Americans slightly; however, these opportunities were overwhelmingly destroyed as the profits from the system of enslavement sharply increased some fifty years later. There were two reasons for the negation of education for Afro-Americans, enslaved or free:

1. the world-wide industrial revolution which gave rise to the establishment of the southern plantation system;

2. the efforts of educated Afro-Americans to publicize to the world the baseness and cruelty of the system of enslavement and the successful Haitian revolution executed by Toussaint L'Ouverture.

Thereafter, Southern statesmen wrote into the statute books laws which prohibited the education of the Afro-American. The laws as related to education were as follows:

1. An assemblage must be in the presence of particular white men.

2. Freedmen were made to leave the area, preventing any aid to education of the enslaved persons they might give.

3. Enslaved persons were no longer to be taught bookkeeping or any type of clerical skill.

4. Private and public teaching of any kind to Afro-Americans was prohibited.

It became clear to holders of enslaved persons that "as intellectual elevation unfits men for servitude and renders it impossible to retain them in this condition, it should be interdicted."[4] In order to keep the Afro-American in a complete service state, it was also necessary to keep him in the state of degradation and ignorance. So serious was the restriction of education for Afro-Americans, there were laws in many states making it a crime for an Afro-American to give instruction to his own child.

As time passed, enslaved persons who could read and write were considered as suspect and "dangerous." The notions against educating the African traveled northward. Hence, fugitives and freedmen who went northward began to experience a severe rejection at every turn. Freedmen were not to be educated in the North either. Freedmen were subsequently forbidden to open schools in some areas of the North. Afro-American teachers were "run out of town" in other areas. In extreme situations, schools were burned to the ground if they serviced black students. Booksellers of African descent were tortured (an excellent example of this is the case of David Ruggles in New York City).[5]

Thomas Jefferson in 1781 described the Afro-American as being of a lower classification than the European, of having body odors, and of having sensuality as the center of his style of life, of being easily humored and having less brain capacity than the European.[6] This early writing by an American statesman has been repeated through the centuries and has found its way into the educational literature and been even "proven" in studies. So heavy is the weight of prejudice it has become a part of educational attitudes.

FINAL STATEMENT

Although the system of enslavement, which dehumanized the African in America, failed finally, a malignant caste system developed which has mitigated against the progress in education for the Afro-American right up to and including the present time. As summarized in the U.S. Riot Commission Report,

> The Negro is in the United States by the very reverse of the democratic principle of free choice. He was seized in his native Africa by force, transported free of charge . . . and compelled to labor as a slave for white masters. He was denied the most basic kind of education, and was separated from his family throughout slavery. (He was denied the most basic kind of education, and was *torn* from his family throughout slavery.) The racism in the country against the Afro-American casts blame on him for those very characteristics the slave owners imposed by rule upon him during the three hundred years of slavery. Any effort on his own part to better his condition educationally is cut down by the malignant racism which has developed over the centuries. The Dred Scott decision formalized his inferiority through the courts, the Supreme Court decision in the case of Plessy vs. Ferguson established segregation by law and by custom.[7]

The report clearly states: "The events of the summer of 1967 are in large part the culmination of 300 years of racial prejudice. Most Americans know little of the origins of the racial schism separating our white and Negro citizens. Few appreciate how central the problem of the Negro has been to our social policy."[8]

The schisms in the country pervaded education to such a degree, it is considered futile by Afro-Americans to resolve conflicts with white participation. The Ocean Hill–Brownsville test case is a classic example of racism in high level operation. The determination for self education follows as a logical alternative. "In the context of professed ideals, Negroes would find more retrogression than progress, more rejection than acceptance."[9]

Dista H. Caldwell states the case for voluntary segregation this way: "At present the survival of the Negro depends upon greater racial solidarity."[10]

The problems of Afro-American education are unique, and they demand unique, distinct, and separate schools in order to be solved. In a real democratic society, separate schools would be unnecessary. However, in a "democratic in name only" society, and in practice, aristocratic, separate schools for the minority denied participation is a sound solution for that minority.

The Afro-American, in the twentieth century, is in reality, struggling for the goals that the Europeans were struggling for in the 1770's.

NOTES

1. Benjamin Quarles, *The Negro in the Making of of America.* New York: The Macmillan Company, 1964.
2. E. Franklin Frazier, *Black Bourgeoisie.* New York: Collier Books, 1964, p. 62.
3. *Ibid.*, p. 63.
4. Carter G. Woodson, "The Education of the Negro Prior to 1861." New York, reprint by Arno Press, 1968, p. 9.
5. The Schomburg Collection of the New York Public Library files on David Ruggles.
6. Thomas Jefferson, "The Inferiority of Negroes," Negro Heritage Library. Yonkers, New York: Educational Heritage, 1965, p. 37.
7. *Report of the National Advisory Commission on Civil Disorders,* U.S. Government, advance copy by *The New York Times,* 1968, p. 214.
8. *Ibid.*, p. 206.
9. *Ibid.*, p. 235.
10. Dista Caldwell, *The Education of the Negro Child.* New York: Carlton Press, 1961.

BLACK STUDIES—

FORECAST FROM HINDSIGHT*

by Nathan Wright, Jr.

THE LATE Dr. Martin Luther King used to emphasize the irresistibility of an idea when its time had come. This has come to be seen as true, perhaps for some significant ill as well as for some substantial good, in the case of black or Afro-American studies.

By now, it is or should be clear to all that Afro-American studies are here to stay. This is so partly because black Americans have decreed that it must be so, at whatever pain the apparent denial of their dignity requires. Black studies are to remain a part of the educational offerings in our schools and colleges because our educators—almost universally, now—are coming to see its need. If the hunger for truth in its wholeness is to be satisfied in the lives of all, then we must go where truth will lead us.

Today the ongoing search for truth has taken us to the most-overlooked area in our nation's rich history. It has led us to the story of black Americans who have played an important part in practically every aspect of the nation's life. Laden with even greater good news is the fact that these bi-cultural black Americans—who have been separated out of mainstream America against their will—have had to develop both critical and creative understandings of white America in order to survive. Hence they have developed in their "black experience" fresh and much-needed perspectives on American life.

I

The lore of the persistently alienated and formerly invisible black Americans now stands ready to be explored and to be unfolded for the enrichment of our total life. Scholars concerned with the positive im-

*Presented at the University of Houston, April 19, 1970.

plications of black studies especially are recognizing a truth of which Gunnar Myrdal wrote some time ago. Gunnar Myrdal emphasized the impossibility of seeing truth whole without viewing it from as many cultural perspectives as possible. To seek to see American life—in any of its aspects—with scholarly integrity while omitting the major marginal perspectives represented by black Americans is thus to engage in a kind of academic folly.

One of the distinguished white historians who participated in the 1969 Annual Meeting of the Association for the Study of Africa, in Montreal, recognized the need for seeing truth beyond the natural barriers raised by culture bias. His published remarks were: "We thought that as white historians we could simply teach history. But we were wrong."

Those who represent the culture of power will see truth in the interests of maintaining that power. Indeed, this is the very meaning of objectivity as it is exercised in every society. Scholarly objectivity in America, until the recent breakthrough of black Americans onto the stage of reality and visibility, has been that which could be seen upon a center stage from which black Americans were absent.

The coming to the forefront of black scholars has a fortuitous dimension which must be examined throughout the nation, particularly at a time when our society has begun to be marked by the phenomenon of continuing change. In sociological and philosophical terms, those who are *in* a society, although not *of* it, are called marginal people. They develop, to the extent that they are self-aware and self-accepting, what technically is called marginal insight. Cast out to the periphery of their society, they are afforded a type of "dramatic distance" where they can see life at the center of the stage with far greater perspective, detachment, rationality, and creativeness than can those who occupy roles at the center of the stage.

The so-called "black experience," is then in a technical sense a marginal experience through which American life can find clearer articulation and more helpful interpretation. For this reason our universities and colleges should be seeking out the ablest self-aware or "pro-black" scholars for the probing of the black experience which is so vital to the academic process at this immediate and fortunate juncture.

Those institutions which are most wise will do much more than this. They will work diligently and self-consciously to create subcommunities of such scholars, as apt specialists by experience and training, who will work together to pool their insights and then share them with the local scholarly community and with others beyond.

There can be no more exciting and potentially rewarding venture in the academic world today than that which is opened up by the focus on black studies.

II

What, then, are some of the problems? And how do we begin to face them?

Without doubt, the first "problem" in black studies is posed by the protesting black students through whose intrepid encouragement the focus on black studies developed.

These students, it must be understood, want to be "in" not "out" with reference to American life. There are none in America presently who want the nation's verbalized ideals to find fulfillment more than do these eager and often angry students. Black anger is heightened idealism which has developed a stubborn and determined will.

For what more can any of us ask who will that only the best be achieved and sustained in our common life? Progress always comes with pain. Hence the black students who strive for change are troublous. Yet it is good that this is so. As we look carefully and thoughtfully at the essential things which black students are demanding, we shall see in their sometimes discordant pleas our own self-interest.

Black students are not seeking to have the educational establishment destroyed. They are insisting that it be inclusive of and that it work in the interests of all who would aspire to the fulfillment of their potential. In our emerging world of the late twentieth-century and early twenty-first-century, continuing or higher education must adapt itself to just this end. The recent studies of student unrest relate campus disorders to perceived lack of relevance or relationship of learning to the life views and aspirations of the learners.

Not a few of the ablest educational administrators in the nation are coming to see black student protest as their last chance to initiate changes which they had yearned for over a period of many years. A part of the "black experience" involves a fresh appreciation of relationship, a recognition of the value of the empathetic or feeling aspects of human life. Students themselves are saying teach *us* not the subjects. They are saying that learning to be relevant must relate to the fulfillment needs or self-concept of those who would learn.

The concern for black studies calls for a change in institutional and classroom style. At heart, our teachers must create a new perception of their tasks as those who relate to persons and facilitate learning rather than as able purveyors of learning. Although the picture here is caricaturized, the spirit is realistic. Our black students in their own way are the advance guard of what will be a growing requirement that all who teach become sympathetic partners in a process of continuous and shared learning.

As we move into the age of the twenty-first-century a major problem will be that of continuously including people on the "inside" in the face of ongoing disorganizing, alienating, and disruptive change. Our black students today—who want the America of today to work—are saying in effect: "Use us as a laboratory for developing the capacities and techniques for change which will be sorely needed for your future survival as well as ours."

The essay "Humanizing Our Schools," which appears elsewhere in this volume, underscores the issues that are raised here. The article in question has been reprinted by the thousands on various college campuses and in school systems. It recognizes that answers given with understanding to the glaring black-student needs will work for benefit of us all.

III

Black students are raising another issue which, from an administrative point of view, may seem to be fraught with difficulty: the issue of student involvement in the control of educational processes.

Until relatively modern times all students controlled the educational process. Plato and Aristotle, Socrates, Maimonides and Christ were all paid by those whom they taught. In medieval European universities— which were the distinguished predecessors of the projected "walk-in" colleges of which we have read of late—students paid teachers and stayed with them in accordance with what they felt the teacher gave to them.

Today our servants are in almost complete control of those whom they are called upon to serve. This is, to say the least, a somewhat odd imbalance. Of course, our young people have much to learn. Of course, our young people do not precisely articulate their aspirations! Yet it is consistent with the station and competencies of trained academicians to understand the sometimes halting attempts of others to verbalize felt needs for changes consistent with their dignity. To be a scholar surely does not confer the right to change from distinguished servant to omniscient master.

One of the best scholars, well-known in the teaching craft has aptly reminded us: "He who would be greatest among you, let him be the servant to all." Our teachers and educational administrators need to be recalled to this ancient truth as well as to the worthy example of the Clerk of Oxford of whom Chaucer wrote: "Gladly did he learn and gladly teach." Our black students today have much to teach all of us in terms of empathetic skills, and all of our students must come to be seen as partners in a never-ending task of cooperative learning in which we have the high privilege to serve as guides.

Concerning "control," this issue is raised for good reason where learnings do not appear to be relevant. We can face this issue creatively in several ways. In our black-studies programs or departments—as well as everywhere in our universities and colleges—the perceived needs of the students must be a starting point for teaching. We must, as educators, begin with where our students are or we shall not teach. Our black students have vastly different perceptions of who they are than do their teachers. This is so because these students have undergone a black metamorphosis overnight, and it is understandably hard for white Americans to catch up.

In some sense, most students *feel* that they are treated as "niggers." Black students *know* that this is so. A simple rule always, in dealing with black students as well as with any others, is to let them know that you have respect for them as persons. This can be disarming, but it is not all that is required. Since learning must serve the fulfillment needs of the learners, it becomes tremendously important that our teachers all come to understand the new black mood of dignity and self-determination.

Even as black students are seeking the kind of self-realization that will equip them to meet the problems of a world of continuing change so also are our students generally. The black students want us to come to see them as persons determined to meet ruggedly and bravely a challenging new world. We must continuously adapt our sights to fit this need.

When students demand seemingly undue measures of control, they are affording us a warning that their persons seem not to be respected. We need not fear their persistence in "undue control" since they cannot presently command the resources for the continuance of the educational task. So fearful reactiveness is not required. Rather, we should take the opportunity to begin adapting learning today to serve human as well as perceived societal needs.

Teachers who are too aloof from those who learn have an unworthy view of what life is all about. Life is for liberation of man and for all mankind. Our students should require that their liberation and fulfillment needs by met. By the same token, our teachers and administrators should know that the older view of realities concerning black and white still will tend to condition their outlook and behavior. We have lived in a white-oriented, white-purposed, and white-controlled world. We should be keenly aware of this and of what this kind of conditioning does to limit our capacities for seeing present realities for what they are. Our time-worn intuitions cannot be trusted to guide us in new situations where "New occasions teach new duties and time makes ancient good uncouth."

In a word, then, we should doubt the validity of our judgments where our reactiveness would tend, naturally, to lead us astray. Openness is clearly called for. In our Afro-American-studies proposals, students will insist upon fullest control where there is the least confidence that they are both understood for what they are and respected for what they see themselves as capable of becoming. Ideally, black-oriented programs should be black-controlled, that is, by black teachers and black students. Until now, blacks have been fully controlled by whites. No longer should they be either dominated or distrusted. Blacks have no significant or equitable control elsewhere in the academic enterprise. We can make at least a humble beginning as blacks control the enterprise where they alone have the capacity to give basic definition to the new and necessary tasks which are involved.

IV

Black studies, as projected by black students and black teachers, have two basic meanings. By black or Afro-American studies is meant the classical disciplines of black anthropology, black history, black economics, black politics, and the like. This is needed even as we begin to "integrate" black subject matter more equitably in our curriculum as a whole. The separate or discreet emphasis is and will remain necessary in order to overcome the overwhelming influence of a culture which daily denies, both in its etiquette and rhetoric, the realities of black life throughout the nation.

Black scholars ideally should teach black-studies courses, at least at the present definition stage. It would assuredly not be proper or reasonable for an Arab to give basic definition to the Jewish experience or for a Russian Communist to give fundamental interpretation of the democratic dream as we are trying to realize it among us in America today. This is not to say that we do not "make do" with what we have when no ideal resources are available. But makeshift or substitute resources should never be confused with what is ideally required.

Black scholars of the highest competence should be employed by all of our major institutions of higher learning to give greatly needed leadership in the reassessment of our whole corpus of social, scientific theory.

Our psychology and sociology, for example, sprung from the womb of colonialism (that is, Darwinian evolution and the Kipling "white man's burden") and were nurtured in an era when the neocolonialist mind was the order of the day. We are all, in a sense, creatures both of our age and of our cultural and historical inheritance. The bi-cultural black scholar, as he seeks his own mental and psychological emancipation, can be of extraordinary value to the academic enterprise as he helps others to open wider vistas upon the world of truth.

On an undergraduate level, black studies will serve primarily a white public. The experience over the past year has been that over sixty percent of those enrolled in black studies have been whites. This serves as a cultural corrective and enriches our total life. For black students this affords a small measure of pride, but general disappointment seems on the increase. The evident cause for this state of affairs is that black students need far more than historical and other social, scientific understandings of themselves, however important these may be.

When black students call for black studies they are speaking on two levels which must be understood. They have been calling for the new courses which are now being offered. Perhaps more important, however, they are using an euphemism for meeting the hard-core human-development needs of those who reside in the center-city environment. Black students realize that somehow their potential is not either recognized or developed so that it may come to flower. Black or Afro-American studies also means, then, urban affairs and human development.

Black-student groups increasingly are aligning themselves with newly forming black-faculty groups chiefly because both black faculty and students want a fresh look at the city from a vastly different point of view than that which exists at present. The phrase, "cities are people" expresses the new point of view. Blacks are saying that an approach to the city in terms of physical fabric or systems does not speak to their own human needs for habilitation, liberation, and fulfillment. Schools from which empathetic relations are lacking, however clever their programs or tools, are not going to help very much. They haven't helped in the past. A focus upon better housing has disorganized black communities and has been accompanied by demoralization and, worse still, pervasive deracination. Black central-city dwellers, under the aegis of an unconsciously inhumane orientation toward supposed "renewal," have come to live of late in a perpetual limbo because of the sense of rootlessness which present "urban renewal" and "model cities" invariably create.

With this condition in mind, some black-studies programs are being organized as departments or institutes of urban affairs. The prospectus for the Afro-American Studies Department at the State University of New York at Albany calls for the change to a Department of Urban Affairs and Human Development with a program of Afro-American studies as one of its components. Puerto Rican students and faculty at the Albany institution have petitioned that a Puerto Rican program be included along with Afro-American and other third-world programs.

The rationale involved is that the human development concerns of the oppressed or powerless peoples throughout the world are of one piece and that they should, at least for the present, be dealt with on a coordinated basis. We know little—or at least apply very little of our knowledge—about human development in reference to the powerless groups among us. Scholars from these groups should direct such programs. It is they who by both personal experience and technical training are best equipped to understand, articulate, interpret, and prescribe in the area of human development for those who are, or sense that they are, oppressed. The scholarly dealing with this area of concern should add significantly to our academic enterprise even as it approaches in potentially far more fruitful ways the unmet needs of our understandably distraught and alienated black and other minority students.

V

On a graduate level, the need to focus upon the use of black scholars under the banner of urban affairs and human developments becomes even more clearly advantageous.

On a graduate basis there needs to be much reworking of older scholarship about the human dimension of urban environment and about the hard-core problems of human life in general. The greatest single pool of underutilized talent for bringing fresh perspectives to such work is represented by our black scholars. Many of these do not have doctorates, although many do.

A program of human development should not simply research the area of concern but should engage in development. Indeed, "research-development" should become a new action term implying the greatest kind of academic responsibility. Hence, such graduate programs throughout the nation should facilitate the sharpening of scholarly tools to be employed by the large number of grossly under-utilized black potential which is at hand. Crash programs which are substantive could and should move to the doctoral level thousands of black bachelor- and master-degree holders throughout the country in less than three or four years' time. Summer programs on an intensive thirty- or forty-hour-a-week basis could provide sufficient residence for such working people or practitioners and take little or no time off from the employment by which they provide for their families' needs.

Equal opportunity for young black students is not enough. We must, in realistic ways, make up for much of the past. When our youth see that we mean business with their parents they will respond with a deservedly far greater trust. When our preschool youngsters, for whom "head starts" become a source of frustration, see their parents rehabilitated, they will find the educatively negative atmosphere which they formerly knew transformed into something beautifully creative.

Hence, not only on the graduate level but also on the undergraduate level, older black adults need to be brought into a process of rehabilitation. At the State University of New York at Albany local citizens and faculty members have joined in creating a tentative program for accelerated collegiate education. They are subsidizing the families of some able black men and women in their late twenties and in their thirties and forties who have demonstrated remarkable capacity for leadership but who may not have completed high school or college. These able persons each have a tutorial or educational sponsorial committee assigned to them. Accelerated studies are being devised for these individuals to be assisted through a bachelor's or master's degree as quickly as possible without compromise to the substantive aspects of the curriculum. Large numbers of such able persons need no subsidy. They need a welcoming facility and substantial encouragement.

If black or Afro-American studies are to meet the felt needs of our black students, then academicians must see that new and effective human-development approaches are made at the same time that black-oriented traditional courses are offered.

Graduate facilities of urban affairs and human development could assist our colleges in the critically needed coordination of social, scientific studies—including economic and business development or administration—and those studies offered by schools of education and of environmental research. Such facilities could greatly assist the entire nation, in the face of rapidly accelerating social and technological change, by exploring new ways of creating or of sustaining a working integration of new and ever-changing alignments of groups which might tend toward alienation and the ultimate fracturing of the nation's life.

Infinite possibilities are before us, if we but open our eyes to see them.

VI

By way of pulling together some of the practical implications of what we have said thus far, the following points are offered:

1. Black or Afro-American studies fill a need, primarily in the white community, by offering new sources of enrichment concerning the nation's heritage.

2. Black studies afford a measure of much-needed pride for black students but do not answer many larger felt needs of black students in the area of human development.

3. Black students are asking, indeed demanding, that their own needs and self-concepts be the center of educational concerns. In this sense, they are affording the educational enterprise an unexcelled, positive opportunity for new and widely needed adjustment in advance of anticipated and widespread student unrest concerning educational irrelevance.

4. Black students want chiefly to make an impact upon black-studies programs rather than to control them. The issue of control decreases as needed openness and good faith increase. All students want to be assured that their needs rather than institutional agenda are the major focus of the educational process.

5. Black or Afro-American studies need to be taught both as separate disciplines and on an integrated basis in order to overcome built-in denials of black value by the culture as a whole.

6. Black scholars who are self-aware and self-accepting are needed to supplement the current academic experience with creative minority (or marginal) insight. Communities of the ablest black scholars should be created for this purpose.

7. Black students are concerned with building urban-affairs and human-development emphases into our educational institutions as a means of dealing with their hard-core needs. Graduate facilities of urban affairs and human development, utilizing the human-oriented (or emphatic) skills and other resources of black scholars in key leadership roles should be created.

8. General, black adult-education rehabilitation is important if black educational needs are to be met reasonably and at minimum costs.

Our forecast for the future is, a bright one, if our educational establishment can use the issues raised by black or Afro-American studies to serve the public good.

What black students are asking for essentially is respect for themselves as persons and the imparting of scholarly or technical tools for their own self-directed growth into self-sufficiency and self-respect. All students are—or soon will be—asking or clamoring for no less than this.

Those who get locked into petty battles over minute, insignificant details of the black rhetoric of aggression miss out on a glorious opportunity to try out change with those who do not presently wish to destroy the establishment.

As our scholars and administrators learn the easy lessons of coping with change from working with our black students, they shall be better prepared to face the greater demands which may come with greater urgency in the five decades of accelerating change which lie ahead.

BLACK POWER AND BLACK HISTORY*

by John Henrik Clarke

"It is not really a 'Negro revolution' that is upsetting the country. What is upsetting the country is a sense of its own identity. If, for example, one managed to change the curriculum in all the schools so that Negroes learned more about themselves and their real contributions to this culture, you would be liberating not only Negroes, you'd be liberating white people who know nothing about their own history. And the reason is that if you are compelled to lie about one aspect of anybody's history, you must lie about it all. If you have to lie about my real role here, if you have to pretend that I hoed all that cotton just because I loved you, then you have done something to yourself. You are mad."—*James Baldwin, "A Talk to Teachers," December 1963.*

FIGURATIVELY SPEAKING, the concept of black power and black history are twins that were fathered by the same historical experience. This concept was created to counteract another concept: that the people of African descent had no history worthy of respect. The Europeans who started the enslavement trade and the colonial system that followed needed to propagate this concept in order to justify their action.

The present-day young black militants are asking, in many ways, why the word *history* is so limited when it is applied to their people. They are beginning to learn (belatedly) that history, depending on how it is manipulated, can be either an instrument of oppression or of liberation. In most cases, what is called "African History" is only the history of Africa's contact with Europe, beginning with the enslavement trade. What is called "Negro History" is generally the history of the American system of enslavement and subsequent effects.

The Europeans who started the enslavement trade in the fifteenth century had to forget—or pretend to forget—all they had previously

*From *Freedomways*, 1st quarter, 1969.

known about Africa's contribution to the development of mankind.

The present-day black power and black history advocates are trying to restore what the enslavement trade and the system of economic oppression took away. Their fight has long roots and it was not started by Stokely Carmichael or H. Rap Brown.

In a formal sense the concept of black power started in the nineteenth century, concurrent with the many attempts to restore black men to an honorable place in history. The concept of black power confuses most people because they are looking for a complicated system. Black power means no more or less than the right to determine your own destiny, starting with the control of your own communities. This is the same thing that every ethnic group in America has—or is trying to get. Black power without a respect for black history is meaningless. Until the essential manhood of a people is respected, no power in their hands is effective.

In a speech made in Cuba last year, Stokely Carmichael, while addressing himself to the subject "Black Power and The Third World," said this:

> Since 1966, the cry of the rebellions has been "Black Power." In this cry, there was an ideology implied which the masses understood instinctively. It is because we are powerless that we are oppressed and it is only with power that we can make the decisions governing our lives and our communities. . . . Black power is more than a slogan; it is a way of looking at our problems and the beginning of a solution. Because our color has been used as a weapon to oppress us, we must use our color as a weapon of liberation. This is the same as other people using their nationality as a weapon for their liberation. . . . This coming together around our race was an inevitable part of our struggle. We recognize, however, that this is not the totality, only the necessary beginning.

Then, while emphasizing the need for the cultural restoration of a people he said:

> Black power recognizes that while we are made to feel inferior, this is only that we can be easily exploited. Color and culture were and are key in our oppression, therefore our analysis of history and our economic analysis are rooted in these concepts. With power we will take our birthright, because it was with power that our birthright was taken from us. . . . Black power not only addresses itself to exploitation, but to the problem of cultural integrity.

The nineteenth-century black militants, and some before them, were saying essentially the same thing in different ways.

The fight against the distortion and suppression of the true history of the Africans and Afro-Americans was started long before the Civil War by "free Negroes" and escaped enslaved persons who had learned to read and write.

The back-to-Africa idea has been a recurring theme in the lives of black Americans for more than a hundred years. The thought was strong during the formative years of the Colonization Society and some of the most outstanding black men of the eighteenth and nineteenth centuries came under its persuasion. In the middle of the nineteenth century, while the issue of the system of enslavement was being debated in most of the country, the feeling for Africa among American blacks was growing stronger. Publications like *Freedoms' Journal* and *Douglass Monthly,* edited by Frederick Douglass, called attention to the plight of the people of Africa as well as the black Americans.

As far back as 1881, the renowned scholar and benefactor of West Africa, Dr. Edward Wilmot Blyden, speaking on the occasion of his inauguration as President of Liberia College, sounded the note for the organized teaching of the culture and civilization of Africa and decried the fact that the world's image of Africa was not in keeping with Africa's true status in world history. I quote from his address on this occasion:

> The people generally are not yet prepared to understand their own interests in the great work to be done for themselves and their children. We shall be obliged to work for some time to come not only without the popular sympathy we ought to have but with utterly inadequate resources.
>
> In all English-speaking countries the mind of the intelligent Negro child revolts against the descriptions of the Negro given in elementary books, geographies, travels, histories. . . .
>
> Having embraced or at least assented to these falsehoods about himself, he concludes that his only hope of rising in the scale of respectable manhood is to strive for what is most unlike himself and most alien to his peculiar tastes. And whatever his literary attainments or acquired ability, he fancies that he must grind at the mill which is provided for him, putting in material furnished by his hands, bringing no contribution from his own field; and of course nothing comes out but what is put in.

The great human drama now being called "The Black Revolution in the U.S.A." has long historical roots, and it cannot be fully understood until it is seen in this context. In his 1944 book, *Capitalism and Slavery,* Dr. Eric Williams places the origin of this revolution in historical perspective and calls attention to its early development:

When, in 1492, Columbus, representing the Spanish monarchy, discovered the New World, he set in train the long and bitter international rivalry over colonial possessions for which, after four and a half centuries, no solution has yet been found. Portugal, which had initiated the movement of international expansion, claimed the new terrorities on the ground that they fell within the scope of a papal bull of 1455 authorizing her to reduce to servitude all infidel people. The two powers (Spain and Portugal), to avoid controversy, sought arbitration and, as Catholics, turned to the Pope—a natural and logical step in an age when the universal claims of the Papacy were still unchallenged by individuals and governments. After carefully sifting the rival claims, the Pope issued, in 1493, a series of papal bulls which established a line of demarcation between the colonial possessions of the states: The East went to Portugal and the West went to Spain.

Though the announcement of the fact came much later, the European "scramble for Africa," and subsequently Asia and North America, started with this act. The labor and raw materials of Africa, Asia, South America, and the West Indies financed the European Industrial Revolution.

The Africans who were brought to the New World against their will were dehumanized and, in most cases, deculturalized. They were neither respected Africans nor accepted New World Americans. They were renamed, and became a marginal branch of the human family now referred to as Negroes. The Europeans needed a rationale for their actions and a rationale was created with supporting concepts. The cruelest concept ever devised by the mind of man was created to support the enslavement trade and the colonial system that followed—the concept of race and the assumption that there are superior and inferior races. The Africans were depicted as a people without a history who had never properly handled power and who, certainly, had made no contribution to the development of human cultures. And thus the seeds of the present-day conflict were planted.

The American Federation of Teachers' Conference on "Racism in Education" held in Washington, D.C., on December 8, 9, and 10, 1966, set in motion much of the present action and the debate about black history and how it should be taught in the public schools.

The noted actor Ossie Davis addressed the conference on the first day. His opening remarks were: "Those of us who are concerned, who are caught up, who really want to be involved in the revolution, must be prepared at this conference to tear aside our most private thoughts and prejudices. . . ."

The tone for the conference had been set. For two days, more than fifteen hundred teachers and educators examined and indicted the American educational system. They were told that a curtain of ignorance hangs over the school systems of this nation and that our children are not being educated to face the realities of this nation and this world. Cases of deliberate distortion of the role that the black Americans have played in the making of this country were pointed out. And it was further stated that everyone from professional textbook writers to missionaries had participated in this distortion.

Ossie Davis cited the English language as a basic transmitter of prejudice. In his speech entitled "The English Language Is My Enemy," he said that he counted one hundred twenty synonyms for the term "blackness" in *Roget's Thesaurus,* half of which were grossly unfavorable.

Davis argued that right from the time a black child learns the English language he learns sixty ways to despise himself, and a white child learns sixty ways to aid and abet the crime.

Keith E. Baird, a New York school teacher, who followed Ossie Davis, talked about the importance of ethnic identification for Afro-Americans. Mr. Baird, who is a teacher of languages, spoke of the respected place in history, as celebrated in the Jewish holiday of Hanukkah, of the Maccabees of Biblical times. He also pointed out that in the process of ethnic identification, not only a person's individual attributes are considered, but the "cultural identification of this group."

Baird presented to the conference a resolution that he urged it to adopt, the wording of which was: "To say that the slavery-connected word 'Negro' should be abandoned, and in its place the words 'Afro-' or 'African-American' be applied to persons of African descent in the United States in all places where such reference to ethnic descent is appropriate."

At a later conference session concerning resolutions, this one was unanimously adopted.

In his presentation, Mr. Baird defined what the cry for black history is about—it is about the search for a people's identity and their need for a new image of themselves. The black Americans are trying to locate themselves on the map of human geography. This explains the growing preference for the words "Black African" and "Afro-American." These words show how the black Americans relate to a land, a history, and a culture.

In a number of other conferences sponsored by the local branches of the American Federation of Teachers, and the UFT, the teachers agreed on plans to implement courses in black history. The main conferences were held in Detroit (May 11-13, 1967) and in Chicago (March 22-24, 1968), and conferences in Denver and St. Louis followed. While many of the white teachers clearly admitted that racism is rampant in the American educational system, very few of them had any basic plan concerning what to do about it. Their reluctance to commit themselves to the correction of this racism caused a lot of black teachers to form separate organizations, some within the framework of the American Federation of Teachers and the UFT. The Chicago Black Teachers' Caucus was one. In New York City the Afro-American Teachers' Association was another.

Still another organization, the Conference of Afro-American Educators, which met in Chicago in June, 1968, shows the best potential of becoming a nation-wide force to affect change in the educational system. At this conference Donald Freeman, who renamed himself Baba Lamumba, defined education as it relates to black people:

> What we understand by education is the application of all one's knowledge for the benefit of the collective which in turn will benefit each individual within the collective. To this end what must constitute a basic part of one's education is the understanding of people rather than things. We realize that once people understand themselves, their knowledge of things is facilitated, that the exclusive knowledge of things does not guarantee knowledge of people and in fact contributes to the erosion, disintegration, and destruction of the creativity of man.
>
> Therefore, education must: (1) teach black people who they are, (2) teach black people what they are fighting for, (3) teach black people who they must identify with, (4) teach black people where their loyalty must lie, (5) teach black people what must be done, (6) teach black people how to do it, and (7) teach black people that the destinies of all black people are inseparably linked whether we are in North, Central, or South America, the West Indies, Europe, Asia, or Africa.
>
> Now, there must be a complete unity of all aspects of one's life and in particular education must be indelibly linked with one's life processes for the benefit of each black man and woman and all black people. Those who have knowledge primarily from books must be linked with those who have knowledge from the streets and vice versa to confront and solve all the problems of black people. Education must assure that all of what one learns can be and will be

applied to concrete practical problems and their solutions. If our people can throw molotov cocktails in white stores, we can certainly throw molotov cocktails in our minds. Mathematics, physics, electronics, sociology, religion, and other sciences must not be viewed as abstractions, but comprehended as the concentrated experiences of man's interrelationships with man, nature, and the universe to mold and control his own destiny.

It is obvious that the American educational establishment is not ready to correct itself and implement these suggestions that it would consider extreme. This would not only be tantamount to correcting itself, it would also be tantamount to repudiating itself. At the base of the grievance of the black teachers and growing numbers of black people is the fact that they have been educated or miseducated in a system that has yet to acknowledge that they are an integral part of American or Western Civilization. Both the clamor for black power and black history are the clamor of people to enter the mainstream of a society and to institute dynamic social reform—or to replace that society. The most far-reaching reforms will be in the field of education. Control is the key word in the school situation because it implies power to act in one's best interest at a time and a place of one's choosing. The educational establishment could digest or tolerate decentralization because the school system would still be run in the main by the educational establishment, which is a force operating outside of the local community. When community control is added to decentralization, a whole new area of power is defined. This means that the community will have the right to hire and fire teachers and to control the massive budge of the school system that is now a major American industry.

In an address in Ann Arbor, Michigan, on May 25, 1968, Dr. Grace Boggs said in effect that the question of black control of the schools has now become a question of survival for all black people. Urban school systems are disintegrating before their eyes to the point where their actual physical and mental safety are at stake. Black children and their parents have lost the traditional respect for the teachers and principals of their schools because of the growing alienation between the school and the community. The mass media, principally television, have taught these children to become suspicious of most large establishments, especially police forces and governmental agencies that make promises which they do not keep.

Many of the white teachers in the large educational systems in cities like New York, Detroit, Philadelphia, Chicago, and Los Angeles, come to the system with preconceived notions about the ability of the black child to learn. Instead of teaching him they spend a lot of time convincing themselves that the children unteachable. They do not bring their best teaching ability to these communities because they do not respect the children or the community well enough to do so. In addition to being poor teachers for the black community, these teachers are not even good baby-sitters. In a lot of cases they are arrogant, unfulfilled and insecure people, long overdue for analysis. Very often the black child and the black community become whipping-boys for their neuroses. Community control would mean that these teachers can be transferred or fired, once their lack of qualifications has been proven.

There is no attempt to drive all white teachers out of any black community. However, teachers who fall within the above description will not be secure under any form of community control.

Keith E. Baird, director of the Afro-American History and Cultural Unit of the Board of Education, gave the following explanation of decentralization and community control at the Summer Forum at Columbia University in August of 1968 on the black experience.

> I am going to talk about decentralization in the public schools and its implications. I use the term "decentralization" largely because it is the one that is generally used. Now, most words that begin with this prefix "de-" suggest a kind of fall from grace, and I think that discussion about the changes that are being sought in the school system suffer somewhat from this semantic difficulty. I rejoice, however, to see that in this booklet the "decentralization" means re-forming the present school system in New York City into largely autonomous school districts, joined with the central education agency into a city-wide federation.
>
> Now this is a fairly decent and workable definition, but what does it actually mean in terms of the "Black Experience," the context in which we have come together to discuss this matter? We seem to have two separate questions before us: "decentralization" and "community control." Of course, the two are not necessarily mutually exclusive: you can have decentralization without having community control and you can have community control without having decentralization.
>
> Now there is no problem about white people controlling the schools, because that, of course, is what has always happened. The schools are run by white people: the majority of the teachers are white, and the people who administer the schools are in great part white. Thus we have what are essentially white schools, reflecting white interests, a white self-concept, and white culture. The question of community control comes in because certain enclaves,

certain new ethnic enclaves, will now be having greater control, or at any rate be in a better position to exercise control over the schools their children go to—provided, of course, that the rules and regulations of the New York City Board of Education actually permit this to happen.

Thus we come to what is really the crux of the situation, namely, the control of schools in Afro-American and Puerto Rican areas by the Afro-American and Puerto Rican communities particularly because these communities have not been significantly represented until now at the policy-making level in educational affairs. What community control boils down to is simply this: Are we or are we not going to let black people and Puerto Rican people really tell teachers what to do? Especially, tell white teachers what to do? And so on. That is really what this whole thing boils down to, and we may as well face up to it.

Because most decentralization and community-control talk in New York City is centered around I.S. 201 in Harlem and Ocean Hill–Brownsville in Brooklyn, it would be well to show the essence of the background of this conflict.

The crucial issue of the I.S. 201 controversy is the poor quality of education in ghettos such as Harlem.

From the first through the twelfth grade, an increasingly larger proportion of ghetto youth perform below their grade level in reading and math. Eighty-seven percent of the pupils in the Harlem school district are below grade level. Better than two thirds of the pupils drop out before graduation from high school. Daniel Schreiber, the former assistant superintendent of District 4, in which I.S. 201 is located, verified these figures.

The parents of School District 4 were willing to accept the promise of the Board of Education that integration would help solve the problem of poor education for their children.

When 201 was proposed as a junior high school as far back as 1958, parents objected on the grounds that construction of a school at the proposed site would create another segregated school. As late as 1965, Dr. Bernard Donovan maintained that 201 would be an integrated school. He even alluded to having the school related to a university, accompanied by special programs. By February of 1966, Daniel Schreiber maintained that 201 would be integrated, but by this time, "integrated" had come to mean representative groups of black and Puerto Rican children.

As early as March 28, community representatives were demanding the

establishment of a community group to which teachers would be responsible in addition to the demand for an integrated school. Parents' opposition to the Board of Education's response (or lack of response) to these
demands canceled the scheduled opening of 201 for the spring term of
1966. The school district was gerrymandered without the consultation of
the community to create a student body of Puerto Ricans and Negroes.

"Integration" gives way to "quality education." By the end of the
summer, the Board of Education had to admit that it had no plan for truly
integrating I. S. 201. The parents, realizing that the Board of Education
had no intention of integrating the schools of Harlem, focused attention
on the basic problem of improving the quality of education in Harlem
with the realization that it would in reality have to be segregated.

There is agreement between the parents and the Board of Education
that the Board has failed to integrate the Harlem schools. There is also
agreement between the parents and the Board that the quality of education in Harlem is low. The disagreement lies in the means used to improve the quality of education. The parents place the full responsibility
of poor education in Harlem upon the Board of Education whose present
structure they feel is incapable of providing or administering a quality
educational system to meet the needs of the ghetto community. The
composition of the Board, how its members are selected, and its source
of power indicate the distance that exists between the body that makes
educational policy and the community for whom the policy is made.

The Ocean Hill–Brownsville decentralization experiment in Brooklyn,
New York was spoiled by success. The local school board, consisting
mainly of parents from the community, took their jobs seriously and
asked that a number of teachers who they deemed incompetent be transferred. This move seemed to have shocked and angered both the Board
of Education and the head of the United Federation of Teachers. This
abrupt exercising of power by the local school board and their unit
administrator came unexpectedly.

The two large black ghettos of Brooklyn merge at Ocean Hill. Its
inhabitants include a growing number of Puerto Ricans. Nothing of a
dynamic nature was expected of these slum dwellers.

In September 1966, the controversy around I.S. 201 in Harlem had a
profound effect on the Ocean Hill–Brownsville School District. That
month a group of parents in Harlem demanded that the Board of Education respect their right to select the principal for I.S. 201. These parents
were asking, for the first time, to have a voice in the administration
of the schools in their community. The contagious cry for community
control was now spreading beyond Harlem. It did not bypass the

Ocean Hill–Brownsville School District in Brooklyn.

After some protracted agitation, the Board of Education allowed the people of Ocean Hill to form an administrative unit, with the understanding that the Board would relinquish some of its authority to this unit. The administrative unit and the local governing board succeeded and began to exercise the authority that the Board of Education never thought it would use. This was the basis of their trouble with the Board of Education and the United Federation of Teachers.

The dispute between the people of Ocean Hill–Brownsville on one side and the Board of Education and United Federation of Teachers on the other side might well be a sad indication of what will soon be a national crisis in education. The cry for black power and black history has rekindled a long smoldering fire that will, no doubt, affect major changes in the educational, political, and economic structure of the United States.

PART V

COMMUNITY INVOLVEMENT

AND ACTION

"COMMUNITY INVOLVEMENT"

IN SCHOOLS*

by Albert Vann

I AM ADDRESSING myself to black people about black people. The community I speak of is the black community, and the black community is where black people are.

Involvement usually connotes participation. However, the black community must redefine participation to mean control. When we speak of community involvement, we must mean that black people must control their schools and school systems. Even when you do not constitute the majority population of a given area, control your schools through coalition. Only when it becomes obvious that you are so few in number that control is impossible should you be a party to involvement as it is traditionally defined. The purpose of this involvement is merely to exert influence so as to protect your most precious resource, your children.

WHY MUST BLACK PEOPLE CONTROL THEIR SCHOOL SYSTEMS?

A cursory glance at the products of the schools that supposedly serve you, a deeper gaze at the plight of black people (and it has been this way for the last 350 years), and then a brief reflection on the role that schools play in this society should provide enough evidence to make blacks realize that they must begin to control their own destiny; they must control the forces that mold the minds of their youth, they must rule the schools. With the knowledge that many of my brothers and sisters are hard-headed, I will give some specifics. Black people must control their schools:

So that we can survive.

*Presidential Address, Afro-American Teachers Association of New York City, June, 1969.

So that we can liberate others (their minds) to ensure our survival.

So that black people can become psychologically, economically, and politically independent.

So that black children can develop self-worth and dignity through knowledge of their history and culture and through the image provided through current community leaders and teachers.

So that teaching personnel will be *accountable* to the community, and, therefore, must really teach if they want to maintain their jobs.

So that curricula, books, literature, and other materials will be relevant to the life experiences and needs of the black child and provide additional motivation to learn.

So that the contracts, jobs, and money that are controlled by those who control school systems will be kept in the black community.

So that we can equip our young to adjust to changing power relationships or prepare them to fight for survival, or both.

Racist America, though a powerful and influential nation, seems bent on a course doomed for destruction. The fear and guilt of white America apparently renders it unable to act rationally in regard to solving the crucial racial problem they created. It will be the insights of the oppressed blacks and their determination for freedom which will probably be the salvation of this nation. A major tool in their struggle for freedom is obviously education. Education for blacks will not become a reality (in a school setting) until black people control their own school systems. It may very well be that such community control will not be possible until there is a revolution in this country, and the establishment of a new order in which different power relationships will develop. Black power? Black power! Of course I am assuming that the white power structure will not respond by sharing decision making or by sharing the wealth of this country, which leaves no alternative but revolution.

In the interim, you must begin to "control" your schools on different levels—the implication being that until you control the purse strings, you never really have complete control. However, blacks can move closer to the money sources by identifying "key" black people who can provide information or exert influence, and making them function on behalf of the black community.

To attain control requires, I think, a multiple approach, as it will afford blacks on different levels of involvement and awareness an opportunity to participate in the fight. Do not hesitate to use your local politicians to dramatize your concerns in state legislatures. Keep pressure on the Board of Education "by any means necessary." Maintain public awareness by *highlighting* the excessive failures of the system and the irreparable damage inflicted upon your children. You must organize parents, students, and community organizations so as to do the following:

Maintain continuous communication.

Make use of community resources.

Develop a structure for governing the schools.

Drive home the realization that only the people in the community directly affected can initiate and maintain (with some sacrifice) the necessary changes in their schools and must not be dependent on other forces.

In the final analysis, however, physical confrontation is inevitable. The community must physically take over the schools, and with that leverage demand control of all policy-making relative to the operating of a school. I view this process as a healthy one. It provides an unparalleled learning experience for the students, as well as giving them a concerted role to play in the struggle. Such a confrontation marks the coming of age of the black man and his community. It further reflects the coming together of segments in the community to form a united front for the purpose of supporting, protecting, or initiating an action for the welfare of the community.

It would seem most appropriate to end this paper with quotations from a noted black historian, Lerone Bennett, Jr., as reported in *Muhammad Speaks,* June 21, 1968:

He who controls images controls minds, and he who controls minds has little or nothing to fear from bodies. This is the reason why black people are not educated or are miseducated in America.

The system could not exist if it did not multiply discrimination.

It is no accident that there is a blackout on the black man's contributions to American history.

An educator in a system of oppression is either a revolutionary or an oppressor.

The question of education for black people in America is a question of life and death. It is a political question, a question of power.

Struggle is a form of education. Perhaps the highest form.

THE AGENCY SHOP*

by Albert Vann

THE UNITED FEDERATION of Teachers realizes that its racism has been exposed and that most black teachers and many white teachers cannot support it in any way—least of all financially. More significantly, the entire black community is aware and therefore despises the UFT. The relevance of any member of the UFT to any community school is highly questionable.

Many teachers who have for a long time disliked being a part of the UFT believed that it was necessary to belong in order to receive fringe benefits. In spite of the fact that at this time the UFT negotiates the contract with the Board of Education for all teachers, all teachers, UFT and non-UFT, receive the same benefits.

Being aware of all of these things, Albert Shanker and his people have already thwarted any attempt for a meaningful decentralization bill, if there is any such animal. Their next move is to obligate all teachers, financially, to support the UFT through this thing called an agency shop.

We of the African-American Teachers Association, with the interest of our black community, will not abide by any such racist, dictatorial mechanism as an agency shop.

Most ATA members have already disassociated themselves from the UFT; except to attack its anti-black community policies.

We have not forgotten the illegal strikes against our communities by the UFT.

We have not forgotten the sabotage activities carried on by its members in Ocean Hill–Brownsville, P. S. 201, and Two Bridges.

We have not forgotten the phony antisemitism issue created by the UFT in an attempt to discredit the black movement as well as some of our black men.

*Position paper, Afro-American Teachers Association, May 6, 1969.

We have not forgotten the job they have done and continue to do in the state legislature to prevent a real decentralization plan for New York City.

We have not forgotten the false issues, created to protect worthless teachers from being transferred from Ocean Hill–Brownsville, which demonstrated no concern for the welfare of black and Puerto Rican children.

We have not forgotten that they have never supported the black communities' demands for black administrators in our schools.

We have not forgotten that even when black people were naïve enough to believe in integration (1964 boycott for integrated schools) the UFT violated its promise to support our demands.

The list of charges against the UFT is inexhaustible. It only serves to remind us that we will fight to the death to defeat the UFT's having the right to tax teachers who are violently opposed to its antiblack policies. We will not accept such a condition, no matter what it takes to prevent it.

THE CIVIL RIGHTS STRUGGLE*

by Samuel W. Allen

CIVIL RIGHTS MAY, in a sense, be a misnomer because the struggle has progressed beyond the narrow concept of civil rights to the wider one of human rights. It is no longer a matter of rights based upon citizenship, but of rights based upon one's identity as a human being. This was made significant by the advent of the United Nations and its Declaration of Human Rights, because it was not a national group, the United Nations focused not upon the citizens but upon the rights of all people. Furthermore, the term "human rights" aids to extend the struggle beyond national boundaries.

I'll begin my remarks by saying something about Daniel Moynihan because he will play an important role in Mr. Nixon's administration; he will be his top man in dealing with urban problems. This means, among other things, that he is Mr. Nixon's expert on black community affairs. Moynihan is considered by some white leaders to be our foremost urbanologist. And that is where the struggle of the black man in America today is focused—in the cities and ghettos—although we must not lose sight of the still vast number who remain outside. You may recall that when Moynihan was in the Department of Labor he prepared a study on the Negro family which was widely read and widely hailed, especially by white leadership, and exercised a great deal of influence. It also aroused widespread ire among black people. His thesis was that the great difficulty in further progress for the black man in America was the disorganization of the Negro family resulting from the system of enslavement and its aftermath and the creation in the Negro of the Sambo syndrome; the Sambo psyche; the emasculation of the Negro male and the loss of his initiative; the loss of his confidence so that he slunk away into oblivion while the matriarchal wife dominated the family and took on the respon-

*An address delivered at Carver Research Foundation, Tuskegee, Alabama, December 18, 1968.

sibility of the family and, indeed, of the whole Negro community.

This approach was at first very widely praised, but soon met with great and intense criticism from many black people, who denied the validity of Moynihan's analysis and who insisted that they were perfectly all right, and you don't have to concern yourself with such alleged insitutional or constitutional defects in the Negro. The problem, rather, is the lack of jobs, housing, and good schooling. I feel—as do many others who severely criticize his work—that Moynihan was essentially correct in his analysis of what has happened to the Negro after three to four hundred years of a system of enslavement and oppression and conscious obliteration of his culture. It was inevitable that something happen to his psyche, to his social organization, something very damaging. But the resistance to Moynihan's correct analysis and tragic prescriptions was essentially correct for another reason, and that was that he didn't mention at all the major pathology in the country—that is, he focused upon the black pathology, but said practically nothing about the white pathology which had created such a problem, which prevailed not only back in the time of enslavement but is a continuing reality: the white pathology which needs a scapegoat—the white personality which is so unsure of its identity that it would exclude significant elements in the community. What is the sickness in the white community that it needs this crutch to lean on? Moynihan said nothing about this. When the report of the National Commission on Civil Disorders came out, it said that the major obstacle to progress here in America is not the Sambo psyche, not the matriarchal family structure in the black community. The trouble in race relations— the reasons why we can't make progress for the black man—asserted the report, is white racism; that's the trouble! It is the white pathology which is the major obstacle to progress. (It is interesting how the name of the commission changed. Up to the moment that the report came out, you may recall that it was known as the President's Commission on Civil Disorders. When the substance of the report was known, it became the National Commission on Civil Disorders, and the President was strangely silent for weeks and weeks.)

It is crucial to recognize the report's emphasis on white racism, a pathology which infects every facet of our society. The trouble with Moynihan's study, which was correct as far as it went, was that, in effect, it led to the conclusion that the victim is the cause of his victimization. The fault is in ourselves, not in our stars . . . that we are underlings. The problem is that if the nation focuses so one-sidedly upon the pathology of the victim, it fails to see the necessity to remove the conditions which cause the minority to be a victim.

Moynihan is a mixed bag, and it seems his approach to problems serves too often as an ingenious justification for a traditional approach to race problems. Not too long ago he issued another statement: the problem in America is not white racism, it's white racialism. White racism, he urged, is a misnomer and fosters confusion. Racism, essentially, he said, holds that another race is congenitally inferior; but this is not the American belief. Americans, rather, Moynihan explains, practice *racialism*, which is, simply, without assumption of inferiority, to exclude the Negro. And what is now true of the Negro has also been true of other minorities: the Irish, the Italians, etc. Well, there may be a difference in degree between American racial beliefs and those of other racist societies (although observers have said there was *less* antisemitism in pre-Hitler Germany than in the postwar United States); but the rejection of the key terminology of the report blunts its impact, and makes easy the assumption that the Negro situation is analogous to that of other minorities, which is certainly not the case.

Well, this, in part at least, is the Mr. Moynihan who will be at the helm in dealing with "the problems of the cities," which is, as we know, largely a euphemism for "black people's concerns." The more I examine what he has been saying, the less is my initial surprise that Mr. Nixon placed him in such a key post. The next several months will tell.

There are two significant dramatic and relatively recent developments in the black revolution which relate to this debate over pathology as well as to each other. (I use the term "revolution" because it reflects the intense and accelerated pace of events, even though it may not be precise, as Harold Cruse has pointed out, in the classic sense of fundamental change in the arrangement of power.) The two developments I refer to are, of course, black power and, related to it, the growing demand for separatism.

I believe that the complex of behavior connoted by the term "black power" is essentially a healthy development. It is the effort of the black man to regain a self-confidence which Moynihan was correct in saying has been largely destroyed by a system of enslavement. It is analogous to what has happened elsewhere; we have heard overseas of the development of negritude. This was largely an aesthetic, which had its beginnings in the literature of Africans and West Indians within the French spectrum. But it, too, has been an affirmation of black values so long denied by the West. Black power has emerged in a more pragmatic society—and is political in its stamp, rather than literary—but its motivation is much the same.

There are as many definitions, of course, as there are definers, but function and purpose of black power remain clear. When people like Kenneth Clark, one of the keenest psychologists on the scene, deplore black power as a cry of desperation and a shabby product of the Negroes' struggle for equal rights, I feel they miss its meaning. Clark laments the fact that black people should be raising the cry of black power in the streets, and he finds in black power the converse of the white racism which took over during Reconstruction. Well, that there is desperation in its origin is true. Black power grew out of the scar tissue of the young SNCC workers who were beaten regularly, with the connivance or active participation of local authorities and without effective intervention from the federal government in Washington. Finally, seeing the futility of the kind of struggle they were waging and the cost in human life, and with the final provocation of the shooting of Meredith on his march to release black people from the continuing reign of terror in the South, Stokely Carmichael raised the cry of black power in Mississippi in 1966.

So black power has grown largely out of desperation, but desperation is not its only attribute. There is also the constructive effort to affirm black values, which, as we remember, has occurred in other parts of the world. Alioune Diop, the Senegalese founder of Présence Africaine, said at Rome in 1959 that it is a sad necessity to have to affirm and extol the values of one's race, but he says in this era, in this time, it is a necessary task; we have to do it. Because three hundred years of domination by the Western world, which has held us in denigration and in a role of inferiority, has made it necessary in order to achieve an equilibrium that we undergo this period of affirmation, I feel that this is very true; it's true for those who are black power advocates, those who are accused of being racists. Basically I feel it is not racism, but if it veers into that area, it is an antiracist racism; it is not going to be permanent. "Black is beautiful" is a very necessary and appropriate cry these days, but it won't exist always, it won't be heard always. I would find it a little odd if white people were going about with a sign saying, "White is wonderful." It's unnecessary, it's implicit in the culture, and when the worth of blackness also becomes implicit in the culture you won't have to affirm it. It would be better not to have to extol racial values. But we are not the only ones to assert group worth. The country has done it in establishing an "I am an American" day. I've never heard of an "I am an Englishman day" or an "I am a Frenchman day," but America in its youthful zeal and its insecurity found it necessary to affirm American values.

The Japanese, while equally if not more certain of their worth, have been different in approach. James Weldon Johnson, in his autobiography, *Along This Way*, tells of a discussion on a ship returning from Japan during the thirties in which he, some American executives, including a Rockefeller, and a number of Japanese were participants. The heart of the controversy, which no one mentioned, was discriminatory racial policy against the Japanese. The Japanese persisted in their silence on the real issue, and Johnson wondered why. Finally he himself described the matter frankly, as he saw it. The Japanese did not utter a word about race either before or after, and Johnson admitted he never did understand their reticence. Johnson was tragically killed in an accident in 1938, but it has occurred to me that if he had been alive on December 7, 1941, he would have understood better the Japanese manner of response.

They did not go about crying Japanese power, but they did react. I suppose many people, black and white, may feel that preferable. They say, If you insist it's necessary to go to whatever ends, do so, but please stop milling about and shouting and sloganeering. Yet the situation is a different one. The Japanese are a separate national group, geographically separated, not part of a larger society with which they are in daily contact. In a sense, the black man's problem is that the white man is always with him, constantly imposing his values, his assumptions, his judgments, and making it necessary therefore to deal explicitly with them in order to resist them.

Let us move on to separatism, which is part and parcel of the black power development. I think Julian Bond made a contribution here at Tuskegee when he urged a voluntary separatism until we were equal in fact. This can't work absolutely, because the process is an interacting one. More precisely, it is necessary to ask, Separatism in what? If we break down this problem into its component parts, there can probably be a far greater degree of agreement. When black people speak of separation, they are focusing on the need to develop and strengthen black institutions and organizations. Most people are not thinking—not yet, at any rate—of taking over the five Southern states. Most people are not thinking of setting up separate governments, but they are thinking of building certain institutions; of building economic institutions, of building social-action organizations, political organizations. There are various areas in the community where it's essential to end the concentration of effort to integrate. We have always been in a position of weakness vis-à-vis the dominant majority. It is necessary to withdraw and develop the strength of our own institutions. And this can lead, itself, to integration ultimately, assuming that it is desirable. Vernon Jordan in Atlanta made a contribution when he said that the two are not mutually exclusive; there can be separation, the development of black institutions, *and* an integrated society; i.e., certain levels at which there can be an open society. It's a pluralistic society, where each group must move from strength, as every other ethnic group has moved from strength. This is particularly true for the black man because no other ethnic group has been as excluded as the black man in this society. So, it's a stage in that direction. It's transitional, hopefully, but whether it's transitional is not that important. We don't have to bank on it. But we build our strength and have a certain independence and still we insist on Title II of the Civil Rights Act, which provides that no man can be denied access to public accommodations because of race, color, creed, or national origin. So the two can interrelate. The point is, we have to think precisely what we are talking about when we say we are separatist. There is a need for black institutions, there is a need for Tuskegee, which should not be so "integrated" (as West Virginia State has been) that there are more white students than black students. There is a place for predominantly black universities. Tuskegee, certainly, has its role.

Now this does not mean that all black students should go to black schools. But even in predominantly white institutions there is a role for black organizations and segments of university activity. I remember Dr. Greenlee saying that at Antioch, where he is this year (maybe this in part is why he's there), there was a concern about getting black students; and so they arranged for scholarships, they scoured the country, and they recruited black students. And they got a huge number, and the first thing the black students did was to form a black students organization and demand an all-black dormitory, which was a great shock and surprise.*
Now everything done in the name of black nationalism or black power or black militancy is not necessarily revealed wisdom. I was discussing the problem with a chap by the name of Pierce, a black psychiatrist on the faculty of the Oklahoma University School of Medicine, and asked him if psychiatric knowledge about the process of change from a psychosis or neurosis afforded any insight. He agreed with my feeling that the movement toward change evident in the assertiveness of black youth is basically a healthy one. He pointed out a danger, however. As a person emerges from a psychotic condition, he throws off the old patterns, which are sick patterns, and this is good. But in the interim, he hasn't yet established the new standards or guidelines, and the danger at this point, the psychiatric profession has observed in the individual at least, is to

---

*My own initial surprise at some of the events on the campuses has been succeeded by an increased awareness of the value of the basic trend. After listening to black students (and white and black faculty) at a number of universities this year, I can see how a measure of separation fits into the overall tendency throughout the society and can be constructive.

stumble or to blunder into suicidal behavior. He has lost the old guidelines and has not yet found the new, and Dr. Pierce felt the same dangerous situation prevails for segments of the black community. There is danger of engaging in aberrant behavior, harmful to itself.

But the main thrust is good; it's a healthy development essentially. The society should remember this fact and not react the way Mayor Daley does when he urges the police to shoot to kill. It should react with a measured restraint, with a balanced realization that the basic development is healthy. The person who exceeds what is termed the "law of the land" against this background is doing so in an entirely different context from that of the average person whom we label criminal when he knocks someone on the head and takes his wallet.

This suggests another aspect of the situation relevant to the pathology of the white community. What happened in Chicago in August was very significant. The emphasis had been completely upon black violence. We see finally from Mr. Walker's report on the events in Chicago that the dominant white community, in the police force, was guilty of violence, of criminal violence. The whole arsenal of tricks and tactics was developed to resist and control black people, following the disturbances in the wake of the King assassination. You remember, after the looting, Daley said he wanted his police in certain cases to shoot to kill. Nobody said it publicly, but it was clear the expectations were for black people to be the object. But there was a surprising turn of events, and the next chapter in the serial involved not black people but white youths coming from all parts of the country. America was amazed and for the first time many were able to understand the reality of the criminal violence visited daily upon black communities. They saw with all the immediacy of the TV screen how ruthlessly the Chicago police acted, how they "rioted" against the demonstrators. There is debate over the alleged "selectivity" of the media, but there is little doubt that some public education was achieved.

There is a perception gap between the black community and the white community. It's difficult for a white person, and for the black bourgeoisie, for that matter, to understand and to realize the oppressive conditions under which the black masses exist. When they are on their way to Montego Bay, St. Thomas, Antigua, they are hard put to realize the desperate plight the black man "enjoys." And so we get, as a result, this breaking through—the early Eldridge Cleavers, the Watts, the Detroits, and the other manifestations of desperation.

Well, what is going to happen? The significant question is whether the society is going to be able to adjust itself to these conditions rapidly enough. I think progress has been made, and I disagree with those who say there has been no progress, with those who say, "What difference does it make if I can get a cup of coffee at a lunch counter when I don't have the money to buy it?" Well, the right to 'enter is progress. It makes a tremendous difference that we can go to a lunch counter, a restaurant, can avail ourselves of any public accommodation (to the extent that this is a reality). I don't think we get anywhere by denying progress—the question is whether it's enough progress, whether it is simply progress for the few, leaving the masses unaffected. To understand what's happening, we must realize that for thousands of years the masses of people have always dwelt in poverty, in suffering, in the midst of vast inequities. We, ourselves, here in this room, did not cause our relatively tolerable fate. Was it because of our individual merit alone that we are sitting here as teachers, professors, students, and are not the people who come here to sweep up afterward. There are vast inequities in the society, and we are just beginning to move to that vantage point from which we can even contemplate a truly equitable and egalitarian society. We are in an embryonic stage, in an infancy. Progress is made, but is it swift enough? Ramsey Clark frequently makes an important point, quoting Anatole France, who was in turn quoting the French philosopher Lamennais, that the stability of societies in the past has rested largely upon the resignation of the poor. I think that is true. The poor have been resigned to their fate, except sporadically, and they have had religion to console them, and so change came about slowly. No major upheavals were caused by the discontent of the poor. But our society has changed. There was the Gutenberg press to begin with, and more people began to get an opportunity to understand what was happening. Now there are the mass media, and everywhere it is known how the rest of the world exists and how other people live. This is the era of rising expectations, as Adlai Stevenson said. It is difficult to judge how and when and where their discontent will speak, but for the first time in human history the poor are not resigned, and, it seems, will not be resigned until a just society is achieved. Although progress is being made, the question is whether it can be sufficiently fast to avoid the kind of cataclysmic upheaval we would presumably hope to avoid. And our domestic problem is also an international problem.

Fortunately for the black American, the problem is internationalized. There is a third world now, and largely because of the media and modern transportation, the plight of the black man is known throughout that third world as well as over the rest of the globe. The Asian and African countries are emerging from domination, and there is a continuing effort to coordinate their struggles, and their struggles with those of minorities in this hemisphere. There is much awareness of the American racial scene, so America cannot deal with its black minorities, with its Mexican-American minorities, as it would before. There is somebody else looking over our shoulder, and this makes a great difference. To what extent there can be effective coordination is questionable. I think so far it's very small, and the other nations are weak—the black American is, in terms of real power, weak. But there is awareness of mutual concern and the groundwork for further coordination.

Well, where do we stand here in this country? My feeling is that we are in a dangerous period. Adam Clayton Powell said recently that he thinks that Mr. Nixon is going to surprise his wealthy supporters and is going to have a much more liberal administration than they expect. I doubt that. I think that Mr. Nixon, himself, may be well disposed. Perhaps he is disposed as the weather vane is disposed. He is undoubtedly aware of his place in history and may want to be known as a great and good president, but he is identified too closely with certain elements. Look at his cabinet and where do you find a man who has had any experience with the ghetto except Romney, who is in a minor spot, really. It is of the greatest significance that there is no black professional—who knows the ghetto experience in both personal and scholarly terms— among his top official advisors. His advisors are men who believe in increasing interest rates to slow inflation, to increase unemployment— an unfortunate incident of sound fiscal policy—to slow inflation. The approach to the ghetto will probably be to ring it with force, the policy of containment, the Kennan and Dulles approach to prevent the expansion of communism. That is the probability, I am afraid. But there have been surprises. Mr. Eisenhower appointed as Chief Justice one assumed to be a "safe" Republican, and we saw what happened. There are surprises. We can be sure the new administration is avidly studying ways to demonstrate that it too is interested in the advancement of the black man. There will be certain showcase appointments, I'm sure. Then, the Republican Party has always been interested in racial equality in the labor unions. That's one area where they are very strong. Howard Jenkins, the one black member of the NLRB, and a Republican, was just reappointed, and he was largely responsible for the ruling that discrimination is an unfair labor practice and is the basis for the withdrawal of certification as a collective bargaining agent. We may see something in this area, and this, indeed, would be no small thing. The unions have been one of the greatest obstacles to the progress of the black working man. This would be very helpful, this would be good; but I think the total picture is not good. And posing that against the determination of the black masses and their growing militancy and Eldridge Cleaver's statement that we shall have our manhood or the earth shall be leveled in the attempt, it is not difficult to see a coming confrontation. Time will tell, but I think the thing we can be aware of, those of us who have had the fortune to have a college education and to have entered into the charmed circle of the black bourgeoisie, and our white sympathizers, is that it is not only our advance which is significant. I should think the black bourgeoisie should fare fairly well under this kind of administration. But it's the black masses who have not had a similar opportunity. They are significant, and the direction the country takes will hinge largely upon the fate of an increasingly politicized black mass, allied with the students —black and white—who are saying that our educational institutions should be much more relevant to the community, and particularly the black community.

QUESTION AND ANSWER PERIOD

Question : How do you interpret Mr. Nixon's proposal on encouraging black capitalism?

Answer (Mr. Allen): Yes, I meant to mention that. This is in keeping with Republican thinking, the emphasis upon free enterprise. I think it's misleading because I don't think a black capitalism can possibly deal with the overwhelming misery of the black masses. Statistics indicated (the most recent ones were issued in November 1967), conditions of the masses of black people in the ghettos were getting worse, not better. The businesses black men develop can't possibly deal with that. The businesses that *white* men have developed haven't been able to deal with it adequately. So, I feel that this is good, I want to see economic strength in the black community, I think this is helpful, but it certainly won't be adequate to deal with the problem.

Comment: I noticed just recently, two things have happened in the *Washington Star*. The black power advocates, like Chuck Stone and the rest, have begun to look into the conditions that exist in the community in crime, they are very much disturbed because of the crime; in spite of the mystique the colored part of the population is suffering a great deal, and I was glad to hear you indicate that the nature of this black power ascendancy will eventually level off and we may get back to the problems that we were trying to solve up until this event.

Response (Mr. Allen): Well, I don't feel that acts of crime are efforts involved in achieving ascendancy in the total society, I don't know if this is what you meant or not. But I do feel the tremendous emphasis here upon black and blackness is something that, once it's achieved, will not continue; it will, as I said, be implicit in the culture. And certainly having black rulers won't solve the problem, although that's better than having white. (I don't agree with this position of "curse on both your houses"; white capitalism is bad and black capitalism is equally bad, that's not true.)

Comment: I lived in Washington, and I know quite a few people connected with the black power movement. It seems that the black people feel that the *Washington Star* doesn't reflect any of their true aspects; however, the *Washington Post* reflects nothing but the truth. I think what's happened in the *Star* is a real reflection of the black power movement.

Response (Mr. Allen): Yes, I would not suspect either paper of reflecting accurately, but the *Post* is better than the *Star*. There is a black columnist in the *Washington Post,* who is keen and intelligent and generally on the ball, right on target, and even he is felt to be an apologist and that he will largely reflect the white liberal view.

Question (the questioner is white): I was wondering if he could pass for an "Uncle Tom" or not.

Answer: I would not call him an Uncle Tom, and I hesitate to call anyone an Uncle Tom; that name is used too freely; I think it's too freely tossed about and it's hard really to know which position to take in this welter, but it is felt that he reflects very much the white liberal view, and not the black militancy.

Question: If we could somehow wipe out the white psychosis, so that everyone, white and black, was treated without any thought of color or national origin, and so forth, even though a man still doesn't have the nickel or fifteen cents to buy the cup of coffee, that would, I gather from what you said, remove most of our problems, if we could just wipe out the white psychosis, or racism, or whatever you want to call it. The other question I would like to ask is, Were you saying in effect that black power is partially good because it's a catharsis, it's an escapism, or were you saying that it's good because basically, in spite of "Come out, you dog" or "you pig," basically, it does mark the right thing?

Response: I think it's a combination of those. It's a reaction, I don't like the term "catharsis" because that suggests that it has *only* a reactionary motivation, is only escapist in nature, but I think it has positive values. I think before you can have a proper relationship between groups or individuals, it must be two entities, two integers before you have integration, and you can't have a weak, deformed, and disabled community and any kind of real equality with the more powerful community. It is also healthy, in a positive sense, not simply catharsis.

Comment: If the white person leveled on this thing, if we wiped out all of the prejudice, we'd still have crime, but it would be crime by criminals, not by black or white.

Response: I would say wipe out the racial problem, but it wouldn't wipe out poverty, it wouldn't wipe out an exploitative society, it wouldn't wipe out the pernicious effect that a monopoly capitalism has upon the rest of the world. It's a coalition of interests in which the order in the world is dominated largely by this country. It was Eldridge Cleaver who said, "Everyone is affected, the lives of everybody in the world are determined by what happens in America." And when we have a presidential contest it's like two, three, or four men fighting up in the cockpit for control of the airplane, while the rest of the world waits back in the passenger cabin having no power whatsoever to determine who's going to control the plane. And so, that would not be wiped out by elimination of a racist psychosis, except to the extent that the international system that we have of industrial nations dominating this world is largely racial in alignment.

Comment: You're thinking this: that twenty million whites and ten million blacks could be working together instead of cutting each other's throats.

Response: I certainly hope so. The racial psychosis is so deep that I think the prospect of collaboration between the white poor and the black poor remains a fantasy. DuBois seeks to develop this in his *Black Reconstruction,* of how there is mutuality of interest between the white dispossessed in the South and the black freed enslaved person. But it never really got off the ground. The racist feeling is just so strong in this country, and it seems to me that it has little prospect at this time.

Question: Do the whites really know, in reference to what happened in Chicago, this course is primarily against the Negro? Are we beginning to realize that?

Answer: I can't say to what extent the white society realizes, but certainly the point has very dramatically been made, and it has been urged upon the society. As a result of Chicago it has been possible to urge it upon the white society as it was never possible before. Whitney Young, just a day or two after this occurred, made the statement, "Now you see" —and his voice is very prestigious in general—"that for the very first time America sees what is happening to the black man at the hands of the police, that there is such a thing as police brutality, and police rioting."

Question: Would you care to comment on J. Edgar Hoover?

Answer: I don't know, I hope he didn't have a twin. I don't know what I could say about Mr. Hoover, except that he is advancing in age.

Question: Well, if the nonviolent blacks had not been treated as they were, the black militantism would not have become necessary. Should I put it that way?

Answer: Yes, I feel that that's true. The militant black is the heir of decades of generations, of violence, illegal violence, visited upon the black man, particularly the black man who was struggling and fighting trying to achieve his rights. For example, it was Stokely Carmichael, when Dick Gregory stepped off the plane in Mississippi in 1964, it was Stokely Carmichael who said, "Now Mr. Gregory, we don't want any violence, we can't stand it, our cause will suffer." It was with the futility, and as I said, the scar tissue of these SNCC workers, out of the terrible experiences of that group, this militant cry "black power" came.

Question: Could Mr. Hoover have done something about that if he wanted to?

Answer: Yes, he could. That's a delicate issue, politically, and that's a long, long story. Our Congress is controlled by these dinosaurs from the South, who are in office for twenty and thirty years. They become the chairmen of the important committees; and in anything that the federal administration wants done, it has to obtain the concurrence of those reactionary parties, and the story of the country has been the story of these antediluvian creatures from the South, collaborating with the Republicans, and since New Deal days it's been an exchange between them; the conservative fiscal policy in return for a reactionary racial policy, so that's the situation which has existed for a long time. I don't know whether they're going to see some change or not. Maybe the Republicans won't need them as much now since they are in control of the federal administration.

Question: Do you think that the future shape of the American society will be such that black racialism might become one of the same problems that we see white Republicans facing?

Answer: I very much doubt it. It's so obviously a reaction against this white racism that has existed for centuries. It scarcely threatens to be the same thing.

Question: Do you see the presence of separatism or black power as being a means to achieving a method rather than a goal?

Answer: Well, I would say yes and no. I would say hopefully, it would be idealistically a means, but if it is the Lord's will and we don't get to what some might consider that happy idealist state of complete integration, it will be sufficient in itself. At least despite what privations he may suffer the black man will have a certain confidence, a certain security, a certain emotional independence, which he has lacked up to this time.

Question: If you were going to give a talk on white psychosis, how would you order your priorities? Would you talk first about economic exploitations, about sexual fears, about psychological gratitude, inferiority, or just what?

Answer: Well, I have spoken to that and I started with the beginning of the Republic; with the Americans coming here to be Americans, coming from England. And the reaction against privilege of Europe, and the whole impulse was to tear down—"You're no better than. . . ." There was a healthy rejection of the privilege of the nobility, they wanted to get away from that, and that was good. But along with it was a tendency to denigrate everybody else and say, you're no better than I am, or get off your high horse, with the loss of that structured society in Europe, again, they were without the guidelines, as the black man threatens to be now, so they had no identity, and if you examine American literature, you'll find the great theme running through it has been the search for identity. This has not been true of European literature. The American novel has been the search for identity, "Who am I?" And so, who is he? He places his emphasis upon three things: upon race, upon money, and upon degrees (formal education), and that'll solve everything. That's the way the American achieves his identity, and Arthur Miller speaks to this; he says the white man little realizes the great psychic income he derives from having a black caste beneath him. Whatever he does he'll never sink so low as to enter that low state. W. L. Cash, in *The Mind of the South*, says the same thing, that the white man gains his psychic income, a kind of guaranteed annual psychic income, from being white, and this sustains him, it always gives him a sense of worth and value. And he lost that when he came over here, he didn't know who he was, but he gets it largely from at least being white. "I may be poor, I may be ignorant, but I'm white." That's one phase of it. I think the others, the sexual, play a great role too, I'm sure. (Freud has been dead too short a time for us to deal adequately with the subconscious.) This is a great fear in regard to other races. There are a number of factors, but I particularly traced and dealt with this sense of identity, and I think the literature bears me out.

Question: In your definition of separatism when it's used with total integration, is there any role at all for any kind of white?

Answer: Yes, I certainly think there is, but not in every organization, not in every group. The late Loren Miller out in California said that there is a role for the white liberal, but as a foot soldier, not as the commanding officer. I think that in many organizations he can participate, it depends upon what the objective is. I was reading an article by Poussaint, the black psychiatrist, who was very active in the Mississippi movement in 1964, and he makes a good study; it depends upon the kind of organization, what they're after. If they're after money, the white sympathizer can play a tremendous role. He says, on the other extreme, if it's an organization that's dedicated to armed combat against white people, they would be completely out of place, usually, not all of them. So it depends upon the goal of the organization, but I don't say that we need to be antiwhite, although I sympathize with what LeRoi Jones and his colleagues are doing. I haven't yet decided what really I feel about it. This antiwhitism in an art form demonstrates the equivalent of the prejedice against blacks. It was interesting to me that Mark Mendel, the young white poet who is instructing here, said, "This is the first time I understood what prejudice against black people means." He said, "Before when I'd read about the way they would mistreat the bad white guy, I would think, Good, he deserves it, or mistreat the Negro, I would sympathize with the Negro, and say, this is too bad, but I never really felt it until this black group began beating this liberal, progressive, sympathetic white person, and why? Simply because his skin is white." So, maybe in the aesthetic realm, there is a role for this sort of thing.

WHY HAVE AN

OCEAN HILL–BROWNSVILLE?*

by Rhody McCoy

I THINK FIRST I'd better tell you a little bit about Ocean Hill–Browns-ville. It is a small community in the middle of what is known as Bedford-Stuyvesant, which is one of the largest black communities in the country. Brownsville is geographically and populationwise almost as large as Har-lem—two ravaged, deplorable ghettos. And we're sitting right in the middle of it. There are eight schools—six elementary schools and two intermediate schools. There are 9000 students in that district, 540 teach-ers, and 35 administrators. Some of our elementary schools have as much as 1200 kids in them. So you see it's a pretty sizable district by compari-son to some school districts throughout the state and country. It's predominantly black and Puerto Rican, and typical of ghetto schools across the country. I've been all across the country looking at those schools, talking to people in them. And they're monumental failures.

If anybody doesn't believe they're failures, I think he's in the wrong place. The problem is so severe that many black people don't understand it. They think it's a way of life, that there's something inherently wrong with the ability of children to learn, or inherently difficult for people to teach them. You may not understand the total significance of this, but we've turned education into one of the prime issues in this country. It's on the tip of everybody's tongue. If you recall, in the heart of our crisis it was front-page, as against the war in Vietnam and some of the other international crises.

We still believe that if we sit quietly and patiently, ask and talk, some great mystique is going to come along and suddenly we're going to be standing side by side with the white society. Out of our nine thousand children, six thousand are better than two or three years academically retarded. And that's a little story in itself, and I think you ought to

*An address delivered at the University of Wisconsin, 1969.

understand that. Once a kid gets past third grade and he begins to go up in age, but he's reading at the third-grade level, he doesn't break that barrier. He can't read.

Well, I attended a PTA meeting with one of the principals of the district when I first came in who alleged to really have the interest of the black community at heart. And a mother stood up in the back of the room and she said to the principal, "Mister, would you tell me how it is that my daughter was pushed on the radiator by a teacher and burned from her hip to the back of her leg?" This principal said to her, "Impossible!" Now there were a group of about eight of what the white establishment like to call militants who were about ready to take that cat outside and take him apart limb from limb, cause here's the girl standing there with the sore of the burn all down her leg. On another occasion here's two teachers, white, who hold a kid, black, pour alcohol on his arm, and set it on fire. The explanation was that they were *playing.* You see, Mr. Charlie's done played with these black people long enough. We may not hold still for more of this. If you let that be threatening to you or frightening to you, depends on how you see it.

There's something wrong with our society and our sense of values; and we, we, we have stood by and let them just give it to us the way they want to give it to us. And it's these kinds of things to which Ocean Hill-Brownsville people said "no more." And they had no idea exactly what they were going to do, they just said we're going to make some complaints and try to start some things operating. And they did. And they got some books, and they got kids off the radiators, off sitting on the floor, all this kind of foolishness. The teachers say the kids can't learn, the kids don't want to learn, the kids fight like dogs, but this parent group got together and they began to move. Finally they got some support, and I have serious questions about what kind of support. But anyway they got some support and they started this demonstration district where parents are involved in their schools. Tell me, man, what do they have to demonstrate when 75 percent of the school systems across this country, and all of the white ones, are community-controlled?

See, under our separate but equal school systems, if you recall, we had black principals and black teachers, but the superintendents and the boards were white. See, we've never had control of any of our community institutions, and surely not the schools, but here was New York City's graciousness giving these black and Puerto Rican people a chance to run their schools. And they built in all the failures. "We are giving you control of your schools," and they pulled the stopper out of the tub, let all the water out. Because the first day we walked in, all the money had been spent the previous year . . . that's the way the system operated. "What am I controlling?" They say you control your budget, 90 percent of which goes to teachers' salaries. Ten percent goes to all the other "committed costs," you know, such as textbooks, transportation, and so forth. So what am I controlling? Pieces of paper that told me what I couldn't do.

Well, we had an election of parents, which has been contested—it's supposed to be illegal. We upset the whole country because we had a large turnout of black and Puerto Rican people. We had about 32 percent of our potential electorate. In other words, only people in the community who had children in the school could vote, so out of about 3500 people, we had about 1500 registered to vote. Most of the Spanish-speaking people said they'd never voted or registered for anything in their lives before. But we'd done such a good job of informing them about what we were all about that they came out to vote.

We went around that community talking to people, just like I'm talking to you tonight, and we began telling them about the horrendous school system, and here's a group of parents—housewives, mothers who want to run their school. Mothers would stand up in the back of the audience and say, "Can you put my children in the right high school?" I'd say "No." They'd say, "Where do you get the decision from?" I'd say, "Down at Central Headquarters." They'd say, "If you still got to go to the white man, forget it. This is a game." See? "Do you have money to put these kids on busses to do something?" "No." "Where do you have to go?" "Have to go to the Central Board." "Whose game you playing? Nothing's gonna change. Long as the Man has control, nothing's going to change." And so they had all kinds of ambivalent feelings about it. They said, "Forget it. This is a joke you're playing, a game they're perpetrating on you." The parents are smart enough to see this, that under a different context, the white man still controls the lives of black people. See, what they really didn't reckon with is that they were dealing with someone who had a little savvy, knew how to pull a few stoppers out of the sink, too.

And so this governing board and this community program were basically launched. I remember going to the superintendent of the school— I had the biggest delight walking in and showing him the election results. I said, "Hey, man, see what we done done to you?" He said, "My God, what have you"—he wanted to say "niggers" so bad I know he could taste it—"what have you *done?*" Caught himself, said, "Well, I guess you did it in good faith." Well, we got off and running and we began to make a few changes. For example, if I say all these people on this side switch onto that side, and you switch onto that side, that doesn't affect anything, does it? So we could make that kind of change. If I say, "Last guy in the last row, you come up front; first lady, you go in the back," they say, "Wait a minute." Now if I say, "Last guy in the back, you go out the door and don't come back," they say, 'Stop that crap." So we made the kind of changes we thought we could get away with. Meantime, we made a few changes that we knew we couldn't get away with. But what we were doing, we were educating the people all along. See, the kind of change that we knew we couldn't get away with was, like we made the statement, "No more children outside our district are coming into our district." Now that takes Central Board action, the white board. But we did it. And we hid behind their own slogans: "We got all these extremists and militants here; if you come in here they're going to get you." Then you sit down and look at them with a poker face.

Well, we got to running the schools, and little by little the kinds of problems we saw coming out were highlighted during the teachers' strike —not our strike, but the teachers' strike. See, they had three issues: more money, the so-called more effective schools (more money), and the black child. See, there's a teacher that would take a kid and put him out of school. See, the New York City school system has approximately 80 to 85 percent white teachers, and the student population is about 55 percent black and Puerto Rican. Well, that was an issue that separated the city.

So around that issue, Mrs. Smith—that's a fictitious lady—used to go into the school and she'd say to the principal, "Will you tell me about my little boy?" And the principal would pass you on to the teacher and the teacher would say, "Mrs. Smith, Johnny is the nicest boy in the world, comes to school neat and clean, it's a pleasure to have him in my class, he's so well behaved," and poor Mrs. Smith! At the end of the year, Johnny can't read his name. See? And I'm trying to tell you in a humorous way, because it's sickening, you understand? It's sickening to see you people stand by and watch this perpetrated on these kids year after year. Don't tell me you don't know what I'm talking about, because all of you've been through it. Wait and tell me about the great genius, the scholar that's sitting in here, that he's made it. He made it because somebody let him make it. See?

But anyway, those were the conditions that we wanted to rectify. But here are these parents, used to feel so bad about themselves, that I'm the cause of my kid not learning because you've been told that you don't care about your kids in school, you're apathetic, you don't come to meetings, if they send for you you don't come, if you come down you got a blade, gonna whup up the teacher, you know. You got all kinds of fictitious addresses, fictitious names, you live under four different names, draw checks under three. You know—they got you. They tell you the story of your life. Don't tell you causes. Those parents went into classrooms and instead of seeing little Johnny, they saw twenty-five little Johnnys, all in the same boat. Man, their whole idea began to change. See, you can see one man with a wooden leg and you say, "Gee, he's in pretty bad shape," but if you look in the room and everybody got a wooden leg you begin to have some concern about it. What's going to happen to these kids? So these parents locked the door on the community and they say, "These kids' education is going to change." And all hell broke loose since that time.

See, New York has about sixty-five thousand teachers in it—that's bigger than this whole town. The largest number they ever fired from these teachers in any one year is twelve. They never fired one for incompetence. So I want to know who's denying who jobs? The twelve they let go usually shot somebody, or went blind or something. And this ties in with the other part—the colleges send all these brand-new young ambitious kids right into the black community and they gain their experience there. The teachers in white schools have their experience. No more jobs over there so they train them in over here, and by the time those of the top retire, these move in. You're always the laboratory, the experimental area. In the Bedford-Stuyvesant area they have yet to bring in an experienced principal to man one of those schools. They get their experience there. At the expense of whom?

We did such things as hire the first Puerto Rican principal in the history of New York City, and the first Chinese principal. And we let the press, the newspapers, the mass media inform the public and we sat back and watched them fool you people. They were all acting, and when the board got tired of them acting they closed the doors and said, "You ain't acting any more," and they take the money and put it back in their pocket. But everybody believes we hired these people and they're our principals. Okay, the community's not going to let you take them away, not unless you want a couple of race riots. That's the way the game is played. They want to subject these principals to their examinations. How many of them you think gonna pass? Especially at eighteen, nineteen thousand dollars a year, right? Have eight of these cats in there at one time drawing that kind of money, they'd think it's a revolution.

Well, that's the sort of thing we did. And we brought in our own teachers, and we began to train our own teachers and do all kinds of things necessary to improve the education of these children. And you see what's happened to us. First, we're anti-Semitic, then we're racist, then we're separatist, then we're extremist. What they failed to say is we're enslaved persons. You go talk to the black professional, he tells you, "Man, don't rock the boat; I don't want to lose my job."

Here in New York it's conceivable that a kid can go from first grade all the way through high school and never see a black teacher. If all these kids coming up today still see the white principal, the white district superintendent, the white Board of Education, white State Commissioner of Education, then their only conception is that in order to be successful and be the boss, you gotta be white. That's not so. At least we don't want these kids to believe that it's so. So we're interested in having success models. And don't get the idea that all the black principals and black teachers are so great, because some of them are just as much oppressors as the whites. Some of the things they teach these kids are just horrendous. As an example, in Stamford, Connecticut, it's against the law to teach Negro history in the school system, and they got Negro teachers working there. There's such a shortage of teachers, they could at least get a job where they teach Negro history, even if they teach it wrong. They *want* to belong to this system that's rotten and decayed. It's so easy, man; it's so easy to sit back and blame everybody for what's going on.

This month I'm required to evaluate two years of my program. In the past, whenever a school system is evaluated, who evaluates it? Black people? You better believe they don't We're going to do something different; we're going to have black people evaluate this year. We're going to pull them from all over the country. And we're going to change.

So now you got inexperienced teachers, poor school plants, poor materials, inferior curriculum, what's a kid going to learn? Fraud and deception. So their hero is the numbers writer, isn't it? Cause he ain't fooling anybody—they know who he is, they know what he's doing. And they applaud as long as as he beats the law. See? That's real to them. And when they ask their parents to take a stand for them, their parents go down and they—what's that expression about the meek shall inherit the earth? When we gonna get our share? So you go in there and the teacher snows you under and you come back and beat hell out of Johnny. Tell him, "You dumb and stupid." Poor guy trying his best to figure out a way. Schools reject him, parents reject him.

Right now, places like Harvard practice their own form of discrimination. They want two from Long Island, two from Wisconsin, two from California; now which two you think are coming? First of all, we can't even afford to send them up there on the train. And also, they got to look right. A cat come up there in his coveralls, they'd throw him out. And they don't make it. But it's not just that they're black. But their parents can't give Harvard a dormitory, can't endow Harvard with scholarships, don't own a great business where he can influence decisions. How you think Harvard stays in the forefront of education? Cause they got the grants.

Now just imagine your local school board all black. A contractor walks in to build a school and they ask him, "How many black people you got in your union?" Then you may make a million dollars off that building yourself. You may have *your* son-in-law that's the architect make a quarter of a million dollars. They're not letting that happen.

When the guy asks me, am I interested in integration, what's he asking me? Do I want to let all the whites into the ghetto? He's certainly not letting me into his place—he's done told me that, he's shown me that over and over again. Howard University—one of the few places where you could get large numbers of black doctors. Then Howard was sold on integration, now 60 percent of the students are white. Integration: all the black people started racing to the white doctors, white dentists. All the black doctors starving to death.

And finally they get around to bussing. But there's something else behind the bussing. How are the parents going to get over there for PTA meetings? For all the important issues that relate to their own schools? So really, what they're doing is they keep fragmenting you, keep isolating you, keep dealing with you. And they keep putting up all these facades and we keep acting stupid, thinking the Man is really sincere. I'm not talking about separatism, because we're already separate . . . we've been separate all our lives. Every other ethnic group has made progress by either stepping on or stepping over us. And you still talk about integration. I just can't understand. What I'm saying is, let's take our own communities . . . make them worthwhile, make them competitive, control them. So then you begin to bite the Man in the hand where it hurts—with money. And once you become an equal partner, then he'll deal with you. He's never going to accept you. But he'll deal with you on equal terms. Till we get to that stage, we adults are fooling our children. And if we wait, you won't have anything to do but just lay down and die, cause those kids are not going to wait any longer.

QUESTION AND ANSWER PERIOD

Question: Did the newspapers portray the fundamental issues in the school dispute?

McCoy: Didn't portray them at all. The situation is in fact that the schools serving black kids have not educated the kids. The press didn't give us that advantage, so that those who needed a reason could say, "I'm with you." What they did say was here's some militants out there. They create pandemonium. No community in the history of the country ever suffered like this one . . . over education, man!

Question: Could black teachers be recruited from those working in industry?

McCoy: You got less than 5 percent of your black students in colleges all across the country. If they all went into industry, I'd still have trouble getting teachers. See, we go where the money is, not where the service is. So we have trouble recruiting. So then they say we got inferior teachers, our teachers are not qualified. You've had a vicious circle of inferior education for blacks for the last hundred years. So if we try to get around the Man's controls he's saying we're buying second-class junk. So I'm saying to the adults, please set up centers where you can help black students, high school and college. At the same time, have some voice at the public school level, like mine, where you have people that are going to fight to see that those kids get educated.

Question: How can you overcome black parents' apathy?

McCoy: First thing is to by-pass the parents. You go set up programs and procedures where you can help the kids. And if you're doing it well enough, where the kids are beginning to have some success, finally the parents will make some moves. You don't even really need them at this point. Because the kids have already demonstrated all over the country that they don't need to wait for their parents. Let's go to the college level now. I'm afraid that most of the black kids on campuses across the country, the ones they call militant, they'll get kicked out and nobody helps them. They're just sitting out there lost. So we need to develop economic bases for those kids. All your college fraternities, all your professional organizations give scholarship money, and what do they ask for? Academic excellence. But the kids who really have the grades don't need the help. Most of the universities are going to have that kind of scholarship. We should help the kids who have not come up to the so-called academic excellence level, which is the mass of our kids.

Question: How can a small community expose false white liberals as Mayor Lindsay was exposed by the Ocean Hill–Brownsville issue?

McCoy: Around certain issues they gotta take a stand, and if the issues are crucial enough, you'll know exactly where they are. We've found that when it comes down to black versus white, on a moral issue, they always vote black versus white. The moral issue stands aside.

Question: What role was played by SNICK, the Black Panthers, etc., in the school crisis?

McCoy: They've been participants, they've had their role to play. It's great for the newspapers to say, "Here's the Black Panthers standing out there in support of Ocean Hill–Brownsville," but they may have been just curious onlookers. For example, Sonny Carlson, a militant, extremely, and they say, "My God, look what he's doing, I'm scared half to death." They never told you he had a son in the school. I'm just saying that each of these groups had a role to play, but more as participants. No one was involved in the policy-making decisions other than the elected body. See, let me give an example. If everybody on this side of the room had halitosis and everybody on this side had one leg, it's still our community. You have no more right to put them out than they have to put you out. They live here. You got to work with all segments. And yet I must say to you that the so-called militant—who's a product of the white press— has been the most effective mover and instrument in bringing about social change. Without them, forget it. You gotta give them due credit.

Question: What can parents do about a school system where there are no black teachers?

McCoy: What do you want to do? If the conditions in that school are bad and you want to change them, then you have to change them. It's just that simple. If you want black teachers, put out a demand for them. But just can't ask for black teachers unless there are some nearby. Maybe you gotta set up housing for them. You may even have to force the Board of Education to make some sort of adjustment in salary. If they couldn't get white teachers at these salaries, you know they'd raise them.

Question: How can we develop solid support here, where the black community does not dominate any sizable geographical area of the city?

McCoy: We had our problems too. Eight or ten parents began demanding such simple things as books, where only half the class had books, where there weren't enough seats for the kids, where there was no heat in the schoolroom, they began pestering the Board of Ed till they got those things answered. And every time these parents gained something, more people joined them. See, the parents don't really understand what's going on in the schools. You can tell them it's bad, but until they really see it for themselves . . . That's when we made our first inroads; we went into the parents' homes and began to tell them and show them and got them into the schools to see for themselves. And that thing had been going on for three years before I came on the scene. I was just able to take it and put it together in some sort of spearhead. So the same problem is true anywhere, black kids have not been educated. I believe youngsters, once they understand what the situation is, in their present state of mind, are probably able to effect more change than anyone else. I'm not suggesting at all that kids be used to get their heads split open—I think that's criminal. But kids can tell you what's going on in school, they can identify the poor teachers, they know what conditions are in the schools, and they have a right to protest.

Question: How can we influence people who still think integration is the solution?

McCoy: Look, I think it's your own responsibility to explain it to them. For instance, if they go into the white schools, isn't there an educational problem being created? What are their images? What are their success models? And I'd almost bet you that of the black teachers there, the largest number are women. And what's that little black boy got to look at? We've got responsibilities. Right now in my district I've got whole lots of men in the elementary school, but they're all white men and I've got all black kids. As they used to say in the South, "There's only two free people, the white man and the black woman."

The school is only one segment of the community. I am afraid that for whatever reasons, we wait till we're forced to react. Just like the poverty program. Okay, one or two good jobs, but the rest is peanuts. And every year we worry about one word: refunding. So I'm saying we're still involved in programs that keep the community from being a community. But there's so many federal programs open to people who have a little savvy, and have learned to put their resources together, you can't tell me any longer that we've been excluded from them. Those kinds of resources got to be pulled together. Somehow we've got to get more students into college and protect and keep those students who are in college. Because we haven't been able to change the requirements for jobs. They tell me that in another ten years there won't be an academic high school in the inner city. They also tell me that in another ten years the school system will be 85 percent black. Then we'll really have integration, because every time you want a doctor, you'll have to go to a white doctor, every time you want a dentist you'll go to a white dentist, every time you want a lawyer you'll go to a white lawyer, you'll appear before a white judge, and you'll go to a white jailer. So if we concentrate only on the school system, which may or may not be vulnerable, and lose sight of everything else, we'll be in trouble. Until we control all the things in the community, you got a problem. We got to look at the community, period.

BUILDING BLACK ECONOMIC EMANCIPATION WITH TEN-DOLLAR BUILDING BLOCKS*

by Rev. Leon Howard Sullivan

THROUGHT THE WORLD things are changing. Old ways of doing things no longer stand up. Ideas people had about others and categories they were placed into are no longer true.

The desire of men to improve their living conditions and to be free is universal. Either nations and governments and communities will help the people change the conditions of poverty, servitude, and helplessness in which they are living, or those conditions will cause the people to do something to change the government, the nation, or the community.

In this respect the replacement of the old by the new in far-off places of the world, as well as at home, should not have come as a surprise to us these past years; for, I repeat, if the nation does not eliminate conditions that create and maintain poverty, these conditions will lead to trouble in the nation.

Therefore, new projects of hope, new programs of opportunity, must spring up in our country and throughout the Western world or trouble and turmoil will continue to grow in intensity and in frequency everywhere. It is not necessary for this to happen. Something can be done.

Leadership for Self-Help

New individuals led and people developed self-help programs. Such programs, economic and social, must become the surge of the times, massively initiated by the people themselves up by their own bootstraps. The programs cannot come from the top down. The leadership for these self-help initiatives must come from the people who live where the problems are. The people must know that the programs belong to them, and that the successes as well as the failures will be theirs, too.

The kinds of projects I have in mind must not be regarded as govern-

*Address at 75th Annual Convention of Savings Bank Association of New York State, 1968.

ment programs, but as people's programs for the inner city (as well as for rural areas), to be supported by the government and by other institutions interested within the community. Thus, the latter must place more confidence in the ability of the people in the concentrated community to plan for themselves, out of knowledge of their own needs, and to utilize public resources effectively.

Contrary to general belief, it does not require uncalculable effort to achieve meaningful breakthrough solutions to inner-city problems. I am convinced that the nature of the problem at this point in our history is as much economic and psychological as racial.

Untie Our Hands

The next great thrust, therefore, in my opinion, must be directed toward the alleviation of economic barriers that prohibit individuals from moving forward into the mainstream of American life, for we cannot expect to enter great suburbs with relief checks. People trapped in ghettos have to develop an economic capability, with will power and green power. It is possible to end discrimination altogether in housing, in employment opportunities, in public school systems and still not reach the problem of the slums. The ghetto may grow yet wider and all of its problems increase in seriousness. Populations remaining unskilled and untrained would be given to greater violence than before, because nothing is more frustrating to a hungry man than seeing a meal before him while his hands are tied.

In America we must untie the hands of our people economically with programs of economic emancipation, so that they can enjoy the democratic process and the free enterprise system.

Economic emancipation of race: this is our new direction for the masses. Our goal is that the black man stand equal to the white man in earning a dollar, in making that dollar work for him, speak for him, and give him security.

Economic emancipation is not the only possible direction; overt militancy, with all of its uncomfortable ramifications, can still be necessary to deal with deeply imbedded prejudices and racism. There are those who will not move except in this way, who will not cut down the rotten tree until limbs fall on their roof. I know the value of militancy, for it was I who created programs of militancy to stir changes in many of the industrial quarters of this land. It was I who created the selective buying program in America, that causes industrial institutions—among them many banking institutions—to open their doors to employ black men and women on the basis of their ability rather than to maintain their invisible walls of racism and prejudice and discrimination against my people.

I could well initiate such challenging programs again, but at this point my direction is to provide creativity and productivity for the masses in the concentrated community. From the integration that has come, we shall move to the next step in the cybernetics of progress. For as important as integration is, I well know that integration without preparation is frustration. No people can ever be respected as long as they have to depend upon others for their livelihood and for their survival.

I have created several new kinds of self-help programs pointed in this direction. I will discuss two of these programs of economic emancipation —one leading to manpower capability and the other to economic productivity. Both will have a significant contribution to make to the development of the democratic process and, hopefully, to the American free enterprise system.

The first is the manpower program called OIC, the Opportunities Industrialization Centers Program, begun in Philadelphia in 1964. It was the first massive, grass-roots manpower program in the United States. It was begun in an old jailhouse in the heart of Philadelphia's main poverty section. It was born in faith and prayer and out of necessity; our problem was recognized and a solution had to found. This is the American tradition.

Skilled manpower had to be found on a massive scale in order to fill the thousands of jobs in industry and in business that almost overnight began to become available in my city.

There were no training programs reaching the needs of the common man. There were manpower programs that had been initiated by the government, but they tended to screen out the people who needed them most. They did not reach into the concentrated community where the most frustrations were.

Therefore, we created a program of the people, by the people and for the people, in the beginning where the people were—where the people themselves would guide and control its destiny: its successes or perhaps its failures.

The program began with only private and community capital, adding $100,000 raised by the people in the concentrated community, to a $50,000 anonymous gift, and with various other contributions I was able to secure; we employed a staff and initiated a training program that began to reach the masses. No vocational books were read as to how to create these programs. No educators were brought in to advise us how. If we had read books about them or brought educators in, we would never have started the OIC.

We started from an idea of what was best for our people, creating and changing as we went along.

Within a few months we found it was important not only to give a man a skill for a job, but to develop in him an attitude, because with a skill but without the attitude the man would still make a poor employee.

Therefore, for the first time within the context of OIC, we created what is called the OIC feeder program, the first prevocational program in America. Every individual who came to OIC went, first, through the feeder program. It was there that he learned all over again the basics of reading, writing, and arithmetic, because most of our people had been out of school for ten or twenty years. We dealt with adults and not with children, but instead of calling it reading, writing, and arithmetic—because no one wants to learn those subjects—we called it communication skills and computational art, and people just flocked there.

We arranged a whole new system of curriculum development with the idea of "curriculumizing" attitude. We also taught consumer values and the value of a dollar, so that an individual would know how to tell a fresh chicken from a stale chicken, a good loaf of bread from a stale loaf by the date on the wrapper, and when a can of tunafish was canned by the markings on the can. We taught the individual to know the value of his money and how to make it stretch further for him.

We taught the individual something about himself. We called it "minority heritage" education, in which black men gain a sense of the relevance of their past and pride in what they are. We taught black men from whence they came, the glories and the benefits of the African continent, and the contributions that black men and women have made to the development of America. We taught the history of the African-Americans. We taught black women that they did not have to be blond to be beautiful, and black men that they did not have to be white to be smart.

We taught men and women to be proud of what they are. We taught them also to respect others; for perhaps the first time in an American educational institution we taught a sense of appreciation for the heritages of others. We taught Italian-American history, and Irish-American history, and Appalachian-American history, and suddenly everyone came to realize that this great country is a compendium of thirty-nine minorities, and that an individual must respect what others are. We find that when a man respects another he does not have to hate him any more.

Then, we taught something that has not been taught much in our schools these days. We taught the value of America and we taught patriotism, because we have found that with all the problems in the world and in America, this country still is the best one can find anywhere. We might as well learn to appreciate this . . . learn to build it up, not tear it down.

We taught the value of a job and what a man must do when he takes a job; that he is to give a good day's work for a good day's pay; that when he does a job well he is to expect advancement; that when he does not do a job well, he can expect the problem of unemployment.

We taught the individual that to an industry he is an investment of dollars, as well as of time, and therefore he must give in effort and productivity the counterpart of the investment that has been put into him as a worker.

Once an individual has been a part of the feeder school from two weeks to three months, we send him to the OIC, where he learns a skill; from there he goes on to a job.

The amazing formula that was created by OIC began to catch on in America. It spread across this country to the extent that today there are OIC centers in seventy-five American cities. There are, at the moment, thirty-five thousand students in OIC training programs. There are programs developing in Senegal, in Ghana, and in Nigeria. There are inquiries about OIC developmental centers throughout Latin America, and there is an OIC being developed at this moment in San Juan, Puerto Rico. The OIC Industrial Advisory Committee was formed to assist and support the work of this new, rapidly developing manpower training program.

The OIC program began in the black community and is a movement whose goal is to serve the needs of the black community, because I make no excuses for the fact that my main concern is still with the African-Americans. I want African-Americans to have a sense of pride in what they are, so that they will know that genius is color-blind, and that man is like a balloon: it is not his color that makes him rise, but what he has inside.

While this is my main concern, OIC has become an American program serving the American people—in San Jose (where 80 percent of the participants are Mexican-American), in Oklahoma City (25 percent Indian), in Roanoke, Virginia (50 percent Appalachian whites) and in Seattle (where large numbers are Eskimos). In the words of Hubert Humphrey, it has become an American program serving the American people.

The ultimate dream of OIC is that in any community of over twenty-five thousand people there will be OIC developmental programs reaching people who never finished grade school, who have lost hope, and who believe there is no place for them in the free enterprise system.

In Philadelphia alone seven thousand people have passed through the OIC program. Ninety percent of those who pass through it have been placed on productive jobs. The evaluation of an expert manpower-evaluation team discovered the fact that 80 percent of those placed on jobs after a year are still on their jobs or have advanced in the job categories in which they were trained. Thirty million dollars in new purchasing power has been added to the Philadelphia economy. Already, in Philadelphia alone, we saved two times in money what would have gone to relief checks. It has brought a new kind of economic prosperity to the concentrated communities of Philadelphia. It bids fair to do the same whereever OIC programs are developed.

Our goal is that by the year 1980 five million people will have passed through OIC training programs, adding $32 billion of new purchasing power to the economy of the country.

Two Hundred Members at Start

The significant fact, though, is that OIC is not a government program, but a people's program which has the support of government and the support of private industry.

The second self-help program, though, is of even greater importance than manpower training, for it moves into the area of entrepreneurship —black people in the world of capitalism.

In 1964, believing that the black community had resources which, if combined, could achieve positive goals for a democratic society, we created a plan called the 10-36 Plan: two hundred members of my church, the Zion Baptist Church, contributed ten dollars a month for thirty-six months, on a people's installment stock market plan, to build together and develop enterprises for the community. Within a year's time we had gathered enough money to begin the building of enterprises.

Six hundred persons ultimately became a part of that 10-36 Plan, and my church in Philadelphia was able to build a million-dollar apartment complex called Zion Gardens.

Because a dollar wisely invested should earn three times, our community had more money available than before. A couple in my church went to rent an apartment in an all-white community. They were refused. They came back to the church, and the next week we bought the apartment house.

Later, with six hundred people still involved in the movement, we continued to combine our resources, and recently we dedicated Progress Plaza, a multi-million-dollar shopping center, controlled solely by African-Americans and built through conventional financing. The whole focus of self-help and the initiative of the black people is dramatically seen on Broad Street in Philadelphia.

Those same six hundred people, with the 10-36 pot that they had organized through the mutual ten-dollar-down installment people's stock market plan, opened Progress Aerospace Enterprises, the first major aerospace enterprise in the world controlled by African-Americans. We now employ 150 people. We have $2.5 million in contracts in the aerospace industry, and parts made at Progress Aerospace Enterprises went to the moon on the Apollo program.

One month after we initiated the aerospace industry, with the same six hundred people at ten dollars down for thirty-six months, putting the money in and turning it over and over again, we created the Progress Garment Manufacturers Company, which grew to employ one hundred workers. Most of the workers came from the concentrated community through the OIC training center; most of them had been on relief, but they are now making up to two thousand garments a week.

And in order to be sure that we would not have to utilize government grants to make up the inevitable losses that occur while a new enterprise is becoming truly competitive, we opened up Progress Retail Store, the profits from which cover these losses. So that no one will have to do me any favors, I will arrange to take care of my own problems.

Through the Progress enterprises project, a new kind of capitalism and entrepreneurial development has been brought into being in the city of Philadelphia. Hundreds of thousands and even millions of dollars will thus be plunged into the local economy and then fed into the mainstream of the nation's economy.

Recently in my church 3000 individuals gathered to augment the 600 that were already participating and broaden the base of the 10-36 Plan. There are now 3000 persons in that plan. There are thousands of people on the waiting list.

The 10-36 Plan is only one new kind of thrust, part of an idea that will continue to grow and spread.

Those in the mutual savings banking industry will be interested to know that the capacity of the African-American community to utilize its combined resources for the good of America is astounding. At this moment the African-American community has $30 billion in purchasing power annually, and by the year 2000 that amount will increase to the astronomical sum of $75 billion in new purchasing.

Those who are involved, therefore, in mutuals or in banking would do well to look in this direction to see how they might contribute not only to the advancement of their industry but to the advancement of the black community. As the black community advances, America advances.

I do not believe in skepticism. I do not believe that the black community can remain in a corner by itself, and the white community by itself. I believe in black power (I am black power—six feet five inches of black power). I believe in the ability of the black man to do what any other man can do, and because I believe this, I have done it.

But I believe also that black power and white power must put their strength together to build American power. It is toward this goal that we work.

Finally, I will never forget the emergence of a vital new Africa thousands of miles beyond our shores, where new dollar investments and values will increase with every succeeding generation, and where new kinds of African export-import ventures and plans will become a rule of the times. It will be of vital significance for those involved in banking or in the mutual savings field to involve African-Americans in their bank staffs and as corporate officers, so that when the lines and the bridges are built between the United States and Africa, there will be black men connected with the enterprise who can communicate with the people there in terms they can understand.

This is the future. It is not a future of pessimism. It is a future of optimism. It is not a future of failure; it is a future of success. It is not a future of cities being burned down; it is a future of cities being built up. For I say, if we support this kind of effort, we shall change the cries in our streets from "Burn, baby, burn!" to "Build, brother, build!"

As a boy, I walked through a cave one day and got lost, in my native state of West Virginia, when only twelve years of age. After hours of wandering through darkness and feeling I would never be found, I looked along the edge of the corridor of the cave and saw a light in a crevice —and I knew freedom was ahead.

In the darkness of our land and our nation, when you are disturbed by the turmoil and the problems around you, when it seems there is no way to get out, keep looking, because there is a light ahead, a light of new kinds of initiative, new productivity. If we work together we will see the new day.

So I say, do not despair, for I think we are going to make it.

OUR SCHOOLS*

by Nathan Wright, Jr.

THE NEW YORK public schools in the fall of 1968 became a battle-ground commanding national and world attention. The mammoth New York City teacher's union was on one side of the struggle. The local residents of the decentralized Ocean Hill–Brownsville district in Brooklyn were on the other.

To say the least, the forces seemed unevenly matched. How could a handful of parents and a few teachers and officials hope to win in a struggle where there were both formidable odds and a lack of local precedent against them?

What were the issues which captured the attention of parents, teachers, and other citizens in cities and towns throughout the nation?

Just how do these issues affect such rapidly changing cities as Newark and such other expanding communities as we have in northern New Jersey?

At issue principally was the crucial question: Who shall teach and manage the nation's schools?

Schools, for young people especially, are at their best when those who teach and manage the schools have a vested interest in the success of each child, when heart and soul are committed to each child's becoming the best person he can be.

This is one of the reasons why often in spite of grossly inadequate resources, our Roman Catholic schools excel in their given tasks. Those who teach and manage the parochial schools by and large are those who feel related to and involved in the lives of those whom they teach.

Both my mother and grandmother were teachers in what are now termed segregated schools. They were good teachers. They worked most diligently, for they knew that upon the success of what they and count-

*From Newark *Star-Ledger*, November 24, 1968.

less others like them sought to do depended the status and well-being of their race.

Black teachers of a generation and more ago recognized that the matter of black survival hung in the balance with the scholastic improvement of each black child.

White parents who speak up for neighborhood schools—contrary to the tide of so much recent opinion—are not necessarily motivated by biased sentiments. Neighborhood schools, no matter what may be said against them, at least have the merit of being under the local parental eye.

This is good for the schools. Those who have children in our schools or who may feel for any number of reasons tied up with the destiny of their students are among the best agents for facilitating the process of learning.

When schools are too largely removed from a sense of immediate responsibility to their clientele, education is in danger. The institution becomes the master rather than the servant of those it teaches.

This does not suggest that local parents, teachers or local school boards (even in such a large system as in New York) should have all the say in the operation of policy making for the schools.

Few of us adults live in the same community in which we were taught as children. With our increasingly mobile population, our education must be geared to preparing our people to serve the nation as a whole. Education is not for local needs only. Yet education must always take cognizance of and show appreciation for local or ethnic needs.

This means that the spirit of decentralization must be accomplished. Local people, at each district level, must have their say.

For the sake of the most effective use of skilled resources, on a second level, there needs to be school district consolidation. There is no good reason why a skilled professional should be under-utilized when there are children, within commuting range, who need his or her help. Nor is there any reason why a classroom seat in one building or district should remain vacant when a child, within commuting range, has no seat to occupy full-time.

Since national self-interest is involved in the productivity of effectiveness of our schools, new, more firm and substantial and far less fussy national involvements are called for as well.

What is required is neither less centralization nor more, but both.

Further, all of our citizens need to be far more involved in the educational process.

Our adults need continuing collegiate-type education in order both to lead fuller lives and to make critical choices at the polls.

Indeed, has not the time come when the whole question of public support of Roman Catholic and other denominational schools needs to be reconsidered? It is to be noted that such education is conducted at public expense in a number of countries.

Perhaps most crucial of all, in terms of issues surfaced in the Ocean Hill–Brownsville affair, is the need for administrators and teachers to be those who identify with those who are taught.

It should be evident that schools essentially are for the children, not for the teachers. Every good teacher knows this all too well.

Unless teachers are those who can identify with those in their classroom in terms of "we," they are not the proper instruments for the education of that particular group of children. Ideally, teachers and administrators who fail to identify with their pupils should be transferred elsewhere and others who can relate more closely to the needs of the pupils should be sought for the task at hand.

Teacher attitudes reflect those of our society. Our society is fractured. Urban change increases our divisions. Hence, while there may be a truce in the New York City schools, for the nation as a whole, and for each of our local communities, the issues raised by Ocean Hill–Brownsville will continue to be with us.

OUR CHANGING SCHOOL
AND COMMUNITY*

by M. Lee Montgomery

MANY OF OUR educators today have had their formal educational experience influenced by John Dewey, a pioneer of new vistas in the educational process. His philosophy relating to the direction and implementation of the pragmatic approach to education penetrated the roots of the educational establishment. His central theme was "that education be used as a lever of change." It can be assumed that many educators today accepted this precept and continue to design, develop and implement those programs which would, indeed, bring about change in the educational process of our children and thereby affect educational institutions.

We know that our educational institutions have been, and to some degree continue to be, the conservers of the mores and values and are dedicated to upholding and protecting the prevailing concepts of the public good. The sheer density of the educational establishment has given ample evidence of its unwillingness to yield to change. However, this has not impeded the rapid design, development and the implementation of numerous innovative programs, all of which are directed at increasing the learning capacity of our children. Technology itself has become a vital component in the educational process with the introduction of computers, television, movies, talking typewriters, and so forth. The hardware (technology) has far outstripped, in development, the whole area of software (materials). There is no question that the innovative programs have had as their objective to prepare young people to learn more about the world around them, to make learning more pleasurable and to acquire a skill which will make them more able to function effectively in their environment. It should be noted here that we are not always clear about what are our goals. For instance, there are many special programs which

*Anna B. Day School Seminar Series, Philadelphia, Pennsylvania, October 17, 1968.

have been initiated, some by government agencies, some by foundations, and some by schools and colleges. "Upward Bound," "Primesite," and "Head Start" are in financial difficulty from the standpoint that the Office of Economic Opportunity has had a problem in securing adequate funds from Congress. Such programs were designed to provide children in inner-city neighborhoods an educational experience prior to entering kindergarten. However, to be perfectly honest about the Head Start program, it is really designed to prepare black and white inner-city children to cope effectively with an educational system which is white-valued and middle-class oriented. In essence it relates very little to the life experience of the child. The problems created by this program may emerge in later years in the form of economic, social or psychological dependence. The basic instructional methods continue to relate to those things, as far as black children are concerned, to those aspects of the society which have been precast by the cominate culture. So that, we will still find that our jobs are to develop those kinds of educational experiences for our children which relate to our culture and our life style. I recall some time ago I had the privilege of spending a few hours with some Head Start school-community coordinators. It was interesting to observe their response to the question, "How many children did you destroy yesterday?" More pointedly, the question related to their behavior, overt and covert; attitudes, expressed and unexpressed and the things which they said in very casual conversation. Thus, we can raise the question: "Do these educational programs serve as levers of change to the educational establishment?"

Our changing schools and community are a fact today. In Philadelphia, Pittsburgh, Chicago, and New York, students, teachers, and parents are in open rebellion. We want to control our schools, say the parents. We want to decide what kind of curriculum will be in our schools, say the students. It's our right, it's our responsibility, say parents and students. Teachers—sometimes they are supportive of local control and students. All groups are in a state of foment. Let us take a look at the changes which are taking place today. The slogan "Black Power" has provided the impetus for the tremendous pressures on educational systems in all large cities. The whole matter of relevancy: What does it mean? How do you get it? Why is it necessary?

What does relevancy mean? It means those things in the educational process which speak to the totality of the black child's life experience. The whole of the black experience today recognizes the cultural differences as a positive factor in our lives and we begin to build and develop positive images which relate to us. Thus, it becomes clear that a person must make every effort to understand the black experience in the United States.

How do you get relevancy? This must be found in the historical background of black people. What it requires is an understanding of the struggle of black people in this nation in relationship to its development economically, culturally, politically, and spiritually. For it is the institutions—more specifically, the educational institutions—that prevent or retard change.

Why is relevancy necessary? The answer may not be so simple in that because of the resistance of the educational establishment to change, it may well be that people may be "burning (the visible buildings) them" down or destroying the system itself completely. Relevancy is necessary in order that every child have the opportunity to fulfill his purpose and acquire a skill which will make him a more effective human being in his environment.

And in response to all of these questions of relevancy, young black students are now demanding recognition of black heroes, black holidays and black studies. This is something that all white people should be able to understand. Perhaps the most significant aspect of this change process which frightens whites and some Negroes involves a shift in the balance of power. The more critical question which comes to mind is how many will opt out—because of fear—and state that I'll have nothing to do with those black militants or what is commonly referred to as the "new left." We must recognize that fear has its foundation in the insecurity of the person and this relates to his mental and physical well-being.

Thus, it is clear that it is a physical and sociological fact that change brings about disorganization. Now, this is not a state or condition which should give you and me any cause for alarm. Earlier we spoke of technological change, and too, we frequently change things which reorder our personal lives, sometimes drastically. But, we know full well that with persistant effort and planning we are able to bring about the kind of order we desire. All of this is to say that change is not a concept nor action to be feared, and in the same way disorganization is not to be feared. If our lives are to be full and meaningful, then we must learn to become advocates of change and encourage change in spite of the fact that it brings about disorganization.

Our personal growth comes from purposeful change in our attitudes and behaviour. Thus, the major problem is that each of us, if we are honest, has done many things which give damaging evidence of our resistance to social change. How do we do this? How often do you hear people talk about the "good ole days"—"things were different when we were young"—"young people today are disruptive"—"in times past we didn't have violence like today"—all clichés which indicate that the speaker is resistant to change. Can any of us here imagine what this country would be like without technological change. We would miss driving our fine plush automobiles, watching our color televisions and the world of miracles which are ours to enjoy. How much do we, as benefactors of technology, enjoy that immense sense of power at the flick of the electric switch, the gunning of gas of the automobile, the take-off in a super jet. We little realize how much we are consumed by power. Yes, power, total control is the essence of life itself—the thrust forward, the awe it inspires, the fear it breeds—this is power in all of its manifestations to you—to me. Can this power relate to the blacker-than-thou concept that is prevalent today? And yet, we see vignettes of power in the name of blackness rearing its ugly head. We must, as a people, begin to develop a collective consciousness of blackness. Our change, as a people, must move us away from those hedonistic western values which embrace power which is dependent upon exploitation in order to perpetuate itself. Let me say here, it is not enough to say we must create a nation of black people based on love, for love can be an expression of power—we can see it in our expressions which are so important to self-identity. However, I feel sure that the love of which I speak and practice is a code which transcends agression. This is what the change process is all about to black people. What I'm talking about are those things which make us resistant to change, specifically social change. It is a matter, it seems to me, of definitions. Our black cultural revolution demands new definitions. It is quite clear that we not only accept, but we adjust to all of the technological changes, i.e., we accept instant prepared foods, instant car washes, and instant service. Our cop-out is that it saves time, so that in spite of our personal resistance, high pressure radio and television commercials, as well as other communications media, have forced changes in our lives to such a point that we can no longer think of doing without these new innovations.

Social change is the most feared by all of us. Social change challenges us to confront ourselves with all our personal prejudices. This is very difficult for any of us to do, but somehow we must. Those of us who haven't made it, are demanding those opportunities which the majority group now has and controls and dominates completely. In order to bring about the change we insist takes place, there must be a substantial reordering of power relationships. There can be no question that black people have been effectively separated and segregated economically, culturally, socially, politically and psychologically and denied equal participation.

Thus, we can look at the struggle which confronts us today and we can see the crisis which faces every large city school system. Black youth are questioning their education experiences. And we too must ask the question whether we are preparing our children to be able to cope with their environment. The issues are well defined and the battle lines are now drawn.

And yet, we have with us all of the new words, phrases and slogans for the scientific 1960's which are supposed to be levers of change. We are reminded of some, such as "dialogue," "coordination," "cybernation," and many, many others. These words, phrases and slogans, in themselves, are representative of a change process, to some degree, which is a part of our everyday activities. I suppose the most controversial aspect of the change process is whether it can be peaceful or must it be violent. As we look at the rebellions in cities across the nation, we have been witnesses of violence which has forced some changes. The question then, "Is or must all social change, and I specifically use 'social change,' be brought about by violence?" How can I be sure, certain conditions for an explosion of anger and frustration are ever present. It is there and nothing appears to affect it. I suppose it is important for us to look at some of the ingredients in social change. It is psychological; it is political; it is cultural; it is economic; and it is spiritual—so that, when we observe the activities and the dynamics of the current social change process all of these elements are involved.

Today, I would say that this nation is witnessing the beginnings of a black cultural revolution. It is within this context that white people and my brothers and sisters must attempt to understand the tremendous forces which swirl around us. It is interesting that most people are unwilling to accept the concept of a black cultural revolution. I am sugesting that all you have to do is to observe what is now going on in all of our large cities. Furthermore, black people at all levels, whether they acknowledge or disavow it, are affected by this black cultural revolution to some degree. A more fundamental point is: What is it that we must do? Dialogue? Keep the lines of communication open with each other? What then?

The first admonition to my dear sisters and brothers is to try to understand the nature of the revolution and upon doing this you will begin to recognize that the very concept of blackness demands new definitions. This is what makes this black revolution a black cultural revolution. It is a redefinition of goals and values. This perhaps is difficult for most people to understand, because the thing we forget is that all of us have been taught by those who have accepted as our educational creed the puritan ethic as well as the value system. The values are those of the majority culture who were the founders of the country. Thus, it should be clear that it is necessary for black people to redefine goals and values, psychologically, culturally, socially, economically, spiritually, and politically. Perhaps the confrontations which are now taking place can be viewed in a different perspective, so that, it is important that not only are black students rebelling and demanding relevancy, but parents must be involved as well. It is a world-wide revolution of students demanding a voice in those institutions of which they are a part. Isn't it time for black adults to raise their voices as well as act positively in developing those institutions which will serve the needs of black people? It is ridiculous for black adults to attempt to retreat in the face of these new challenges. It borders on the brink of being sacrilegious as we continue to treat young people today as we were treated ten, fifteen, twenty years ago. We ought to be able to understand that this nation's new technology has not only changed and reordered many of the structures in travel, leisure, and employment opportunities, but it has reordered our social behavior and is now affecting our attitudes and feelings about each other.

We are a part of a society which has placed its full emphasis on individualism and it has developed accordingly. An example, not only the get ahead in industry or government, but the emphasis of all social benefits are geared to meet the needs of the individual. Is there any wonder that there is a breakdown in family structures. As a nation, we do not consider group collectiveness. Look at our cities and their many problems. What you really find are numerous programs operating independently of each other, all geared to some individualized accomplishment and never really looking at the whole. It is for this reason that the crisis in the school and community that we find massive uncoordinated changes taking place with conflicting goals as students identify them. The problem, as I see it, is that the students are ahead of the parents in expressing their concerns regarding the purpose and function of education. Parents have sat and pretended that all is well with the kind of education their children are receiving. Certainly, it must be clear to all of us that this just is not so. Therefore, the challenge before us is whether we can effectively become a resource in the design of future meaningful educational experiences for our children or do we, as adults, opt out by saying, "What is needed is better administrators and more teachers to take over." For much too long parents have placed the responsibility for the education of their children in the hands of others. The time has come for all parents and community to accept their rightful role and share in the education of their children.

COMMUNITY BUILDING AND

LEARNING CENTERS*

by M. Lee Montgomery

BLACK AMERICANS are caught up in a process of change without the majority understanding the impact and the direction of that change. Even so, fewer still are aware of what this change is doing to black youth and adults. Many who are searching for identity, self-determination, and human dignity do not understand the scope of these concepts nor have they taken time to develop a sense of purpose, a sense of direction and designed a strategy to achieve these objectives.

We are taught to think within the framework in traditional methods and techniques to accomplish a given task. Because of this, the black artist, dancer, musician, playwright, and poet have failed to create meaningful experiences which emphasize the culture of black people. Our artists have a responsibility to the black community to dramatize, in words, songs, paintings and dance, the actions of our youth. We, the black intellectuals, continue to accept explanations, methods, and techniques as fact without making an effort to question and analyze events in depth. In our educational experience we have not been encouraged to probe and to question. The method which has been established is to let the "critic" or "evaluator" or "commentator" do it for us. We know full well that today's educational systems "train" youth as well as adults to fit into the existing society. The intent of the system, then, is to "train" every individual in such a manner so that he will not question any part or facet of the economic, social, political and spiritual systems of this society. We see the evidence of the aforementioned statements when we reveiw in depth the curricula currently in use in schools with all of the deliberate omissions and disorganized presentation of information. This is especially true in the areas of social, economic, political and spiritual aspects of black peoples' struggles for survival in this nation. It goes

*Presented at Emergency Conference of the Philadelphia Black Community, Radnor, Pennsylvania, January 14, 1968.

without saying, that black people have become confused and frustrated in their efforts to adapt the folkways and mores of Americanization in the United States with its materialistic goals which have their foundation in this nation's birth on a white minority power structure in a capitalistic society. Black intellectuals, in years past, have not taught the black masses techniques of ethnic group survival under the American system. Intellectuals are bankrupt of ideas and have satisfied themselves with repeating old mistakes with some minor innovations. The question is then: What will black intellectuals do about this deliberate genocide of young black minds?

The gauntlet has been passed by our great black leaders of days past to the black intellectuals today. We must search our historical past in order that we can plan for today and tomorrow. Do we have the courage to define and develop our own black value system? Can we and do we want to develop an educational system whereby every individual can develop to his full potential in dignity? Can we see the necessity for the development of ethnic cohesiveness? Can we develop new economic systems (cooperative self-help) for our survival? Can we develop group cultural self-education? We must become the creators of these new systems. Let me say, when we speak of "systems," we are talking about the interacting and interdependent complex of ideas and principles which form a coherent whole which are founded in economic, social, political and spiritual divisions of life. In order that we, as black people, develop these complex ideas and principles (systems), we must begin to formulate a "base"—a "foundation." And this "base," as many of us see, is to be founded in a different kind of educational system. A system which will function in the reality of the American capitalistic system. Indeed, we recognize that black people need many and varied skills and knowledge in order to survive. And today these skills and knowledge are not forthcoming from the current educational establishment. And we know, all too well, that current educational establishments do not prepare young black minds to assume effective leadership roles in the black community. The reason is that young black people are taught the classic examples of individualism with little or no emphasis on man's relationship to man. Yet, we must be concerned about the destiny of all our brothers and sisters. It is for this reason that many of us share these very strong determinations that there must be established a black people's institution which can prepare young black minds for effective leadership in black communities. It is so important that the black intellectuals immediately address themselves to the task of initiating a program to achieve this purpose.

Community building and learning centers are a vehicle by which black people can begin to prepare black youth and adults to work more effectively in black communities. The centers are designed to develop the whole individual by nurturing him in a humane community of truth so that he is free to determine his own potential. In the development of community building and learning centers, the philosophical foundation is humanism, a concern for the well-being of man. We recognize that for ethnic group survival, we must develop new techniques to communicate to the masses. Thus, it becomes incumbent upon all of us to refine our perspective, direction and philosophy as we strive to understand our role, the nature of our being, the purpose of our life and our future.

There are many of us already working to develop community building and learning centers. We recognize the need for the kinds of curricula which will develop the whole person and that public education, as we know it, will not share this concern. The present economic system of this nation has not been designed to benefit the needs of all mankind. It does not provide the climate in which human beings can explore, in depth, the very nature of the being and the purpose of that being. It is with this in mind, that we are compelled to develop the kinds of curricula which will facilitate the growth of black youth and adults. We, then, recognize the need for the development of curricula in history (African, American, World), the social sciences, natural sciences, community building (philosophy, religion) and fine arts, considering the whole person and relating each part of this curricula to each other.

Therefore, the goal of the community building and learning centers is: To prepare black people to master and control all of the material (economic, political and social) and the non-material (intellectual and spiritual) means necessary to seek truth. To rid society of all untruths and thereby moving to create a more humanistic society for all people. To encourage all people to affirm their being without exploiting their fellow man.

The goal, so stated, is another way of saying that we've got to develop skills and techniques with which the masses of black people can survive in the capitalistic system of the United States.

In order to achieve these goals we have developed and are implementing a schedule of activity. The community building and learning centers, in order to become what they are conceived to be, must be the result of the labors of every black person in the black community. More specifically, we say that the black intellectual has an undelivered commitment —that he has given the black community a "blank check." And that the black community now demands that the black intellectual honor his commitment. He can no longer hide nor can he sit passively—he must return to the land from whence he came. This kind of development by black people must be a commitment based on a sincere desire to share his experience in educational forms and models, as well as his creative talents. It is with empathy and love for black people's intrinsic worth which will be the source of strength to facilitate our push toward the growth and development of the whole person, the family and the community. And too, in order that black people survive, we must emphasize and put into action learning that ties all skills and information together.

Community building and learning centers must become the cornerstone in the growth and development of black people. We, who are working in the development of community building and learning centers, recognize that black people's survival in capitalistic systems means that we must create a new kind of group economic, group cultural expression and group politics. We understand that the present systems approach, "integration," will not solve the problems of black people. However, the value of a systems approach in problem solving can be an effective tool for the development of ethnocentricity. Thus, we see the centers as providing a thrust in the direction of that self-determination.

Community building and learning centers are already in operation. Initial efforts are being confined to history with emphasis on African-American History. The need to know one's past is important, for it gives us roots—the answer from whence we've come. At present, there are more than twenty-five "learning partners" participating in an "in-service training program" in history. These "learning partners" are being prepared to share experiences with youth and adults in our established centers. We will continue to recruit "learning partners" for all divisions of the curricula. In case you ask, why are the people called "learning partners," let me explain the reason. It is because they are willing to share in a meaningful exchange of knowledge and because where there is verbal communication between two people a learning experience occurs.

At work, concurrently, are the various curriculum committees. The centers are in need of those with skills and expertise in the areas of natural sciences, community building, social sciences and fine arts. With the goal of community building and learning centers in mind at all times, we will continue to work to develop curriculum, audio and visual materials for use in the centers.

We have found, since time does not wait, that it was necessary to move toward the development of an all black people's institution which will serve as the intellectual base for the growth and development of black people. The community building and learning centers have established a time table to achieve a black people's institution by 1973. Preliminary steps for such an institution have been initiated. We recognized that, as black people, we must do whatever is necessary to achieve this goal. Thus such an institution deserves the highest of our priorities. We must plan now and for the future.

The community building and learning centers need your skills on all of the curriculum committees as well as "learning partners." It is of the essence that black people of whatever skill become actively involved in the development of these centers. We *must not forget* the purpose of the educational establishment in white society. We must come to grips with the realities of this massive change. We must remove our blinders in order that we can see that black people are being programmed into annihilation by our own lack of cohesion. These centers will serve as a cohesive force to strengthen the black community. For those who stand on the fringe of this massive change, can any of them deny that our black youth are consistently and persistently shortchanged, that the design of this change is deliberately confused by the establishment so that it affects our thinking? This, in turn, points out our severe lack of understanding and willingness to define for ourselves the differences between desegregation, segregation, separation and aggregation. The centers will create an atmosphere in which our youth and adults can think creatively. This is a necessary ingredient in the development of the whole man. May we remind you that these centers are *Community Building* and *Learning Centers*. There is no other name for them. This name was selected because we are building a community in which an atmosphere for creative learning can take place based on our mutual respect of the dignity of the person.

ABOUT THE CONTRIBUTORS

Dr. Preston Wilcox is President of Afram Associates, an urban education consulting firm in New York City, founder and President of the National Association for African-American Educators, and a trained social worker. Long an activist as well as a scholar, he has served on the Planning Committee for the National and International Conferences on Black Power.

Dr. Olivia Pearl Stokes is currently Director of Urban Education for the National Council of Churches and was formerly Director of Religious Education for the Massachusetts Council of Churches. An Africanist and a feminist, Dr. Stokes has concerned herself professionally with issues relating to the powerless.

Leslie Campbell's name has come to be synonymous with the struggle of black people in the field of education: the Malcolm X Memorial at I.S. 201 in New York City, the Bedford-Stuyvesant Heritage School, the African Studies Institute at Pratt University, the Ocean Hill-Brownsville community action, the African-American Teachers Association, and Brooklyn CORE. He attended Long Island University on a four-year athletic scholarship and majored in Western History and Culture (or, as he says, "How to exploit and steal and apologize for it").

Dr. Jesse J. Johnson is a practicing psychologist who serves as an educator and as a consultant to industry. He is a founding member of the Association of Black Psychologists, an athlete, and a saxophonist affiliated with the American Federation of Musicians. His educational concern is the underutilized potential of the black professional as reflected in his article in this volume.

Dr. Nathan Wright, Jr., is Professor of Urban Affairs and Chairman of the Department of Afro-American Studies at the State University of New York at Albany. He is also President of Empowerment Incorporated, a consulting firm for urban, educational, ethnic, and population problems. Dr. Wright served as Chairman of the 1967 and 1968 National and International Conferences on Black Power.

Lawrence Hawkins is Dean of the College of Community Services of the University of Cincinnati and formerly served as Assistant Superintendent for Student Development in the Cincinnati Public Schools. Dean Hawkins is a humanist who feels deeply that education must awaken in all students the universal will for self-realization and fulfillment.

M. Lee Montgomery is Director of Urban Affairs at Temple University in Philadelphia, Pennsylvania. An organizer of the National Association of African-American Educators, he served in 1969 as Dean of its summer "Black University" in Atlanta, Georgia. The focus in his articles upon community involvement, attitudes of teachers, and relevance of learning to pupil needs and aspirations suggests the breadth of Lee Montgomery's interests and commitments.

Dr. Edward K. Weaver is Dean of the School of Education of Atlanta University in Georgia and has been a teacher in the field of education for more than twenty years. Dean Weaver believes that far more can be gained for all in education by learning from undereducation in our black minority.

Dr. Norma Jean Anderson is the consultant for intercultural education in the St. Paul Public Schools. A clinical psychologist by training, she has worked as a marriage counselor. She earned her bachelor's, master's, and doctorate degrees at the University of Illinois at Urbana, Illinois. She is a founding member of the National Asssociation of African-American Educators.

Frank Kent is now Director of Civil Rights for the Office of Economic Opportunity. Prior to his Washington appointment, Mr. Kent was Commissioner of Human Rights for the State of Minnesota. A businessman by training, Mr. Kent's extensive involvement with education came through his work with the Commission on Human Rights.

Robert S. Browne is Assistant Professor of Economics at Fairleigh Dickinson University in New Jersey and serves as a consultant to the Phelps-Stokes Fund. Between 1955 and 1961 Mr. Browne was an economist for the International Cooperation Administration, serving in Cambodia and Vietnam. He is an organizing director of the Institute of the Black World and served as an organizer for the 1967 National Conference on Black Power.

Dr. Darwin T. Turner entered the University of Cincinnati at the age of thirteen, was elected to Phi Beta Kappa Honor Society at the age of fifteen, and graduated with a Bachelor of Arts in English at the age of sixteen. Presently Dean of the Graduate School at the University of

North Carolina at Greensboro, he is a specialist in black American literature and serves on the boards of many professional organizations.

Dr. Benjamin E. Mays is perhaps the best-known black educator in America. He retired from a long tenure as President of Morehouse College in Atlanta, Georgia, and immediately went into politics, serving presently on the Atlanta Board of Education. He is the author of a number of books in the field of education and is Distinguished Visiting Lecturer in Afro-American Studies at the State University of New York at Albany.

Dr. Elizabeth Duncan Koontz is Director of the Women's Bureau in the U.S. Department of Labor and served formerly as President of the National Education Association. She serves as U.S. Delegate to the United Nations' Commission on the Status of Women. She has specialized as a teacher in work with slow learners and disadvantaged children.

Dr. Andrew Billingsley is Assistant Chancellor for Academic Affairs at the University of California at Berkeley. A specialist on the black family, he is author of *Black Families in America* (Prentice-Hall, 1968) and serves on boards of directors of numerous scholarly and civic agencies.

Dr. Franklin H. Williams has had a long and illustrious career in government and in the field of education, serving at ambassadorial rank in the Johnson administration and recently serving as Director of the Urban Center at Columbia University. Dr. Williams is presently Director of the Phelps-Stokes Fund in New York City.

Dr. C. Eric Lincoln, perhaps the most eminent young black social historian in America, is Professor of Social History at Union Theological Seminary in New York City, and Visiting Professor of Black History at the State University of New York at Albany. He is author of numerous books on black Americans, most notably *Black Muslims in America.* (Beacon Press, 1961).

John E. Churchville is a thoughtful activist who symbolizes the new mood of younger black Americans who want no more of outworn warp. He attended Temple University where he majored in music, spent two years as voter-registration worker in Southwest Georgia and Mississippi, and founded the Freedom Library in Philadelphia in 1964 and the Freedom Library Day School in 1967, of which he is the Director.

Dr. Grace Lee Boggs received her A.B. from Barnard College in New York and her M.A. and Ph.D. from Bryn Mawr College in Pennsylvania. She has been active in the Freedom Movement since the days of the first March on Washington, which extracted Executive Order 8802 from the Roosevelt administration. Born in New England of Chinese parents, she is the wife of James Boggs, author of *The American Revolution: Pages from a Negro Worker's Notebook.* (Monthly Review Press, 1963).

Edwina C. Johnson is Acting Chairman of the Black Studies Department at Fordham University in New York, founder of the National Association of African-American Educators, and editor and publisher of *Guide for Teachers,* which is circulated widely among educators in thirty-five states.

John Henrik Clarke is associate editor of *Freedomways* and President of the African Heritage Association. Mr. Clarke, who has studied African history in this country and at the Universities of Ibadan in Nigeria and of Ghana in Accra, has been the nation's foremost champion of Afro-American studies. He is author of six books in Afro-American history. His latest book is *Malcolm X: The Man and His Time* (The Macmillan Company, 1970).

Albert Vann is President of the African-American Teachers Association in New York City and is editor of its publication, *Forum.* He is an assistant principal in the Ocean Hill–Brownsville community of New York and is an articulate exponent of community control, which he sees as a process whereby black people will attain the attitudes and skills to resolve their problems.

Samuel W. Allen is a distinguished poet and lawyer who has become deeply involved in education. His legal career includes general practice in New York City, Deputy Assistant District Attorney in New York City, and Associate Professor of Law at Texas Southern University. He holds degrees from Fisk University in Nashville, Tennessee, and Harvard University. He has served most recently as Avalon Professor of Humanities at Tuskegee Institute in Alabama.

Rhody McCoy has commanded national attention as administrator of the controversial Ocean Hill-Brownsville experimental school district in New York. He is a founder of the Institute for the Advancement of Urban Education and has worked throughout the nation in the interests of community control as the door to improvement of the nation's central-city schools.

Rev. Leon Howard Sullivan is Pastor of Zion Baptist Church in Philadelphia and founder of the nationwide Opportunities Industrialization Centers. Dr. Sullivan holds that technical skills must be combined with black-purposed community action, if blacks are to enter into the mainstream of American life. Protest and education are his bywords.